Teachers' Guides to Inclusive Practices

Behavior Support

Third Edition

by

Linda M. Bambara, Ed.D.

Rachel Janney, Ph.D.

and

Martha E. Snell, Ph.D.

with contributions from
Raquel M. Burns, M.Ed., and Dolly Singley, M.Ed.

Baltimore • London • Sydney

Paul H. Brookes Publishing Co.
Post Office Box 10624
Baltimore, Maryland 21285-0624

www.brookespublishing.com

Typeset by Scribe Inc., Philadelphia, Pennsylvania.
Manufactured in the United States of America by
Sheridan Books, Inc., Chelsea, Michigan.

All of the vignettes in this book are composites of the authors' actual experiences. In all instances, names have been changed and identifying details have been altered to protect confidentiality.

Library of Congress Cataloging-in-Publication Data
The Library of Congress has cataloged the print edition as follows:

Bambara, Linda M., 1952-
    Behavior support / Linda M. Bambara, Rachel Janney, Martha E. Snell. — Third edition.
       pages   cm. —(Teachers' guides to inclusive practices)
    Previous editions entitled Behavioral support and entered under: Janney, Rachel.
    Summary: "A concise guide for educators to implement positive behavior support in the classroom and across an entire school"— Provided by publisher.
    Includes bibliographical references and index.
    ISBN 978-1-59857-886-7 (paperback) — ISBN 978-1-59857-943-7 (epub3)
    1. Behavior modification—Case studies. 2. Inclusive education—Case studies.   I. Janney, Rachel. II. Snell, Martha E. III. Janney, Rachel. Behavioral support. IV. Title.

    LB1060.2.J36 2015
    371.39'3—dc23   2014044897

British Library Cataloguing in Publication data are available from the British Library.

2019   2018   2017   2016   2015

10   9   8   7   6   5   4   3   2   1

Behavior Support

Contents

About the Forms

This book contains 14 forms for educational use. Purchasers of this book have permission to photocopy and use the blank forms found in Appendix A (pp. 176–198). Larger, printable versions of these blank forms are available for download online, and filled-in examples are also available online for easier viewing. Please visit **http://www.brookes publishing.com/bambara** to access these materials.

About the Authors

Linda M. Bambara, Ed.D., is a professor and program director of special education at Lehigh University, where she also directed two university field-based programs serving adults and transition-age youth with developmental disabilities and autism to participate in inclusive community settings. She has been involved with individuals with disabilities for more than 35 years as a teacher, teacher trainer, advocate, researcher, and director of research and training projects. As a productive author, she has published numerous books, chapters, and articles, including three additional books on positive behavior support. She has served on national boards of professional organizations such as TASH, the Association for Positive Behavior Support, and the editorial boards of six journals. She is former Editor-In-Chief of *Research and Practice for Persons with Severe Disabilities.*

Rachel Janney, Ph.D., is an independent scholar and consultant who has worked with and on behalf of children and adults with disabilities in a number of capacities, including special education teacher, educational and behavioral consultant, technical assistance provider, teacher educator, researcher, and author. For a number of years, she was a professor in the School of Teacher Education and Leadership at Radford University in Virginia, where she taught courses and supervised student teachers in the special education program, specializing in the inclusion of students with extensive learning and behavior support needs. Dr. Janney received her master's degree from Syracuse University and her doctorate from the University of Nebraska–Lincoln.

Martha E. Snell, Ph.D., is Professor Emerita in the Curry School of Education at the University of Virginia, where she has taught since 1973 and directed the graduate program in severe disabilities. Dr. Snell's focus has been the preparation of teachers with a particular emphasis on those working with students who have intellectual disabilities and severe disabilities. She has been an active member of the American Association on Developmental and Intellectual Disabilities, TASH, and the National Joint Committee on the Communication Needs of Persons with Severe Disabilities.

CONTRIBUTORS

Raquel M. Burns, M.Ed., is a doctoral student at Lehigh University. She worked with Linda Bambara for 4 years as a lead program coordinator for one of Lehigh's field-based programs, where she coordinated supports for adults with developmental and intellectual disabilities in community settings in the areas of choice making, community integration, relationships and social network building, daily living skills, and self-determination. She also supervised the field training experiences of master's students specializing in special education in the areas of systematic data collection, social integration and long-term natural supports and relationships, and positive behavior supports in community settings. Ms. Burns currently works as Assistant Director for a nonprofit community supports program for individuals with disabilities.

Dolly Singley, M.Ed., is a doctoral student at Lehigh University. Ms. Singley worked closely with Linda Bambara for 7 years as a project coordinator for one of Lehigh's field-based programs, working with transition-age youth and adults with developmental and intellectual disabilities to provide them with meaningful inclusive community experiences, such as employment and postsecondary education. As project coordinator, she trained master-level students in special education on how to design and implement community-based instruction, positive behavior supports in community settings, and social skills instruction in natural environments. Ms. Singley currently works as a disability support specialist at Cedar Crest College.

Acknowledgments

Many colleagues and friends deserve thanks and recognition for their contributions to our understanding of positive ways to support people with difficult behavior and the development of evidence-based practices to put our values into action. These people include Rick and Angela Amado, Fredda Brown, Ted Carr, Glen Dunlap, Mark Durand, Ian Evans, Rachel Freeman, Tim Knoster, Rob Horner, Herb Lovett, Luanna Meyer, and Robert O'Neill.

We also wish to thank Johnna Elliott, Cynthia R. Pitonyak, Christine C. Burton, and Kenna M. Colley for their contributions to a previous edition of this book and for their ongoing and untiring efforts to improve the lives of individuals who have disabilities and need positive behavior supports.

We would also like to acknowledge our editors at Brookes Publishing—Rebecca Lazo, Steve Plocher, and Kimberly Beauchamp—and Project Manager Janet Wehner for their excellent guidance, editing, and persistence in completing this book and others in the series.

Finally, we wish to acknowledge the hundreds of individuals with disabilities and their families, our students, and educators and direct support professionals with whom we have worked over the years. Direct experience and collaboration are the best teachers.

To all the educators, direct support professionals, parents,
and students who are working to create and maintain
inclusive school environments: places where all students have
membership, enjoy social relationships with peers, and have the
needed supports to learn what is important for them to be successful in life

1

Positive Behavior Support

FOCUSING QUESTIONS

- What are the core features and principles of positive behavior support (PBS) that distinguish it from traditional behavior management approaches?
- What is the research base for PBS?
- What are the three tiers of support that make up a schoolwide positive behavior support (SWPBS) network?
- What teaming structures are used to implement school-based PBS?

This book is primarily designed for use by teachers and other members of educational teams who are working together to educate students with learning and behavior problems and their peers in inclusive classrooms and schools. Before the 1970s, many of these children were removed from their families, local schools, and communities and placed in special schools or in institutions. In contrast, inclusive schools welcome all students and provide special education supports and services from a base within general education classrooms. Teaching students who sometimes behave in ways that can be difficult for educators, classmates, parents, and siblings to cope with and understand is one of the challenges of inclusive education (Baker, Blacher, Crnic, & Edelbrock, 2002). Some students are disruptive, noncompliant, and aggressive and appear unable to control

their feelings and behavior, whereas other students are disengaged, are withdrawn, or may even hurt themselves.

In addition to the serious behavior problems that some individual students may display, educators, parents, and other citizens are concerned about the existing and potential lack of safety and discipline in schools (National Center for Education Statistics, 2006). In 2011–2012, about 38% of teachers agreed or strongly agreed that student misbehavior interfered with their teaching, and 35% reported that student tardiness and class cutting interfered with their teaching (Robers, Kemp, Rathbun, & Morgan, 2014). As more is learned about programs and strategies that improve schoolwide discipline, it has become evident that both individual students with behavior problems and the student body as a whole benefit most from proactive, positive, instructionally based approaches (Didden, Korsilius, Van Oor-souw, & Sturmey, 2006). Students need effective instruction and supportive and well-managed schools and classrooms to learn academics; the same holds true for learning social interaction skills and self-control. Furthermore, everyone—students without behavior problems, students with behavior problems, teachers, parents, and administrators—benefits when time that might have been spent responding to dis-ruptive, antisocial, or destructive behav-ior is spent instead in productive teaching and learning activities.

This book describes and illustrates processes and strategies that teachers can use along with parents, administra-tors, and other educators and school staff to provide schoolwide, group, and indi-vidual supports. The framework includes supports to improve the overall social climate in schools as well as supports to address the needs of students with exist-ing or potential behavior problems. The approach is most effective when class-room educators, administrators, school staff, and parents work collaboratively and in concert to create integrated sys-tems for social and academic support that extend along a continuum from less to more specialized. The types of inter-vention applied will differ depending on the students addressed and the degree of specialization required, but school-wide, classwide, and student-specific approaches to improving school disci-pline and student conduct are based on similar conceptions of behavior problems and behavior change and similar perspec-tives on the roles and responsibilities of teachers and schools in addressing them. The interventions and supports employed should not only be confirmed as effective by sound research and practice but also should be suitable for the students, teach-ers, and classrooms involved. In addition, any practice adopted should be consistent with the values on which inclusive educa-tion and PBS are based.

This book helps faculty and educa-tional teams become better collaborative problem solvers; it is not meant to pro-vide a cookbook approach to behavior intervention. Although the principles and many of the practices described are useful in many educational settings, the exam-ples and case studies provided come from our work in inclusive schools.

THREE-TIERED MODEL OF SCHOOLWIDE SYSTEMS FOR STUDENT SUPPORT

This book's organization and content reflect a three-tiered framework for cat-egorizing the systems of behavior inter-vention used in schools that implement PBS (see Figure 1.1). The framework—originally based on the three-tiered model of prevention in public health—provides a way to classify the three tiers of inter-vention strategies required to provide a full continuum of behavior supports in schools (Sugai, Sprague, Horner, & Walker, 2000; Walker et al., 1996). The three tiers of interventions—primary, sec-ondary, and tertiary—are based on their intended prevention outcomes.

Primary prevention (Tier 1) uti-lizes universal supports that are part of a broad, schoolwide system of well-defined, consistent discipline policies, effective aca-demic instruction, and social skill devel-opment. Universal interventions that are applied to all students in a school are effective in inhibiting the development of problem behavior in an estimated 80%–90% of the student population. Secondary prevention (Tier 2) focuses on students (estimated at 5%–15% of students) who exhibit risk behaviors such as poor school performance, affiliation with violent peer groups, and poor social skills. The selected interventions (e.g., adult mentors, self-management support, social skills train-ing) designed for these students often are delivered to small groups of students with similar emerging behavior problems

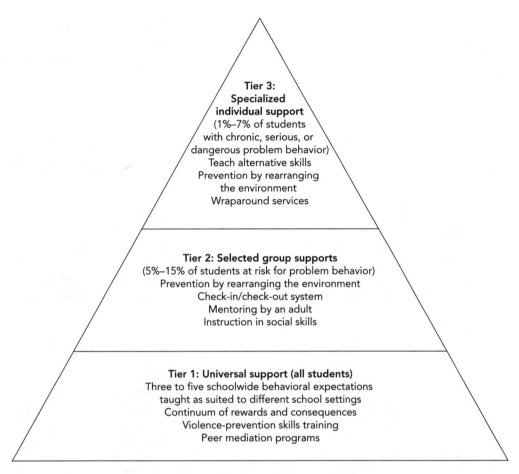

Figure 1.1. Framework for a three-tiered system of school-based positive behavior support. (*Source:* Walker, Ramsey, & Gresham, 2004.)

in order to prevent those problems from worsening or becoming chronic. The goal of tertiary prevention measures (Tier 3) is to reduce the harm inflicted and experienced by the 1%–7% of students who display chronic, severe problem behavior. These students require specialized interventions that are more individualized and intensive; they benefit from comprehensive PBS at school but will often need out-of-school services as well (Walker, Ramsey, & Gresham, 2004).

Chapter 1 focuses on the basic principles underlying PBS and its use in schools. Chapter 2 examines a schoolwide systems approach to discipline and universal behavior supports that help create and sustain an environment in which behavior

problems are prevented or more effectively ameliorated. Chapter 3 describes classroomwide practices to enhance academic and social-behavioral outcomes and also addresses ways to provide selected supports for students whose behavior problems are not adequately improved through schoolwide interventions or who experience risk factors for developing more serious problem behavior.

Chapters 4 and 5 address the more specialized, individualized level of PBS required for students who exhibit the most serious problem behaviors. Chapter 4 outlines the process of gathering and analyzing functional behavior assessment (FBA) information to develop individualized behavior support plans. Chapter 5 details intervention strategies and other supports that compose a behavior support plan and ways to monitor and evaluate the plan's effectiveness. Some of the chapters include Student Snapshots or case studies to illustrate how the chapter's topic has been used in schools. When worksheets or other planning tools are described, examples of completed worksheets are included within the chapter. Blank, photocopiable worksheets are provided in Appendix A and are available as a forms download.

This book, like others in the Teachers' Guides to Inclusive Practices series, is designed to be practical and user friendly and provide information about research-based practices that have been effectively applied in typical schools by typical teachers and other members of school teams. The primary intent is to provide teachers, along with the administrators, other educators, support staff, and parents with whom they work, with the foundational and applied knowledge needed to fill their vital role in planning, implementing, and evaluating PBS for the students in their schools and classrooms. Teachers should feel confident that they understand the purposes and general methods being used, even when the guidance and assistance of outside experts is needed, such as when conducting FBAs (see Chapter 4). And, teachers need to know how to advocate for the leadership, resources, and backing needed to empower them to effectively fill their own roles when administrative support is required to put positive behavior approaches into practice.

USING POSITIVE BEHAVIOR SUPPORT IN SCHOOLS

Anyone who has been a teacher knows that there are always some students who have difficulty following the rules, getting along with others, controlling their emotions, or staying focused on the task at hand. Some students seem to get into trouble on purpose or seem to do things that make it difficult for others to want to spend time with them. Some even hurt themselves or others or become involved in gangs and other subcultures that encourage destructive and violent behavior. Why do some children and youth behave in ways that can be so difficult to understand and so damaging to a school's atmosphere?

There are many different theories, models, and approaches to addressing behavior problems. This book describes a PBS approach to helping students with behavior problems. This approach evolved in the 1980s as a movement away from traditional, mechanistic, and even aversive behavior management practices that were being applied to individuals with disabilities and toward behavior intervention grounded in person-centered values and socially valued outcomes (e.g., Donnellan, LaVigna, Negri-Shoultz, & Fassbender, 1988; Evans & Meyer, 1985; Horner et al., 1990; Lovett, 1985). The movement sought to use the principles of behavior change that had been demonstrated through applied behavioral analysis in contrived, isolated laboratories or segregated schools within effective yet practical interventions that could be implemented by educators in regular school settings (Carr et al., 2002). The movement also insisted that behavior-change practices for people with disabilities must be respectful and individualized and result in quality-of-life improvements, instead of only focusing on reducing targeted behavior problems (Evans & Meyer, 1985; Horner et al., 1990).

Contemporary applications of PBS in schools incorporate integrated, school-wide efforts to prevent problems and improve all students' behavior and learning. "Schoolwide PBS (SWPBS) is a set of intervention practices and organizational systems for establishing the social culture and intensive individual behavior supports needed to achieve academic and social success for all students" (Horner, Sugai, & Anderson, 2010, p. 4). Although many features of SWPBS are not novel (e.g., applying behavioral and social learning principles, using direct instruction to teach approved behavior), it is unique in its focus on the whole school as the unit of analysis and the systematic use of the three-tiered approach to improving learning and behavior (Sugai & Horner, 2002). SWPBS emphasizes using collaborative teaming and problem-solving processes to create supports, programs, and other interventions that stress prevention and remediation of problem behaviors by providing effective educational programming and creating a supportive environment. As previously noted, support practices are implemented at three levels of intensity so that the intensity of the supports provided matches the student's level of need.

Although PBS is a complex, multifaceted approach to behavior intervention and therefore challenging to study scientifically, the research base has grown dramatically since the mid-1990s. Implementing SWPBS entails not only an array of evidence-based intervention practices but also a system of procedures and processes (Horner et al., 2010). Evaluating the effectiveness of SWPBS requires examining the three tiers of support practices as well as the systems used to design, deliver, evaluate, and sustain the network of interventions and supports (see Figure 1.2). The use of PBS also has been incorporated into the Individuals with Disabilities Education Improvement Act (IDEA) of 2004 (PL 108-446), strengthening the support for practices such as conducting FBAs and developing individualized PBS plans based on FBAs (see Figure 1.3).

Research is still needed to develop specific guidelines for the most efficient and effective ways to implement and evaluate PBS in schools. Research on punishment-based interventions, however, clearly shows their limited effectiveness on generalization and maintenance of behavior improvements (Strauss, 1994) and their ineffectiveness in reducing the antisocial behavior (e.g., aggression, vandalism) of students with emotional and behavioral disorders (Mayer & Sulzer-Azaroff, 2002). Furthermore, punishment-based interventions run counter to the deep-seated values of equality and respect cherished in our schools and society.

CORE FEATURES AND PRINCIPLES OF POSITIVE BEHAVIOR SUPPORT

The support methods and intervention techniques incorporated within school-based PBS are those that have demonstrated effectiveness, are suitable for implementation by teachers and others in a school setting, and are consistent with values of equality and respect. Several distinct features and principles about the causes of behavior problems, the most appropriate and helpful ways to alter behavior, and the desired outcomes of behavior intervention are at the foundation of a PBS orientation. PBS incorporates five core features and principles that distinguish it from other approaches to behavior intervention. These features may be given slightly different names in various writings on PBS (Bambara & Kern, 2005; Carr et al., 2002; Crone, Hawken, & Horner, 2015), but the underlying concepts remain consistent. The features apply to each of the three levels of behavior support—primary, secondary, and tertiary—but are implemented differently depending on whether the support is schoolwide, for a smaller group of students, or for an individual student.

1. Behavior Is Learned and Can Change

The question "Why do some children and young adults act in ways that are difficult to understand, disturbing to others, and even destructive to self, others, and property?" can be answered this way from a PBS perspective: A person's behavior is a function of the interaction between the person and the environment. According to this theory,

What the Research Says

Effectiveness of Positive Behavior Support and Future Research Needs

Schoolwide positive behavior support (SWPBS) has been effectively implemented in a wide range of contexts—urban, rural, and suburban settings; elementary and middle schools; and both public and alternative settings (Goh & Bambara, 2012; Horner, Carr, Strain, Todd, & Reed, 2002; Snell, Voorhees, & Chen, 2005). Given training and technical assistance, typical intervention agents, including teachers, administrators, and school psychologists, have demonstrated accurate implementation of research-based intervention practices, along with the organizational systems required to sustain them. Literature reviews and individual studies supported the following findings about the effectiveness of the continuum of supports that compose SWPBS and the research that is still needed to promote the most effective applications of positive behavior support (PBS) in schools and community settings.

Universal Level

Case studies and quasi-experimental studies have suggested that SWPBS can have the following outcomes: 1) reduced office disciplinary referrals, 2) reduced out-of-school suspensions, 3) improved academic achievement, 4) increased perceptions of school safety, and 5) reduced rates of disruptive behavior (Curtis, Van Horne, Robertson, & Karvonen, 2010; Lassen, Steele, & Sailor, 2006; Luiselli, Putnam, Handler, & Feinberg, 2005; Medley, Little, & Akin-Little, 2008; Nelson, Martella, & Marchand-Martella, 2002; Simonsen, Britton, & Young, 2010; Solomon, Klein, Hintze, Cressey, & Peller, 2012; Swanson, 2011; Warren et al., 2006).

Randomized controlled studies comparing accurately implemented SWPBS with typical school discipline practices report a significant reduction in office disciplinary referral levels and student suspensions, as well as an increase in overall perceived school safety (Bradshaw et al., 2010; Horner et al., 2009), and a higher proportion of third graders passing state reading assessments (Horner et al., 2009). Training and technical assistance were functionally related to implementation fidelity and improved results in both of the aforementioned studies.

Secondary Level

Research suggests that secondary-level supports that effectively prevent or decrease problem behaviors include classroom practices such as increased daily progress monitoring, adult attention, positively stated expectations, explicit social skills instruction, group-based contingencies, and positive reinforcement for desired behaviors (Simonsen, Myers, & Briere, 2011).

The most evaluated secondary-tier intervention is a check-in/check-out system (McIntosh, Kauffman, Carter, Dickey, & Horner, 2009; Simonsen et al., 2011). The check-in/check-out system is designed to give students with nondangerous behavior more contact with adults who provide additional instruction, feedback, and reinforcement regarding expected behavior (Campbell & Anderson, 2011). Check-in/check-out is efficient and inexpensive to administer and has proven effective in decreasing off-task behavior and increasing academic engagement as compared with typical practice (McIntosh et al., 2009; Simonsen et al., 2011). Check-in/check-out is described more fully in Chapter 3.

Tertiary Level

Reviews of research on individualized PBS found function-based interventions that employed antecedent manipulations, teaching replacement behaviors that match the function of the problem behaviors, and positive reinforcement for appropriate behavior or use of alternate skills consistently demonstrated positive results (Horner et al., 2002; Snell et al., 2005).

PBS interventions consisting of antecedent manipulations, teaching alternative skills, and function-based consequences were found to be equally effective across diverse student populations and educational settings, including inclusive classrooms, in a meta-analysis of function-based interventions conducted in school settings (Goh & Bambara, 2012).

Figure 1.2. Effectiveness of positive behavior support and future research needs.

Critical Features of SWPBS that Have Not Been Adequately Researched

Few experimental assessments of SWPBS have been conducted (Horner et al., 2009). Therefore, it is difficult to know precisely which aspects of the supports provided to students precipitated the social and academic improvements associated with implementation. In particular, further examination of the relationship between SWPBS implementation and effective instruction is needed to tease out the links between improved student social behavior and academic achievement (Horner et al., 2009).

Identification of mediators (i.e., variables that are influenced by PBS implementation and, in turn, influence outcomes; examples include teachers' sense of efficacy and schools' organizational health) and moderators (i.e., variables that affect the direction or strength of the relation between PBS implementation and outcomes; examples include school size and implementation quality) are needed to increase the understanding of the impact of SWPBS on students and school personnel (Bradshaw et al., 2010).

Although a basic assumption of the three-tiered model for SWPBS is that quality implementation of Tier 1 practices will reduce the need for Tier 2 and Tier 3 supports, research has not confirmed this theory. There is a general absence of studies that demonstrate that implementation of SWPBS as a whole model reduces the need for intensive individualized supports. Furthermore, there is an absence of research that examines how the entire model affects the performance of students with disabilities.

Research on SWPBS implementation in high schools is limited. Research that has been conducted suggests that achieving and sustaining high-fidelity implementation, particularly of targeted and individualized supports, presents unique challenges (Bohanon et al., 2006; Warren et al., 2003).

---

which is sometimes referred to as an *ecological theory* of behavior, behavior problems are not just a reflection of some emotional or mental disturbance that dwells within the person (Hobbs, 1975). Although it is true that behavior is affected by individual biochemical, cognitive, physical, and psychosocial characteristics, behavior also is strongly affected by the environment in which one functions. Factors in the environment that influence behavior include the physical space, the people present, the

---

The Individuals with Disabilities Education Improvement Act (IDEA) of 2004 (PL 108-446) includes several requirements concerning school disciplinary procedures and strategies for addressing behavior problems of students with disabilities.

1. The use of positive behavior support (PBS) must be considered in two situations:
    a. During the development, review, and revision of an individualized education program (IEP) for a child whose behavior impedes his or her learning or the learning of others, the IEP team must consider, if appropriate, strategies to address that behavior.
    b. When a child with a disability violates a code of student conduct and is removed from his or her current placement for more than 10 consecutive school days (unless the removal is due to certain specific reasons, such as behavior that resulted in bodily injury or other zero-tolerance offenses) and if the local education agency, the parent, and relevant members of the IEP team determine that the conduct was a manifestation of the child's disability, the IEP team must conduct a functional behavioral assessment (FBA) and implement a behavioral intervention plan (BIP) for the child. If a BIP already has been developed, the team must review the BIP and modify it as necessary to address the behavior.
2. The IDEA does not specifically prohibit any particular behavior intervention strategies, but it does require that the behavior support plans developed for students who receive special education be based on an FBA process such as the one described in this book and that PBS be considered.

Figure 1.3. Individuals with Disabilities Education Improvement Act (IDEA) Amendments of 2004 (PL 108-446) and positive behavior support.

social atmosphere, the events and activities, and the rules and norms. The environment can elicit as well as inhibit certain types of behavior. For example, most people behave quite differently at a soccer game and in a library. The atmosphere at a soccer stadium elicits enthusiastic cheering and conversation, whereas the atmosphere in a library discourages such loud activities. Some people feel more at ease at a soccer game, whereas others feel more comfortable in a library because of the personal traits and previous experiences that each person brings to a situation. Personal factors, however, can interact differently with the environment at different points in time: A person who typically enjoys soccer games may leave early rather than remain at a game when she or he gets a migraine headache.

Some children and youth have been taught effective social interaction and self-control skills. Such skills are weak or lacking, however, for some students, including those with and without disabilities. Students with weak self-management skills may use immature, impulsive ways to accomplish their goals when the environment presents a situation calling for tolerating frustration, coping with hurt feelings, or delaying gratification. Students who are frequently off task, disengaged, disorderly, and noncompliant either may not have learned the rules for deportment at school or may not share the values behind them.

In addition, some children and youth have unintentionally been taught to use problem behaviors as a way to communicate their wants and needs (e.g., the desire to remain at recess rather than go to math class, the need for help in completing a difficult assignment, the wish for someone to sit with them at lunch, the desire to be left alone). Serious problem behaviors such as tantrums, aggression, and self-injury may be disturbing to others, and educators certainly want to help students to stop doing them. Some students who exhibit these behaviors, however, literally do not have better ways to get their wants and needs

met. Also, the disturbing behaviors must be working for the student in some way—that is, they are being reinforced at least some of the time or the student would probably stop using them.

The good news about both of these behavior problems—those that reflect a lack of teaching and those that result from having been inadvertently taught the wrong behavior—is that students' behavior reflects the interaction of their biology and previous learning with the current context. Problem behavior can be learned, and it also can be changed through learning. Educators and other members of educational teams cannot completely control the school environment, but they can make numerous adjustments to the environment that will elicit approved behavior and inhibit problem behavior. They can teach the school rules as well as social skills and self-management strategies that will help students get along during their school years and in the future. And, they can identify the specific skills they need to teach as replacements for serious problem behaviors. This point leads to the second core feature of a PBS orientation: Behavior problems cannot be simply removed; instead, students can learn other ways to achieve their wants, needs, and desired outcomes. Appropriate behavior must be increased to reduce problem behavior.

2. Support Is Based on the Function of Behavior

Understanding the way the environment or context interacts with students' biology, psychology, and learning experiences is a major principle underlying the PBS approach and is crucial when designing effective supports. If a class of first graders who have not learned school rules and basic self-control strategies is left unsupervised in the cafeteria, then the result is predictably problematic. If Roberto craves adult attention and repeatedly receives more attention for acting out than for sitting quietly and doing his schoolwork, then it is not surprising that Roberto continues to act out. If Jewel, who has disabilities that make communication very difficult for her, is given a series of challenging tasks and is uncomfortable from sitting too long, then she may cry or shriek in protest.

Analyzing the patterns and relationships among students' problem behaviors, the conditions in the environment that precede them, and the ways the behaviors are reinforced can reveal the function of the behavior. It is helpful to think of problem behaviors as having one or both of two broad purposes: obtaining something or escaping or avoiding something. Problem behavior most often serves a social-communicative function: It serves as a way to influence people and the external world. Problem behavior is controlled less often by internal factors such as having too little or too much internal stimulation. The purposes or functions of behavior problems are

- Obtaining attention, nurturance, comfort, or help

- Obtaining something tangible or a preferred activity

- Obtaining sensory stimulation (e.g., deep pressure, visual stimulation, endorphin release)

- Escaping or avoiding tasks or activities

- Escaping or avoiding attention or other social interaction

- Escaping sensory stimulation (e.g., noise, itching, pain, hunger)

Effective PBS requires understanding what people obtain or avoid by using problem behavior. This is not to say that people necessarily use problem behavior intentionally to achieve these purposes; however, research has shown that these are the consequences that commonly maintain problem behavior (Horner & Carr, 1997).

All three tiers of PBS use a function-based approach to intervention but with degrees of specificity and rigor that correspond to the relevant intervention focus. Tier 1's supports are universal, so they are not based on analyzing the purpose of problem behavior for an individual student. Universal supports are designed, however, to be sensitive to predictable patterns in students' behavior and the ways behavior varies according to factors in the environment, such as the amount of structure and supervision present. Universal supports primarily focus on teaching approved behaviors to all students and then ensuring that the environment supports their use.

Tier 2 interventions targeted to students with emerging behavior problems or at-risk profiles are designed to match students with similar needs for environmental structure, social-behavioral skills, and reinforcement. These matches may be based on a simple FBA that relies on indirect methods, such as a teacher interview or self-reflection, to determine antecedents that are predictive of problem behavior, behaviors that should be improved, and what the student gains or avoids when using the problem behavior (see Chapter 3). Interventions at this level are applied in similar fashion for groups of students but may be somewhat customized based on functional assessment results. For example, an intervention such as a check-in/check-out system that uses adult attention as reinforcement would need to be modified for students whose problem behavior is motivated by gaining peer attention (see Chapter 3).

In contrast with the secondary tier's simple FBA, a plan based on a comprehensive FBA is implemented when a student has serious, chronic behavior problems that require an individualized plan for PBS. This assessment process is used to develop and sometimes test hypotheses about the ways the environment is setting the stage for and then reinforcing problem behavior (see Chapter 4). This FBA involves gathering data through indirect and direct observation methods and analyzing those data for patterns of behavior for the student. One of the most important findings of research on PBS is that the likelihood of success significantly increases when systematically collected information about a person's moderate-to-severe problem behavior and the environmental variables associated with the behavior is used as the basis for behavior support interventions (Carr et al., 1999; Didden et al., 2006; Ingram, Lewis-Palmer, & Sugai, 2005; Newcomer & Lewis, 2004; Scotti, Evans, Meyer, & Walker, 1991).

The following Student Snapshots describe children and young adults the authors have known who were members of general education classes in inclusive schools and whose educational teams conducted FBAs from which to build individualized PBS plans. Their behaviors help illustrate the varied purposes of problem behaviors.

Student Snapshot

Abby is 6 years old and in first grade. She has a significant intellectual disability and mild cerebral palsy. She speaks only a few words and has no other conventional communication system. When Abby wants more juice at snack time or does not want to put the books away when it is time to clean up after recess, she points to the thing she wants and shrieks. Her teachers and the classroom instructional assistant often feel that there is virtually nothing that Abby likes to do except eat snacks and look at books. It is quite clear that Abby is saying, "I want juice" or "I want the books" when she shrieks and cries. Her shrieking serves to get something tangible.

Student Snapshot

Austin is a second grader who has a difficult time coping with frustration. It sometimes seems like he is walking a tightrope and any little breeze can knock him off balance. His teacher has noticed that Austin often "loses it" when he is given independent activities that take more than about 3–5 minutes to complete or when the class is doing learning center rotations and Austin has to switch from a center he likes to one he does not like. Austin can communicate quite well when he is calm and engaged in an activity; however, when he becomes frustrated, he quickly escalates from loud complaining to destroying and throwing materials to trying to leave the room. These behaviors seem to be a way for him to say, "This is too hard! I can't do this!" Austin's behaviors serve the function of escape or avoidance of a difficult task.

Student Snapshot

Sophia is a fourth grader with autism. She uses a few words and signs and has some very basic reading, writing, and number skills; however, she is not adept at communicating her wants, needs, and feelings. Sophia sits and rocks back and forth when she is in a place where there are a lot of people, noise, and confusion. She appears to use this behavior as a way to shut out the noise and confusion, the same way that other people might put their hands over their ears and close their eyes. These behaviors enable Sophia to escape stimulation that is aversive to her.

Student Snapshot

Harley is a 10th grader who is classified as having a behavior disorder and obsessive-compulsive disorder for which he takes medication. He has good general knowledge and basic skills and can communicate quite well with the adults in his life; however, Harley lacks skills for initiating social interactions and making friends with peers. When he wants to interact with peers, he may approach them and make a rude or off-color comment as he laughs loudly, or he may become physically aggressive. Although these behaviors do not help Harley to make friends, he usually gets a dramatic reaction from his peers. Harley seems to crave attention so much that he wants any type of peer attention, whether it is positive or negative.

Coping with the behaviors displayed by some students is a difficult task for teachers and parents; the goal is to teach these students other ways of expressing themselves and getting their wants and needs met in legitimate ways. Teachers and parents will not be able to help the student meet his or her needs, however, unless they understand the purpose or purposes that a problem behavior serves. Once teachers and parents understand the consequences that are maintaining the behavior and how the behavior works for the student, they are in a better position to develop a plan for change that will help the student learn and use more appropriate behaviors that will serve the same purpose (Bambara & Kern, 2005).

3. Support Emphasizes Prevention and Teaching

The intervention practices used in PBS focus not on manipulating consequences to manage or suppress problem behavior but on preventing problem behavior by improving the environment and teaching 1) school rules, 2) skills that give students the tools to navigate the school context, and 3) ways to accomplish their needs without having to resort to difficult behaviors.

A PBS approach emphasizes using the strategies that educators and other members of school teams have available to them to prevent problem behavior by changing the environment and teaching students the skills they need to be more effective as individuals and as members of their families, schools, and communities. It is the responsibility of educators and other adults whose role is to help students grow and develop to take the first steps to improve behavior. Intervention typically begins with teachers and other adults who have created the settings in which students are required to function. Creating an environment for success is a fundamental intervention strategy when using PBS.

Although PBS uses principles of behavior analysis, it is a much broader and more comprehensive approach than traditional behavior management, which focuses on manipulating contingencies to control behavior. Multiple supports, which vary in intensity across the three intervention tiers,

are used to achieve the meaningful outcomes that are the goal of PBS. As indicated in Figure 1.1, at the primary tier, all students are provided the following supports:

- Active efforts to create a positive, inclusive school climate

- A unified, schoolwide system of discipline that includes positively stated behavior expectations, lessons to teach those expectations as suited to different settings, and a continuum of rewards and consequences

- Teaching additional social interaction and self-management skills (e.g., violence-prevention skills, self-awareness, self-monitoring skills)

- Prevention by changing the environment to alter antecedents that predict problem behavior (e.g., increased supervision of hallways, cafeteria, playground)

- Use of peer-mediated instructional and behavioral strategies (e.g., classwide peer tutoring, peer mediation programs)

At the secondary tier, these multiple supports are somewhat intensified, with increased structure, richer reinforcement, and frequent monitoring of academic and behavioral performance (see Figure 1.1). Students also may receive supplementary instruction in schoolwide behavioral expectations and/or other social-behavioral skills.

At the tertiary level, these multiple supportive features are still more personalized, intensive, and enduring. Individualized PBS plans may include

- Modifications to the classroom environment (e.g., seating in a low-traffic area, quiet place to read)

- Visual supports for classroom participation and self-management (e.g.,

self-monitoring systems, visual schedules, picture cues)

- Individualized scheduling (e.g., plac-
ing student in classes with particular
peers, alternating easy and difficult
subjects or courses, providing additional movement breaks)

- Support of peer buddies, partners, or
tutors

- Instruction in communication and
choice-making skills

PBS plans will indeed include consequences or responding strategies, but
the emphasis is on preventing problem
behaviors from occurring and teaching
new behaviors that are more personally
and socially effective.

4. Supports and Outcomes Are Personally and Socially Valued

The goal of a three-tiered SWPBS system is
to prevent or minimize behavior problems
both currently and in the future. Other
objectives include enhancing social skills
and overall social competence, developing personal responsibility, and pursuing
academic success. The goals of individualized PBS for students with the most serious behavior problems are not limited to
improving specific behaviors of concern
within particular settings, although such
changes constitute one desired outcome.
A PBS approach takes a much broader
view of the possible outcomes of behavior intervention and support—to improve
quality of life.

Goals of PBS include helping students to 1) develop new communication,
social, and self-control skills; 2) increase
and improve interactions and relationships with peers, teachers, and other community members; 3) take more active and
autonomous roles in their classrooms,
schools, and communities; and 4) gain
further educational opportunities and,
eventually, employment. These outcomes

may be preceded by, accompanied by,
or followed by improvements in academic achievement. In addition to the
positive outcomes for the individual student, PBS can result in improved family
quality of life, as indicated by measures
such as improved family interaction (e.g.,
enjoying spending time together) and
increased feelings of safety at home, work,
school, and in the neighborhood (Smith-
Bird & Turnbull, 2005).

The practices described and illustrated in this book were selected based on
their proven effectiveness in preventing or
reducing problem behavior and increasing socially acceptable behavior through
means that are respectful, normalized,
and suited to the age, culture, and gender of the target student or students (Carr
et al., 1999; Horner, Carr, Strain, Todd,
& Reed, 2002; Snell, Vorhees, & Chen,
2005). Along with other criteria, PBS
interventions are judged by the extent to
which they achieve good contextual fit,
meaning the following:

- The procedures are consistent with
teachers', parents', and students' values and beliefs about how students
should be treated.

- Teachers, parents, and others assisting
with implementation have the skills to
implement the support.

- Parents and teachers view the support
as potentially effective and efficient
because the procedures are feasible
and can be implemented within typical routines and activities.

- Adequate resources are available to
implement the support (e.g., staff
time, material resources).

- Administrative support is provided
to ensure that intervention plans are
effectively managed and monitored
(Albin, Lucyshyn, Horner, & Flannery,
1996; Lucyshyn, Kayser, Irvin, & Blumberg, 2002).

In short, schoolwide interventions and supports must be acceptable to the school community, be easy to implement, and yield noticeable results (McIntosh, Filter, Bennett, Ryan, & Sugai, 2009). Individual plans need to include strategies based on the FBA and specifically chosen to suit the context and be acceptable to the student and his or her PBS team. Otherwise, school team members may not willingly and competently implement interventions (Walker et al., 2004).

5. Comprehensive, Integrated Support Networks Require Schoolwide Systems

A clear finding from research on problem behavior in schools is that multiple systems of support are required to create and sustain safe schools with a positive climate and high levels of academic achievement (Bradshaw, Mitchell, & Leaf, 2010; Carr et al., 1999; Safran & Oswald, 2003). A continuum of least-to-most special or universal-to-individualized supports is needed, including universal interventions for all students, selected interventions for some students, and specialized PBS for a few students. Using effective multitiered PBS requires systems and processes to ensure sustained high-fidelity implementation, including staff buy-in and commitment to the values and practices associated with PBS, administrative support at the district and school levels, collaborative teaming by school-focused teams and student-centered teams, family and student involvement, ongoing professional development, effective horizontal and vertical communication, technical assistance, and data-based decision making (Bambara, Nonnemacher, & Kern, 2009; Coffey & Horner, 2012; Mathews, McIntosh, Frank, & May, 2013).

Supports for students with severe, long-standing emotional or behavioral disorders may need to extend outside of school and involve multiple agencies and individuals other than those who typically serve on school-based teams. The needs of students with severe emotional or behavioral disorders for services and supports outside the school setting also are addressed through wraparound systems of care that address both the student's and the family's needs and strengths. Person-centered planning may be the process used in these cases to develop strategies for improving the student's quality of life (see Chapter 5; Scott & Eber, 2003).

POSITIVE BEHAVIOR SUPPORT TEAMS

Preventing or ameliorating any level of antisocial, disruptive, or destructive behavior calls for a team effort involving parents, teachers, psychologists, administrators, and other knowledgeable and committed people, whether the problem is minor misbehavior that frequently occurs schoolwide or the severe, chronic behavior problems of a few students. A team approach brings together different ideas, knowledge, and skills. Educators know how to teach and manage classrooms; parents know their child best; psychologists and behavior specialists have expertise in behavior change principles and practices; and administrators understand how to deploy resources, garner political support, facilitate communication, and maintain data systems. Used alone, these different skills are not enough for a successful schoolwide approach to behavior support; however, each person's skills are more powerful when they are used together.

Schools that implement effective PBS systems use various team configurations. Creating three separate teams to facilitate each level of intervention (i.e., universal, selected/group, specialized or student specific) is one possible approach. Other schools, however, institute two permanent teams: 1) a SWPBS planning team (sometimes called a SWPBS leadership team) that coordinates the comprehensive schoolwide effort and 2) a student-focused PBS team (sometimes called a student support team or behavior support team) that coordinates selected or Tier 2 interventions and lends support and expertise to individual student teams (Todd, Horner, Sugai, & Sprague, 1999). Whereas some members of the student-focused PBS team take the lead responsibility for planning and facilitating selected group interventions, others focus more on providing guidance to individual students' support teams, if needed.

The specific activities undertaken by the schoolwide planning team and student support team are described in detail in the ensuing chapters. What follows here is an overview of the composition of the two teams and the collaborative processes they use to meet, make decisions, and develop action plans.

Schoolwide Positive Behavior Support Leadership Team

The membership of the SWPBS leadership team should provide broad representation of stakeholders within the school and community—administrator, general education teachers from multiple grade levels, special educator, paraprofessional or other support staff member, parent, school psychologist, or counselor. Many school systems have behavior support coordinators or specialists who are assigned to assist several schools' leadership teams. SWPBS leadership teams are most efficient and effective when there are no more than 8–10 members (Todd, Horner, Sugai, & Sprague, 1999). The schoolwide planning team is most familiar with the data that can indicate the prevalence and distribution of office discipline referrals (ODRs) and other student data that are reported at the administrative level.

The roles and responsibilities of team members must be clear, which is true for any efficient and effective educational team. The SWPBS team should determine a facilitator or coach who will make sure the team meets regularly and follows agreed-on meeting processes and team-developed action plans. Administrators may not necessarily attend every team meeting, but they should ensure that team members have access to adequate professional development, time for meetings, and consultative support if needed. Administrators also need to communicate the importance of the PBS initiative to the school community (it is recommended that the initiative be one of the top three priorities in the school's strategic plan [Todd, Horner, Sugai, & Sprague, 1999]) and acknowledge the team's efforts and the resulting successes.

All leadership team members do not need the same level of knowledge and expertise in behavioral assessment and intervention, but all members need to be supportive of the PBS approach. All members are responsible for learning the fundamentals of FBA and the collaborative problem-solving process needed to create and sustain SWPBS, regardless of their baseline level of experience. Training is available in most states through the U.S. Office of Special Education Programs' National Technical Assistance Center on Positive Behavioral Interventions and Supports (http://pbis.org).

Student Support Team

The PBS team that coordinates selected (or Tier 2) supports also must include an administrator, general education and special education faculty, parents or guardians, and members with FBA/PBS expertise such as a behavior support specialist, school psychologist, or counselor. The team may sometimes invite ad hoc members with expertise in particular programs or strategies being implemented (e.g., social skills, conflict management). Supplementary team members or consultants from the school district office, a nearby university, or a technical assistance center may be needed to round out the team's expertise, particularly in the area of conducting FBAs (Horner, Albin, Sprague, & Todd, 2000).

A student support team needs a team coordinator to manage the screening of students for selected interventions, planning FBAs, and developing and monitoring interventions. This person might be a school psychologist, special education teacher, consulting teacher, or behavioral consultant. The coordinator is typically responsible for organizing team meetings and ensuring that all team members are informed about team decisions and serves as liaison between school and out-of-school team members.

Individual Positive Behavior Support Teams

An individual PBS team for a student with serious and/or chronic behavior problems often has two iterations: The whole team, which plans for the FBA and makes major decisions about services and intervention, and the core team, which implements and monitors FBA assessments and the PBS plan on a day-to-day basis. When the student receives special education services (which is likely to be the case), the whole team will include the members of the student's individualized education program (IEP) team—the student's special education and general education teachers; the parent(s); and, if necessary, related services providers, counselors, psychologists, and paraeducators. If the student receives support from outside mental health agencies, then representatives from these organizations may be included as needed.

In addition to being required by IDEA and principles of best practice in behavior support, involving family members and other people who have an ongoing

relationship with the student leads to more effective interventions and supports (Carr et al., 1999). Families have important knowledge about their children's lives and are deeply affected by behavior problems and supports (Dunlap, Newton, Fox, Benito, & Vaughn, 2001).

The individual student team members may need assistance in conducting the FBA and designing a PBS plan, depending on their level of expertise. Students with significant intellectual, emotional, or behavioral disabilities who have severe, long-standing behavior problems can have needs so complex that additional expertise is needed. A member of the student support team may be able to lend expertise to the team. If not, a school district behavior specialist or an outside technical assistance provider may be needed, at least to conduct an FBA or functional analysis. Many school support teams, however, find that as they gain skill and experience in using the process detailed in Chapters 4 and 5, they are able to address many problems with limited outside expertise.

Team Approach to Decision Making

Developing and implementing plans for schoolwide, group, or individual behavior support requires a commitment to regular team meetings and ongoing communication among team members and others involved in or affected by the plan. Many teachers have had frustrating experiences with meetings and group decision making. Teams can spend too much time sharing stories and never arrive at any decisions or action plans. A member who controls the discussion and does not give others a chance to contribute sometimes can dominate the team. Collaborative teams function more effectively and efficiently when they establish norms and standard operating procedures. The following are some strategies for making team meetings and the team decision-making process both cooperative and efficient:

1. Begin and end the meeting on time.

2. Develop an agenda either before each meeting or at the beginning of the meeting. Begin each meeting by setting time limits for each agenda item.

3. Adopt or develop a team meeting form to use for writing down the agenda and the decisions made by the team. A sample Team Meeting Agenda and Minutes form is shown in Figure 1.4. If the Team Meeting Agenda and Minutes form is completed on paper, then make photocopies and distribute them at the meeting's end. Or, if all team members have access to computers, then an electronic template can be created so that minutes can be entered during the meeting and the completed form can be electronically distributed.

4. At each team meeting, ask team members to adopt specific roles. If a group has more than four members, then some members may not have a particular assigned role at each meeting. Consider rotating roles at different meetings in order to distribute leadership among team members and ensure that the team's decisions reflect everyone's contributions. Some roles that many teams have found necessary are

   - *Facilitator:* Keeps the meeting moving, making certain that each agenda item is addressed and that the team stays focused on the tasks at hand

   - *Recorder:* Records team decisions and makes certain that all team members receive a copy of the minutes

   - *Timekeeper:* Keeps team members aware of time spent and time remaining in the meeting; makes certain that the team sticks to time limits agreed on for the meeting

   - *Observer:* Gives team members feedback on the group process (e.g., "It seems like we are making decisions before we have evaluated all of the possible solutions we generated," "We need to remember to listen to one another's ideas more carefully")

5. Use an explicit series of problem-solving steps when making decisions about how to solve problems or issues the team has identified:

   - Clearly identify the problems or issues that need to be addressed.

   - Gather information about the problem in order to develop a hypothesis about why the problem is occurring and an observable, measurable goal statement.

   - Generate potential solutions and then evaluate the pros and cons of each potential solution. Cross off ideas that do not meet the team's agreed-on criteria (e.g., feasible, good contextual fit, only as specialized as necessary).

   - Organize the best ideas into an action plan that specifies who agrees to do which specific tasks and by when.

6. Establish accountability. It is important that everyone pitches in and helps, and team members should not only accept responsibilities but also gently hold other team members accountable. Many plans have failed not because they were bad ideas but because they were never actually used, or not used as intended. One way to reinforce accountability is to begin each meeting by reviewing the tasks that were assigned to each team member at the previous meeting. It also is crucial to evaluate the impact of any supports or interventions that were implemented. If the desired effects are not evident, then it is time to cycle through the

Team Meeting Agenda and Minutes

Team: _Valley View Middle School positive behavior support (PBS)_   Date: _9/22/2014_
leadership team

People present/role today: Absentees:

Josh Randall (facilitator)   _Nadia Wells_   _Shania Whittaker_

Rosa Oyos (timekeeper)   _Anne Marie Dotson_

Mike McDonald (recorder)

Gabe Bennis (observer)

Purpose of meeting: _Schoolwide PBS training year_

Agenda items	Decisions/actions	Who and by when?
1. Report on action items from last meeting.	• Faculty and staff agreed to three schoolwide behavioral expectations at Friday's workday: respect yourself, respect others, respect property. • A graph was created to display office discipline referral (ODR) data.	Everyone keep up the good work!
2. Office behavior expectations for different settings: halls, classrooms, cafeteria, bathrooms, bus and bus stop, locker room, media center, auditorium.	Created matrix and began listing expectations for each setting.	Will complete the matrix as a team at next meeting.
3. Review data on ODRs and attendance.	ODR forms show inconsistencies in reporting. Need clearer instructions for using office forms.	Josh and Nadia will draft written instructions by next meeting.
	Date: _9/29/2014_	Time: _3:15 p.m.–4:00 p.m._

Agenda items for next meeting

1. _Complete matrix with behavioral expectations for different settings._
2. _Review and finalize instructions for office forms._
3. _Discuss lesson plans for teaching behavioral expectations._

Figure 1.4. Sample Team Meeting Agenda and Minutes. (A blank, photocopiable version of this form is available in Appendix A, and blank and filled-in versions are available in the forms download.)

problem-solving process again. See King-Sears, Janney, and Snell (2015) for more detail on collaborative teaming.

CONCLUSION

SWPBS is organized into three tiers—primary, secondary, and tertiary—creating a continuum of intervention practices and operating systems matched with the intensity of students' needs. The intervention practices at each tier are evidence based, focused on preventing problem behaviors and teaching approved behaviors, and feasible for use by teachers and other school staff in typical school and classroom contexts. SWPBS requires effective organizational systems to ensure that student needs are identified early, matched with suitable supports, and regularly monitored. The organizational systems essential to effective and efficient SWPBS include team-based planning and implementation and ongoing in-service professional development for faculty and staff. In addition, teams use data to ensure that interventions are accurately implemented and students are making the intended social-behavioral and academic progress. The intervention practices and organizational systems essential to each tier of the SWPBS framework are described in detail in the ensuing chapters.

2

Schoolwide Positive Behavior Support

FOCUSING QUESTIONS

- What are the benefits of primary-tier SWPBS?
- What are the elements of an effective schoolwide discipline approach?
- What are research-based programs for teaching students to solve social and behavior problems, including prevention of bullying?
- What steps do schools use to establish primary-tier SWPBS, and how do schools ensure that these interventions are implemented with fidelity and sustained over time?

> Every school must make the creation of a safe and supportive learning community one of its highest priorities. Each component of this phrase—safe, supportive, learning, community—is critical. Schools may be safe and orderly, but if they fail to build a supportive community and press for high academic expectations, students learn little. Similarly, schools may be warm and supportive, but if they have low expectations for their students, little learning takes place. (Learning First Alliance, 2001, p. 1)

SWPBS is conceived as a continuum of tiered supports that vary in intensity, complexity, and the number of students targeted (see Chapter 1). The universal interventions and prevention programs that are the subject of this chapter are used with all students in the school and are estimated to prevent antisocial behavior for 80%–90% of a school population (Walker et al., 2004). The processes, structures, and practices designed to prevent behavior problems at the broadest level have come to be known as universal supports within SWPBS (Sugai & Horner, 2002). These interventions are designed to create a safe, healthy learning environment where behavior problems are avoided or prevented from worsening and students learn self-discipline and effective interpersonal skills. To be maximally effective, the universal supports are implemented within SWPBS and are a part of a comprehensive system of behavior support delivered at three levels of intensity, from broad but low-intensity universal supports, to selected practices for students at-risk for behavior problems, and finally to individualized, intensive supports for the few students with chronic and/or dangerous behavior problems. Tier 1 of SWPBS, as a primary prevention system, has the important goal of improving the school's overall behavioral climate and limiting the number of students who require more individualized, specialized (and resource-intensive) supports. Primary-tier supports are delivered by all adults in the school to all students in all settings (Sugai & Horner, 2002). The design, implementation, and evaluation of those universal supports are guided by a SWPBS leadership team (which was introduced in Chapter 1 and whose work is described more fully later in this chapter).

Effective primary-tier SWPBS efforts entail four components: 1) a safe and responsive school climate, 2) a unified approach to school discipline, 3) active development of students' social and emotional competencies (e.g., problem-solving and conflict resolution skills), and 4) effective academic instruction (Sugai & Horner, 2002). Each of these four key components incorporates using interventions and support strategies that are evidence based, suited to the context, and efficient. Organizational systems to create action plans, make decisions, and ensure that strategies are accurately and sustainably implemented are also necessary.

This chapter first details the rationale for primary-tier SWPBS, then describes three of the four components of primary-tier interventions—a safe and responsive school climate, a unified approach to school discipline, and active development of students' social and conflict resolution skills. Effective classroom management and academic instruction are briefly discussed in Chapter 3, in the context of classwide supports at the Tier 2 level, but it should be noted that effective behavior management and effective instruction most likely complement one another in generating positive effects on students' academic and social development. The final section of the chapter examines the systems-change aspects of initiating and sustaining SWPBS.

RATIONALE FOR PRIMARY-TIER SCHOOLWIDE POSITIVE BEHAVIOR SUPPORT

Before the advent of PBS approaches, and continuing today in many schools, school discipline programs tended to be reactive and exclusionary, focusing on using negative consequences for misconduct. Since the emergence of zero-tolerance policies in the early 1990s, more rigid and extreme applications of suspension and expulsion policies have been mandated, often resulting in applying the same negative consequences for all offenses, from firearms, drugs, alcohol, and fist fighting to showing disrespect, swearing, and bringing nail clippers to school (Skiba, 2000).

There are a number of reasons why reactive, exclusionary, zero-tolerance approaches to school discipline are ill advised. First, there is little evidence to support their effectiveness in improving student behavior or improving school safety (Maag, 2012; Skiba & Peterson, 2000). Exclusionary discipline practices (e.g., suspension, expulsion) ignore the function of behavior and, for some students, act as reinforcement (Tobin, Sugai, & Colvin, 1996). Using punishment and disciplinary removal not only does not work for students with chronic antisocial behavior, but it is also likely to result in a greater intensity and frequency of antisocial behavior (e.g., aggression, vandalism) and a greater likelihood of academic failure and dropping out of school (Bowditch, 1993; Mayer, 1995). Without intervention that actually helps them to improve their behavior and achievement, these students have a high likelihood of experiencing numerous negative life outcomes, including involvement in the correctional, welfare, and mental health systems (Sprague et al., 2001). An additional drawback to using punishment and exclusion is the negative effect on students' social and emotional states, the relationships between the students and the adults in a school, and the culture of the school (Shores, Gunter, & Jack, 1993; Thorson, 1996).

Second, even if punitive "get tough" approaches to school discipline were able to make schools safer by ridding them of violent behavior, they do not effectively address the most frequent types of behavior problems facing educators. Serious violations such as drugs, weapons, and gang activity occur much less frequently in schools than minor disruptive behaviors, disrespect, bullying, and verbal abuse (Heaviside, Rowand, Williams, & Farris, 1998). Although any victimization (e.g., theft, assault) of other students or school personnel is cause for concern, the rates of such behaviors are not as alarming as some might assume. In 2012, the total rate of victimization at school for students ages 12–18 was 52 victimizations per 1,000 students. Thefts accounted for 24 of those offenses, and serious violent victimizations occurred at the rate of 3 per 1,000 students (Robers et al., 2014). Therefore, expelling the relatively small number of students who do commit serious, violent offenses in school does not rid schools of the more frequent problems of disruptive behaviors or incivility.

Third, reactive, exclusionary discipline practices are administered in a biased way (Skiba et al., 2011). African American students, students who live in poverty, and students with certain disabilities (e.g., behavior disorders, learning disabilities) are consistently disproportionately suspended and/or expelled (Achilles, McLaughlin, & Croninger, 2007; Fenning & Rose, 2007; Skiba & Knesting, 2002)

By contrast, since the 1970s, evidence has shown the success of positive and prevention-oriented approaches to disruptive, violent, and other antisocial behavior in schools (e.g., Sugai &

Horner, 2002). Research on schoolwide disciplinary practices associated with PBS (e.g., actively teaching behavioral expectations and social skills, rewarding appropriate behavior, increasing supervision in problem-prone locations) provides convincing evidence of the success these strategies can have in reducing disruptive and antisocial behavior and creating a positive social climate (Horner et al., 2010; Solomon et al., 2012). Preventing serious violent behavior in schools requires a comprehensive approach that also prevents disruptive and disrespectful behavior, is educationally focused, and maintains the dignity of students, teachers, and other school personnel. The central belief of SWPBS that schools should be places that reduce students' exposure to risk factors while also increasing their exposure to protective factors has strong empirical backing in research on the prevention of emotional and behavioral disorders (Forness, Kavale, MacMillan, Asarnow, & Duncan, 1996; Nelson et al., 2002). Prevention and early intervention for antisocial behavior not only keeps behavior problems from worsening but also impedes the development of academic failure, impaired mental health, social rejection, and social maladjustment (Forness et al., 1996; Lane, Gresham, & O'Shaughnessy, 2002).

Positive, prevention-oriented approaches to school discipline are increasingly advocated by educators, psychologists, parents, university educators, and others who are familiar with the research supporting their effectiveness in increasing behavioral and academic success. Support also comes from the U.S. Department of Education's (2014) guidelines for improving school climate and discipline, which recommended creating positive school climates; using tiered, prevention-oriented supports; promoting social and emotional learning; and involving all school personnel, families, students, and community services.

SAFE AND RESPONSIVE SCHOOL CLIMATE

> School climate refers to the quality and character of school life. It is based on patterns of school life experiences and reflects norms, goals, values, interpersonal relationships, teaching, learning and leadership practices, and organizational structures. A sustainable, positive school climate fosters youth development and learning necessary for a productive, contributing and satisfying life in a democratic society. (Dary & Pickeral, 2013, p. 1)

Creating and sustaining a safe and responsive school climate is a foundational component of SWPBS and requires taking active steps to shape a community where everyone belongs and feels connected. Teaching children and youth to be socially responsible, caring individuals who are adept at forming and maintaining social relationships and who demonstrate good character can seem like a daunting responsibility to educators who also are responsible for their students' academic success. Disorder decreases and academic achievement is facilitated, however, when students' academic experiences occur in classrooms and schools where they feel safe, valued, and cared for (Zins, Weissberg, Walberg, & Wang, 2004). In addition, the social and emotional skills that enable students to be self-directed, make responsible decisions, effectively communicate, and work well with others are essential not only to success in school but also to future success in the workplace, the home, and the community (Elias et al., 1997). A safe and responsive school climate is a universal support that contributes to decreasing students' exposure to risk factors and increasing their exposure to protective factors.

Schools with a positive social and behavioral climate typically evidence these indicators: 1) perceptions by students, teachers, staff, and parents that the school is safe; 2) perceptions by students that they belong and are cared for; 3) clear, unambiguous, and fairly administered rules, rewards, and consequences; 4) effective communication and problem solving among administrators and faculty; 5) high attendance rates; 6) minimal general student misbehavior; 7) low rates of juvenile delinquency and serious behavior problems; 8) student engagement, academic success, and social adjustment; 9) orderly classrooms and public spaces; 10) positive interactions among teachers and students; and 11) high teacher morale (Gottfredson & Gottfredson, 2001; Hernandez & Seem, 2004; Irvin, Tobin, Sprague, Sugai, & Vincent, 2004). Accordingly, the rate of behavioral incidents warranting disciplinary action by administrators is low. School improvement activities that focus on climate enhancement go hand in hand with improving the schoolwide discipline program and teaching social and conflict resolution skills; these efforts all seem to be reflected in a more positive school climate and decreases in disorderly and antisocial behavior (Irvin et al., 2004).

When a school undertakes the development or enhancement of universal-tier PBS, it is crucial that goal statements, support practices, and discipline systems be culturally responsive and inclusive of all students and their families (Sugai, O'Keeffe, & Fallon, 2012). For example, school handbooks and hallway posters should use language, images, and messages that are appropriate for all cultural groups. Schoolwide screening practices should consider possible cultural factors that have a bearing on norms for behavior, and data systems should be structured to enable scrutiny for disproportionality in race and gender in office referrals and the application of negative contingencies.

UNIFIED SCHOOLWIDE DISCIPLINE APPROACH

Safe, responsive, and effective schools have schoolwide discipline systems that are prevention oriented; well defined; clearly communicated to all students, families, teachers, and other school personnel; and consistently implemented. An effective schoolwide discipline approach typically includes the following seven elements (Simonsen, Sugai, & Negron, 2008; Sugai & Horner, 2002):

1. A purpose statement that relates the goal and rationale for the discipline system

2. Three to five clearly defined, positively phrased schoolwide expectations for appropriate behavior, along with observable examples of expected behaviors for different school settings and routines

3. Procedures for directly teaching those behaviors as well as monitoring, prompting, and correcting them

4. A variety of ways to acknowledge appropriate, expected behavior

5. A consistently used continuum of consequences for correcting rule violations

6. Strategies to increase structure and supervision in nonclassroom and classroom settings

7. Procedures for record keeping and decision making

Research showing that schoolwide discipline systems incorporating these features are associated with significant reductions in disruptive and antisocial behavior and the increased perceptions of positive school climate is quite compelling (Lewis, Sugai, & Colvin, 1998; Luiselli, Putnam, & Sunderland, 2002; Nakasato, 2000; Nelson, Martella, & Galand, 1998; Taylor-Greene & Kartub, 2000). Each of these elements—presented as seven steps to follow when creating an effective schoolwide discipline system—is briefly described and illustrated in the following section. The school's overall PBS action plan, which is developed by the school staff under the guidance of the SWPBS leadership team (the work of the SWPBS leadership team is described in the final section of this chapter), guides the implementation of these steps. A series of figures in this section will illustrate aspects of the schoolwide discipline plan used by an elementary school known to the authors. To maintain the school's anonymity, we have changed its name in this book to Mountain View Elementary School. This discipline plan incorporates the components and steps described here.

Step 1: Generate a purpose statement that relates the goal and rationale for the discipline system. Most schools have a mission or purpose statement, but that statement may not be used for ongoing guidance in fostering a positive school climate. The statement should be positively phrased, focus on all staff and students, and relate the desired outcomes of social and academic success for all students. For example, "Mountain View Elementary School is a community of learners. We are all here to learn and grow together and to become good citizens."

Step 2: Identify positively phrased expectations for appropriate behavior, along with observable definitions of the expectations for different school settings and routines. A schoolwide discipline system begins with three to five simple, positive phrases that guide behavioral expectations for the entire school. These essential expectations for behavior emphasize key values on which the school's social and behavioral climate is based. Schools often give a name to their expectations, which might be based on the school name or the mascot. For example, a school whose mascot is the honeybee named its expectations the "Three Bs: Be respectful, Be responsible, Be safe" (Taylor-Greene & Kartub, 2000). These student expectations were called the Steps to Success in another middle school:

1. Be responsible

2. Be respectful

3. Be ready to learn

4. Be cooperative

5. Be safe (Warren et al., 2006, p. 191)

One function of the key expectations for behavior is that they contribute to the sharing of a common language among staff and students so that they can easily communicate about their school's social-behavioral climate. The expectations should be seen in many places and spoken or heard often. For instance, posters using a selected format should be posted in classrooms and in numerous locations around the school (e.g., hallways, library or media center, cafeteria, gymnasium). A school pledge that incorporates the school expectations could be recited each morning. For example, the pledge in a school that has adopted the "Three Bs" might be the following: "As a Hometown Elementary School student, I will be respectful: I will honor all people and their ideas. I will be responsible: I will use my time wisely and do all tasks that are assigned to me. I will be safe: I will keep myself and others from harm."

The general expectations for behavior must be defined as observable examples of behaviors that can be identified by all staff and students. Students cannot learn the approved behaviors if the adults cannot describe and demonstrate them. The definitions must preclude those behavior problems that are of the greatest concern and identify alternative, suitable behaviors for various settings in the school. An assessment of behavior at the schoolwide level enables SWPBS teams to identify common behavior problems that are of greatest concern and their predictable relationships with antecedents in the environment, such as places, times, student groupings, and the context (e.g., the degree of structure and adult supervision provided; Scott & Caron, 2005). For example, the lunchroom, hallway transitions, playground or gym, and bus area

often are likely to set the stage for behavior problems when they are crowded and unsupervised or when helpful physical arrangements and routines have not been established. The general expectations for behavior should be defined more specifically for each nonclassroom and classroom setting or routine.

Figure 2.1 shows Mountain View Elementary School's mission statement, its three major expectations for behavior, and the specific behaviors that define those expectations so that all students and staff can know what behavior that is respectful of self, others, and property looks like in all nonclassroom settings.

Step 3: Design procedures for directly teaching expectations and behaviors and for monitoring, prompting, and correcting them. Initially, all teachers in the school directly teach the specific behaviors that evidence each general expectation through a direct instruction sequence: 1) introduce the expectation (e.g., "Be respectful to self, others, and property in the cafeteria") and give the rationale for being respectful (e.g., "Everyone here is an equal; as equals, we are all equally worthy of respect"; students can help generate reasons why it is important to be respectful); 2) provide clear examples of respectful behavior and nonrespectful behavior within the target setting and ask the students for examples and nonexamples (these can be listed on a T-chart and posted in the classroom); 3) the teacher (and possibly another adult) demonstrates the behavior for a specific setting, pointing out critical features; 4) students practice the behaviors in role-play situations or other activities and are given immediate performance feedback; and 5) the teacher assesses students' overall skill levels and provides feedback.

After delivering initial lessons to teach behavioral expectations, teachers continue to facilitate accurate and fluent performance by cuing and prompting the use of appropriate behavior both in and

Mountain View Elementary School is a community of learners. We are all here to learn, grow, and become good citizens.		
	Respect self	Respect others	Respect property
Hallways	Walk quietly. Stay in self-space. Stay right and face forward.		
Cafeteria	Stay seated. Stay in self-space. Use inside voices. Keep clean.		
Playground	Be safe. Take turns and share. Stay in safe area. Report problems.		
Bathrooms	Keep clean. Report problems. Flush toilet and wash hands.		
Bus room Busses	Stay seated. Stay in self-space. Use inside voices. Stay packed.		
Assemblies	Listen quietly. Stay in self-space. Stay seated.		

Figure 2.1. Key behavior expectations for different school settings. (From the Mountain View Elementary School 2005–2006 Staff Handbook.)

outside the classroom. For example, an elementary school teacher reviews the cafeteria expectations before leaving the classroom to go to lunch: "Remember the four cafeteria expectations: stay seated, stay in self-space, use inside voices, and keep clean." Teachers often add gestures to match each key behavior or provide a quick model; teachers also may remind students of reinforcers that will be available for meeting behavioral expectations.

Schools may decide to emphasize teaching one expectation per week for the first several weeks of the school year, such as during morning announcements or teacher advisory periods. This approach helps to remind all adults in the school to be consistent as they supervise target environments (e.g., hallways, restrooms) and provide positive reinforcement or corrective feedback. If skills are only taught in the classroom and not followed by prompts, active supervision, and positive or corrective feedback, then the levels of

problem behavior in target environments in the school may not decrease (e.g., Lewis et al., 1998).

In order to increase consistency in the schoolwide discipline approach, schools prepare lesson plans for teachers to use when teaching the expectations for each setting. The schoolwide PBS leadership team can take this responsibility, or the larger faculty might develop the plans during an in-service professional development day devoted to the schoolwide discipline system. Figure 2.2 shows a sample lesson plan for teaching hallway expectations at Mountain View Elementary School.

Step 4: Develop a variety of ways to acknowledge appropriate, expected behaviors. A schoolwide reinforcement system should include an array of ways to acknowledge expected behaviors—tangible and social, predictable and unpredictable, frequent and infrequent (Sugai & Horner, 2002). Effective praise—that is, praise that is contingent,

---

1. Discuss the schoolwide expectations for the hallway:

    Walk quietly   Stay in self-space   Stay right and face forward

    Ask the children to tell what they think respectful hallway behavior looks like, sounds like, or feels like. Contrast it with a similar discussion of what disrespectful behavior in hallways looks like, sounds like, or feels like.

2. Present several scenarios to them, and ask them to identify the respectful aspects of each (focusing on the positive examples rather than the negative).

3. Just before going into the hallway, review the expectations of respectful behavior (either as teacher prompts or selecting children to reiterate).

4. Actively teach (not just verbal teaching—go out in the hallway), practice, monitor, and reward (use Buck-a-Roos) appropriate behaviors.

Practice activities

1. Role play: Groups of children demonstrate what respectful hallway behavior looks like, either in an organized line (walking as a class with the teacher) or walking individually without the teacher (e.g., taking a note to the office). Have a few children demonstrate the wrong way to walk in the hallway (in an organized line and walking individually). Cue them to use average misbehaviors (e.g., trying to pass others in line, pushing, walking by a friend so they can talk, touching artwork, kicking walls), not extreme misbehaviors.

2. Students write stories or draw pictures that indicate both the respectful ways to move in the hallway and the inappropriate ways to move about.

3. Practice! Go somewhere as a class; students discuss with peers the respectful behaviors they have practiced.

Figure 2.2.   Sample lesson plan for teaching expected behaviors in the hallway. (From the Mountain View Elementary School 2005–2006 Staff Handbook.)

specific, and genuine—is the centerpiece of a schoolwide reinforcement system. Effective praise communicates exactly what the student did well, and it is given immediately after the desired behavior occurs. Acknowledging positive behavior is one of the best methods for improving prosocial behavior (Ialongo, Poduska, Werthamer, & Kellam, 2001) and contributes to establishing the positive student–teacher relationships that help protect young people from future academic and behavioral problems (Hamre & Pianta, 2001).

A school will also often use a token or ticket system and a range of activities or goods that students may trade for their reward tickets. Each classroom teacher uses these rewards with his or her own students, but all teachers and other staff members may and should bestow reward tickets on any student in the school for engaging in behaviors that demonstrate the schoolwide behavioral expectations (Scott & Caron, 2005). Some examples of acknowledgement or reinforcement systems follow:

- The reinforcement system used in the middle school whose expectations were called High Fives incorporated a High Five coupon that could be redeemed for products or entry into school activities, including raffles, open gym, classroom visits, and Gold Card night (Taylor-Greene & Kartub, 2000).

- Public recognition was given to students at another middle school who successfully demonstrated one of the school's universal behavioral expectations (which were dubbed the Five Steps to Success). For example, students who were successful in demonstrating "being safe" behaviors in the hallways were acknowledged as "certified hallway walkers" via a school announcement over the public address system (Turnbull et al., 2002). A schoolwide ticket or positive referral system was also developed to reinforce desired behavior. Teachers and other school staff would issue a positive referral ticket when they caught a student displaying behaviors related to the Five Steps to Success. Students would then place these tickets in boxes, which were separated by grade level, in the school office. The vice principal pulled a ticket from each box each day and announced the student's name and the universal expectation the student had followed over the school's intercom system. The winning students were called to the office, and the vice principal took their pictures, escorted them to a display case where they selected a prize, and then mounted their pictures with a statement of what expectations they had followed (Turnbull et al., 2002).

- Teachers in one middle school rewarded students with positive behavioral referrals, which were tickets that could be submitted to participate in frequent drawings for special prizes. Prizes included a wide array of desirable items (e.g., stuffed animals, school supplies) and activities (e.g., extra gym time). The names and photographs of students who had won prizes were displayed in a trophy case near the cafeteria (Warren et al., 2006).

Mountain View Elementary's ticket system is described in Figure 2.3. The system utilized tickets that could be bestowed by any teacher or staff member in the school whenever students were witnessed enacting the schoolwide behavioral expectations. A list of the *opportunities* (the term the school community preferred over *rewards*) offered to students is also shown in Figure 2.3. The value given to social interaction opportunities is one thing that stands out about the opportunities available to students in this school. For example, eating lunch with a teacher or the principal was viewed as a special opportunity that carried a high ticket cost.

Step 5: Establish a consistently used continuum of strategies for responding to rule violations. The schoolwide discipline plan must 1) provide clear definitions of behaviors that are to be corrected; 2) give guidance in preventing, interrupting, and correcting behavior problems so that they do not escalate; and 3) specify which consequences are administered by teachers or by school administrators (Horner et al., 2004). The behavior–consequence relationships must be well defined. On-the-spot corrections delivered by teachers for minor misbehaviors (e.g., a brief incident of teasing, running in the hall) are

---

"Buck-a-Roos" are tickets that students earn for demonstrating behaviors in our school that are consistent with our teachings and expectations: respect self, respect others, and respect property. Students will save Buck-a-Roos they earn throughout the school and exchange them later for special opportunities.

Buck-a-Roos are a means for recognizing positive behaviors being used by our students. This is not a deficit-based system. Buck-a-Roos are never taken away from students to punish misbehavior. They are given only to reward positive behavior. It is critically important for us to use positive language and praise along with the Buck-a-Roos to reward students meeting our school expectations. We do not use them in a negative fashion—such as threatening not to give them out.

Things to remember:

- Have around 10 choices
- Mix choices throughout the year
- Set some opportunities high, some low (Note: *High* means a person or schedule change is involved; only use these one to two times per year. *Opportunities* is the term we use instead of *rewards*.)

Figure 2.3. Guidelines for using Buck-a-Roos, a ticket system to acknowledge appropriate behavior. (From the Mountain View Elementary School 2005–2006 Staff Handbook.)

at the lower level of the continuum of consequences. For example, "I saw you running in the hall and almost bumping into other students. I need to see you walking quietly, staying in your self-space, and staying to the right. Please show me that you can do that." A second instance of the same behavior would call for reteaching hallway expectations to the student. Somewhat more serious violations (e.g., a heated verbal exchange between students that stops when a teacher intervenes) are still handled by a teacher and might include mild consequences such as loss of free time or use of a disciplinary technique such as completing a Student Problem Report (see Figure 2.4). The Student Problem Report is designed to help students reflect on their behavior and the schoolwide expectation that they violated and make a plan for how to be more successful in the future. In elementary schools, at least two versions of the report would be needed for different age groups. The report shown in Figure 2.4 is developmentally appropriate for students in the upper grades but not for students in the primary grades.

The school, with facilitation by the SWPBS team, needs to develop a predictable response that is consistently applied by all school staff when more serious offenses (e.g., physical aggression, a heated verbal exchange with threats) and chronic behavior problems occur. If the response includes ODRs (as often is the case), then it is especially important that the referral system include clear definitions of the applicable behaviors, the procedures teachers are to follow when making a referral, and the steps administrators are to follow in response.

The instructions for using office forms and procedures at Mountain View Elementary School are provided in Figure 2.5. An example of a completed office discipline referral form is included in the school's staff handbook, as is a sample copy of the letter sent to parents/guardians to inform them if their child receives a discipline referral.

Step 6: Use strategies to increase structure and supervision in nonclassroom and classroom settings. What school locations tend to be associated with the greatest challenges to behavior management? It has been estimated that 50% of all problem behaviors resulting in discipline referrals occur in nonclassroom settings such as hallways, cafeterias, restrooms, and playgrounds (Colvin, Sugai, Good, & Lee, 1997). Even when schoolwide behavioral expectations have been identified and taught, these unstructured, crowded settings may lack clear behavioral expectations or may be inadequately supervised. The SWPBS team can examine ODRs to detect problem-prone settings, times of day, or student groupings. In addition to uncovering these antecedents of problem behavior, the team can consider the consequences that might be achieved by the problem behaviors occurring in those settings. For example, pushing, running, or verbally harassing peers may work to gain the attention of peers or adults or may enable students to be first in line at lunch. This function-related information can be used to help design routines and structural arrangements to assist in preventing problem behavior and increasing the likelihood of desired behavior (Scott & Caron, 2005). The solutions developed to improve discipline in nonclassroom settings may involve strategies such as the following (see Figure 2.6).

• *Developing, teaching, and reinforcing orderly routines for students to follow:* For example, an assessment of factors contributing to problem behavior in the cafeteria might reveal that too many students are arriving at the cafeteria at once, the location of utensils or condiments interferes with the movement of the line, or there is not a sign on the wall listing the expected cafeteria behaviors. Changing the lunch dismissal schedule, improving the movement of students through

Student Problem Report

Name: _Jonah_ _____   Class: _Ms. Diaz, 4th grade_ _____

Date: _Friday, 10/3/14_ _____   Time (start and stop): _1:30 p.m.–1:40 p.m._ ____

Description of the problem

1. Location and activity or routine:

   _x_ Classroom: _indoor recess_ _____   ___ Playground: _____

   ___ Hall: _____   ___ Cafeteria: _____

   ___ Gym: _____   ___ Bathroom: _____

   ___ Music: _____   ___ Other: _____

2. People involved: _Jonah, Dmitri, Eli, Kayla_ _____

3. Witnesses: _Pretty much the whole class_ _____

4. What happened first:

   ___ Someone told me to do something I did not want to do.

   ___ My work seemed too hard or I made some mistakes in my work.

   ___ I broke a rule or did not listen to adults.

   _x_ I did not get my choice.

   ___ Other: _____

Explain or add details: _I wanted to play dominoes with Eli, but Dmitri got them first because I had_
to finish my math homework before I could have recess. _____

5. What did you do?

   ___ Said inappropriate or disrespectful words   _x_ Yelled or screamed

   ___ Left my assigned area without permission   ___ Refused to participate

   ___ Used physical aggression   _x_ Threw, broke, or destroyed something

   ___ Took something that was not mine   ___ Other: _____

Explain or add details: _I kicked over the domino structure and threw some of the dominoes_
across the room. I was not trying to hit anyone, but one hit Kayla on the leg. I sort of screamed,
"It's not fair." _____

6. How did you feel about what happened?

   ___ Angry   _x_ Frustrated

   ___ Disappointed   ___ Afraid

   ___ Sad   ___ Other: _____

7. How do you think the other student(s) involved felt? _Scared and maybe angry_ _____

Results or consequences of the problem

8. Did your behavior help or hurt you and the others involved? How? _It hurt everyone. I still did_
   not get to play dominoes, I lost recess time, and I scared my friends. _____

9. Did you forget a schoolwide behavior expectation during this incident? Which one(s)? What
   specific respectful behavior did you forget?

   _x_ Respect self: _Do your personal best._ _____

   _x_ Respect others: _Keep everyone safe. Take turns._ _____

   _x_ Respect property: _Use things the way they're supposed to be used._ _____

Figure 2.4.   Student Problem Report.

Figure 2.4. (*continued*)

---

10. List two things you might have done to prevent this incident from happening or to make things turn out better.

   1. *I could ask Eli and Dmitri if I could play dominoes with them.*

   2. *If I did not get to play dominoes, I could choose another game.*

11. What will you do next time to improve your self-control?

   ___ Count to 10.

   _x_ Tell myself something such as, "Calm down. You can handle this."

   ___ Think about the consequences of making a bad choice.

   ___ Other: _____

Student's signature: *Jonah Smithers*

Teacher's signature: *Ms. Diaz*

---

the line, and providing students and supervisors with a visual reminder of cafeteria expectations might improve the situation.

- *Increasing active adult supervision:* Although few teachers want more duty periods, the impact of increased active supervision on student behavior can be significant. Active supervision strategies include scanning the area to signal to students that you are aware of everything that is happening, moving around the setting, and frequently interacting with students (Sugai & Horner, 2002).

- *Using precorrection strategies before students enter the setting:* After teachers have signaled for students to line up to leave the classroom, they review setting-specific rules, verbally prompt and possibly model desired behaviors, and remind students of reinforcers that will be available for meeting expectations.

Figure 2.7 provides the plan devised to improve behavior in the cafeteria at Mountain View Elementary School; the plan clarifies the routines and procedures that teachers, cafeteria aides, and students are to follow.

Step 7: Establish procedures for record keeping and decision making. It is essential for the leadership team to establish

---

There are three office forms:

1. Health/general concern (green form)
2. Celebration (gold form)
3. Discipline referral (blue form): Use this form to send students down to see an administrator for an office offense. Be sure to complete the entire form, explain the incident in detail at the bottom of the form, and use one form for each student. It needs to be kept on file for records. Thank you.

Please note that

- A student should not be sent to the office without a form in hand.
- Students are only to be in the office for health/general concerns or for discipline—no "chill time."
- Teachers are encouraged to use a team or buddy teacher for minor offenses ("chill time").

Figure 2.5. Office forms and procedures. (From the Mountain View Elementary School 2005–2006 Staff Handbook.)

What the Research Says

Universal Interventions Targeted to Nonclassroom Settings

What school locations tend to be associated with the greatest challenges to behavior management? It has been estimated that 50% of all problem behaviors resulting in discipline referrals occur in nonclassroom settings such as hallways, cafeterias, restrooms, and playgrounds (Colvin, Sugai, Good, & Lee, 1997). These unstructured, crowded settings often lack clear behavioral expectations and may be inadequately supervised. Research has suggested several efficient, low-cost interventions that schools can incorporate into their schoolwide unified discipline system to reduce behavior problems in these troublesome settings. The practices include precorrection (e.g., reviewing behavioral expectations for the setting, modeling of desired behaviors), active supervision, and individual and group contingency systems.

Playground

- Lewis, Powers, Kelk, and Newcomer (2002) found that active teaching of playground behaviors and use of group contingencies were effective in reducing problem behaviors on an elementary school playground.
- Lewis, Colvin, and Sugai (2000) examined the combined effects of precorrection by classroom teachers and active supervision by paraprofessionals trained as playground monitors on elementary students' playground behavior. The researchers noted that the intervention was not associated with change in the level of problem behavior because low levels of problem behavior occurred during structured playground activities. The researchers, however, supported the effectiveness of the two antecedent strategies in reducing problem behavior during unstructured playground activities.

Hallways and Other Transition Settings

- Colvin et al. (1997) implemented a 15-minute in-service training session with staff in one elementary school to prepare them to use precorrection and active supervision in transition settings (e.g., entering and exiting the building, going to the cafeteria). Results suggested that the intervention was generally effective and that although the number of supervisors present during a transition did not affect the frequency of problem behaviors, the more times a supervisor interacted with a student, the fewer times problem behavior occurred.
- Johnson-Gros, Lyons, and Griffin (2008) provided school staff with a 30-minute in-service professional development session on using active supervision in hallways during class changes in an effort to reduce unexcused tardies in a high school. The intervention was associated with a decrease in office discipline referrals for tardiness. The specific component behaviors of active supervision that appeared to have the greatest effect on decreasing the number of tardies were 1) being on post, 2) escorting students through the transition area, and 3) briefly interacting with students.
- Kartub, Taylor-Greene, March, and Horner (2000) successfully used active supervision, verbal reprimands, and negative contingencies (detention for continued excessive noise), along with a training exercise, to teach students to distinguish loud from quiet to reduce hallway noise during lunch transition in a middle school.
- Oswald, Safran, and Johanson (2005) demonstrated that precorrection, praise for appropriate behaviors, and active supervision achieved a 42% reduction in problem hallway behaviors after 5 weeks in a middle school implementing schoolwide positive behavior support.

Figure 2.6.   Research on universal interventions for nonclassroom settings.

record-keeping and decision-making procedures that are consistently used. The procedures must be as efficient and user friendly as possible or they will not be used regularly and there will not be sufficient reliable information to evaluate whether the schoolwide discipline system is being used as designed and achieving the desired impact on students' behavior and the school's social-behavioral

1. Teachers will walk students into the cafeteria threshold (doorway) of the serving line.
2. Students entering the serving line will be quiet except for when they are talking with the servers.
3. Students will be reminded by teachers and posted signs to get all of their lunch supplies (forks, spoons, milk, ketchup, napkins, and so forth) while going through the line.
4. Students will proceed to the tables and sit down and eat.
5. Students will raise their hands to request help from an adult.
6. If students ask to go to the bathroom, then the instructional assistant will respond, "Can you wait until after lunch? It will be over in __ minutes." If the student says "no," then the student will be given permission to go to the bathroom. Teachers need to provide time for students to use the bathroom before lunch.
7. Students will be reminded throughout lunch to follow the cafeteria expectations:
   • Stay seated
   • Stay in self-space
   • Use inside voices
   • Keep clean
8. Students will dump their trays when an instructional assistant calls their table.
9. Students will return to their tables to wait for their teachers and talk quietly.
10. Students will quietly line up and leave the cafeteria when teachers arrive to get them from their tables.

Figure 2.7. Cafeteria routines and procedures. (From the Mountain View Elementary School 2005–2006 Staff Handbook.)

climate. The SWPBS team should regularly communicate the results of record keeping and data analysis to all staff using a consistent method and format (e.g., the team facilitator presents graphed data at monthly faculty and staff meetings). Data should be presented in ways that allow the team and other school staff to analyze patterns across students, locations, times, types of behavior, and consequences (Horner et al., 2004). In addition to analyzing student data for individual, classroom, and grade-level rates and types of infractions, trends in disciplinary referral data may indicate when teachers and staff need booster training with respect to issues such as supervising particular locations in the school or consistency in determining which behavior problems warrant office referrals (Taylor-Greene & Kartub, 2000).

ACTIVE DEVELOPMENT OF SOCIAL AND EMOTIONAL COMPETENCIES

Social and emotional learning (SEL) involves the processes through which children and adults acquire and

effectively apply the knowledge, attitudes, and skills necessary to understand and manage emotions, set and achieve positive goals, feel and show empathy for others, establish and maintain positive relationships, and make responsible decisions. Social and emotional skills are critical to being a good student, citizen and worker; and many risky behaviors (e.g., drug use, violence, bullying and dropping out) can be prevented or reduced when multiyear, integrated efforts are used to develop students' social and emotional skills. (Collaborative for Academic, Social, and Emotional Learning, 2012, p. 4)

Schools that embrace PBS seek to bolster students' resilience and affect conditions that promote learning by creating a safe, caring, and supportive school climate and by teaching students the skills they need to meet the school's basic expectations for behavior. Once their schoolwide unified discipline approach is being implemented with fidelity and efficiency, schools should consider how to integrate additional focused efforts to support students' social, emotional, and academic growth. A number of effective programs to teach students how to manage their own behavior, understand their own and others' emotions, make responsible decisions, and deal positively with the social challenges that arise in schools and elsewhere are consistent with the values, practices, and systems of SWPBS. Schools may consider integrating universal conflict resolution, peer mediation, bully prevention, violence prevention, or other social and emotional learning programs into their system of support.

Conflict resolution programs are curriculum-based programs designed to teach prosocial skills, empathy and perspective taking, bias awareness, and anger management skills that give students the tools to use positive alternatives to violent conflict resolution. Johnson and Johnson (1996) reviewed 15 studies of the types of conflicts in which students engage in schools. Physical violence that results in serious injury is infrequent although, of course, still of concern. The most common conflicts between and among students were gossip, physical fights, dating/relationship issues, rumors and gossip, harassments and arguments, and name calling and insults. Without explicit training, students tend to use strategies such as withdrawal or suppression of the conflict, intimidation and force, and/or win-lose negotiations (Johnson & Johnson, 1996). Students trained in conflict resolution face the problem, engage in problem solving, and use integrative or win-win negotiations (Johnson & Johnson, 1996).

Peer mediation programs use trained student mediators to resolve a conflict that has already developed (Johnson & Johnson, 2005). Students can be referred by students, teachers, or administrators, or they may come voluntarily to their peer mediators to work to create solutions that are acceptable to everyone involved. Both conflict resolution and peer mediation programs can utilize a cadre of trained students or involve training the total student body. Effective implementation of a peer mediation program can be quite complex because it requires 1) training of the peer mediators and the school team guiding the program, 2) establishing a referral protocol, 3) scheduling the mediations so that academics are minimally disrupted, and 4) ongoing monitoring of the program (Johnson & Johnson, 2005). Conflict resolution and peer mediation programs can improve students' ability to resolve conflicts through negotiation and discussion, decrease discipline problems, and improve students' attitudes toward school (Aber, Brown, & Henrich, 1999; Daunic, Smith, Robinson, Miller, & Landry, 2000). Students are able to learn the procedures for negotiation and peer mediation, retain that knowledge over time, and transfer the procedures to nonclassroom and nonschool environments (Johnson & Johnson, 1996). These programs also have been useful in supporting the development of students' self-direction, self-esteem, sense of personal control, and other aspects of their psychosocial health. As a result, rates of student-to-student conflict, physical violence, office referrals, and suspension have been found to decrease (Johnson, Johnson, & Dudley, 1992).

Figure 2.8 provides a description of Teaching Children to Be Peacemakers (Johnson & Johnson, 2005), a program that goes beyond developing social problem-solving skills to address a broader spectrum of the attitudes and skills necessary for constructive conflict resolution. Peacemakers also includes broad efforts to affect school climate and encourages schools to use an integrated curriculum approach that builds program content into core subject area instruction.

Bullying is a widespread concern in schools. Twenty-three percent of public schools reported that bullying occurred among students on a daily or weekly basis during the 2009–2010 school year, with the problem being greatest in urban middle schools and high schools (Robers et al., 2013). The imperative to prevent bullying pertains to victims as well as perpetrators.

Teaching Students to Be Peacemakers seeks to reduce violence in school, create supportive school communities, enhance academic achievement, and teach conflict resolution and mediation strategies (Johnson & Johnson, 2005). Peacemakers is a K–12 program that begins by creating a cooperative school climate in which students view themselves and their peers as interdependent rather than independent or in competition. The program then systematically teaches all students in the classroom or school the steps of the constructive conflict resolution process, which involves learning how to create constructive integrative agreements or win-win solutions to conflicts. The classroom instruction in conflict resolution, which can be integrated with academic subjects, typically takes 10–20 hours over several weeks.

Next, teachers implement the peer mediation component in which each student gets experience serving as a mediator of their classmates' conflicts. Once all students understand these processes, particular students are selected to serve as official mediators to whom their peers can turn if they have been unable to resolve a conflict themselves. The peer mediation aspect of the Peacemakers program can be implemented with a cadre of peer mediators, a classroom group, or an entire student body. Weekly training in negotiation and mediation procedures continues from 1st through 12th grades, at more complex and sophisticated levels each year (Johnson & Johnson, 2005). The Peacemakers program has well-documented experimental effectiveness in teaching students to use constructive conflict resolution and negotiating strategies and to maintain use of those skills over time (Johnson & Johnson, 1995, 2002).

Figure 2.8. Teaching Students to Be Peacemakers. (*Source:* Johnson & Johnson, 1995.)

Victims of bullying are more likely to avoid school through truancy or by dropping out altogether and may develop psychosocial problems such as depression (Espelage & Swearer, 2003). Students who demonstrate bullying behavior are more likely to continue violent behavior as adults (Nansel, Overpeck, Pilla, Simons-Morton, & Scheidt, 2001). Schoolwide efforts to address bullying include programs specifically dedicated to bully prevention (e.g., Olweus Bullying Prevention Program [Olweus, 1993]) and broader social and emotional learning programs such as Open Circle (Wellesley Centers for Women, 2014) and Second Step (Committee for Children, 2014), which give users the option to incorporate an antibullying unit. Research using control groups and quasi-experimental designs showed promising results in some bully prevention programs. Research on program effectiveness, however, has primarily used self-report measures of students' knowledge of the antibullying curriculum and their perceptions of how they might respond to future incidents of bullying. Few studies have employed direct observations of student behavior to determine if bullying and victims' responses to bullying improved as a function of the program (Merrell, Gueldner, Ross, & Isava, 2008), and none of the programs has achieved

a model program designation (Center for the Study and Prevention of Violence, 2014; Osher & Dyer, 2006). In addition, implementing some stand-alone bully prevention programs can require a substantial infusion of resources and suffer from a lack of integration with other schoolwide initiatives, making them difficult to sustain (Good, McIntosh, & Gietz, 2011; Ross & Horner, 2009). The following section describes a universal-tier bully prevention program specifically designed to fit within the SWPBS framework.

Evidence-Based Social and Emotional Learning Programs

A number of universal social and emotional learning programs have been recognized by governmental, educational, and professional organizations as model, effective, or promising programs. Programs with these designations have documented effectiveness in helping schools prevent violence and other antisocial behavior, improve students' problem-solving skills, create positive solutions to students' emotional and behavior difficulties, and enhance achievement. The social and emotional learning programs listed in Table 2.1 met the following criteria—documented effectiveness

Table 2.1. Universal programs with documented effectiveness in promoting student achievement and preventing behavior and emotional problems

Program	Brief description	Designations and research
Project ACHIEVE (preK–12; Knoff, 2008) 49 Woodberry Road Little Rock, AR 72212 http://www.projectachieve.info	This comprehensive school improvement program strengthens resilience and self-management skills. Its focus is on social skills, conflict resolution, self-management, academic progress, positive school climate, and safe school practices. The program uses a collaborative team approach to problem-solve ways to support individual students with challenging behavior, early intervention services for students who are at risk, and decision making based on data.	SAMHSA's NREPP Harding et al. (2008)
Caring School Community (formerly called the Child Development Project) (K–6; Developmental Studies Center, 2014) 1250 53rd Street, Suite 3 Emeryville, CA 94608 http://www.devstu.org/caring-school-community	This comprehensive school improvement program focuses on good citizenship, school bonding, academic success, and social-emotional learning. The purpose is to build a caring school community and foster academic, social, and ethical development. It has four program components—class meetings, cross-age buddies or peer mentoring, schoolwide community-building activities, and home or family involvement activities. The program also includes optional cross-curricular components.	CASEL SELect program SAMHSA's NREPP Chang and Munoz (2006) Solomon, Battistich, Watson, Schaps, and Lewis (2000)
I Can Problem Solve (preK–8; Shure, 2014) Myrna Shure, Ph.D. Drexel University Department of Psychology 3141 Chestnut Street Stratton Hall, Suite 119 Philadelphia, PA 19104 http://www.thinkingchild.com	This program focuses on interpersonal problem solving to prevent antisocial behaviors (e.g., physical and verbal aggression, impatience, social withdrawal) and help children learn to generate nonviolent solutions to everyday problems. It provides extensive guided practice in using constructive conflict resolution skills (e.g., recognizing and labeling emotions in oneself, considering the other's perspective, generating alternative solutions before acting).	CASEL SELect program SAMHSA's NREPP Boyle and Hassett-Walker (2008) Shure and Spivack (1982)
Olweus Bullying Prevention Program (K–8; Olweus, 1993) Center for the Study and Prevention of Violence University of Colorado Boulder Box 442 Boulder, CO 80309 http://www.colorado.edu/cspv	This program was designed to reduce the opportunities and reward structures for bullying and to reward positive, prosocial behavior. It uses an anonymous bullying questionnaire to assess bullying at the school; a bullying prevention coordinating committee coordinates the effort. Interventions include increased supervision at "hot spots" for bullying, firm limits on unacceptable behavior, and consistently applied nonhostile, nonphysical negative consequences for violations.	CSPV Blueprints Promising program Bauer, Lozano, and Rivara (2007) Melton et al. (1998)

(continued)

35

Table 2.1. (continued)

Program	Brief description	Designations and research
Open Circle (K–5; Wellesley Centers for Women, 2014) Wellesley College 106 Central Street Wellesley, MA 02481 http://www.open-circle.org	This program focuses on equipping teachers with effective practices for creating a cooperative classroom community and establishing positive relationships. Teachers use structured lessons to teach skills in relationship building, communication, problem solving, and understanding and managing emotions. Classroom lessons provide skill practice and homework/extension activities and suggest connections to literature. A separate unit on bullying is available, as well as separate components to support schoolwide implementation and family involvement. The program provides suggestions and reminders regarding cultural sensitivity and ethnic norms. Required on-site trainings are spread across the school year.	CASEL SELect program SAMHSA's NREPP Hennessey (2007)
PeaceBuilders (K–8; PeacePartners, 2014) PeacePartners, Inc. 741 Atlantic Avenue Long Beach, CA 90813 http://www.peacebuilders.com	This program seeks to create a positive school climate by developing positive relationships between students and school staff; directly teaching nonviolent attitudes, values, and beliefs; and providing incentives for students to display these behaviors. Activities and rewards are designed to create a common language and weave peace-building behaviors (e.g., helping others, righting wrongs, avoiding put-downs) into the school's everyday routine with the participation of all staff.	SAMHSA's NREPP Flannery et al. (2003) Vazsonyi, Belliston, and Flannery (2004)
Promoting Alternative Thinking Strategies (K–5; Greenberg, Kusché, & Mihalic, 1998) Channing Bete Company One Community Place South Deerfield, MA 01373 http://www.channing-bete.com/prevention -programs/paths/paths.html	This program is designed to promote social-emotional competence, including expressing, understanding, and regulating emotions. It focuses on developing self-control, frustration tolerance, anger management, and emotional understanding through affective, behavioral, and cognitive strategies. It has been proven to be useful with students who have language or cognitive delays and is taught throughout the school year. The program can be used as either a universal or targeted intervention approach.	CASEL SELect program CSPV Blueprints Model program SAMHSA's NREPP Domitrovich, Cortes, and Greenberg (2007) Greenberg, Kusché, Cook, and Quamma (1995)
Responsive Classroom (K–5; Northeast Foundation for Children, 2014) Northeast Foundation for Children 85 Avenue A Post Office Box 718 Turners Falls, MA 01376 http://www.responsiveclassroom.org	This program is designed to create classrooms that are responsive to children's physical, social-emotional, and intellectual needs through developmentally appropriate experiential education. It teaches competencies in self-awareness, self-management, relationship management (especially cooperation and negotiation), decision making, and social awareness (especially appreciating human differences). It does not use structured lessons but is based on six essential components: 1) classroom organization, 2) morning meeting, 3) rules based on respect for self and others and logical consequences of violating these rules, 4) academic choice, 5) guided discovery, and 6) family communication strategies.	CASEL SELect program Elliott (1995) Rimm-Kaufman (2006)

Second Step (preK–9, ages 6–12; Committee for Children, 2014) Committee for Children 2815 Second Avenue, Suite 400 Seattle, WA 98121 http://www.cfchildren.org	This classroom-based social skills program includes school curricula, parent training, and skill development. It is designed to reduce aggression and promote social competence and targets the skills and behaviors of empathy, impulse control, problem solving, and anger management. The instruction emphasizes taking responsibility for actions, being honest, recognizing feelings, and communicating in respectful and assertive ways to solve problems. Students learn strategies to manage anger, fear, and stress, as well as refusal techniques. A unit on bully prevention is also available.	CASEL SELect program SAMHSA's NREPP Frey, Nolen, Schoiack-Edstrom, and Hirschstein (2005) Grossman et al. (1997)
Teaching Students to Be Peacemakers (K–12; Johnson & Johnson, 2005) Interaction Book Co. 7208 Cornelia Drive Edina, MN 55435 http://www.co-operation.org/	This program aims to develop social-emotional competence to reduce antisocial, aggressive, and violent behavior. Students learn skills for problem solving and how to mediate peers' conflicts. Skill lessons involve role playing with two peers serving as mediators per lesson so that all students have equal opportunities to be leaders. Each spring, booster sessions prepare students for the next grade, in which weekly follow-up lessons are delivered.	SAMHSA's NREPP Johnson and Johnson (1995, 2002)

Note: The first column provides the name of the program, relevant ages, author(s), and a source for more information. The second column provides a brief program description. The third column provides expert evaluator designations and key research.

CASEL: Collaborative for Academic, Social, and Emotional Learning (2012) designates programs as CASEL SELect if they are well designed and classroom based, deliver high-quality implementation supports, and are evidence based (researched using a control group as well as pre- and postmeasures).

CSPV: Center for the Study and Prevention of Violence at the University of Colorado Boulder designates programs as Blueprints Model or Blueprints Promising: Both promising and model programs are evidence based and replicable; model programs have evidence from an experimental design, a sustained impact, and are ready for widespread use (available at http://www.blueprintsprograms .com).

SAMHSA's NREPP: Substance Abuse and Mental Health Services Administration's National Registry of Evidence-Based Programs and Practices (U.S. Department of Health and Human Services) includes programs in its NREPP if they meet these minimum criteria: 1) achieved one or more positive outcomes in an experimental or quasi-experimental study that has been published in a peer-reviewed publication and 2) implementation materials, training, support, and quality assurance procedures are available to the public (available at http://www.nrepp.samhsa.gov).

based on research using experimental or quasi-experimental design, sound theoretical underpinnings, easily integrated into existing school practices, multiple site replication, and sufficient technical assistance or other resources available to support effective implementation (Collaborative for Academic, Social, and Emotional Learning, 2013; Osher, Dwyer, & Jackson, 2004). Most of these programs require professional development (e.g., workshops, institutes, follow-up coaching) from specialized trainers and purchase of training and implementation materials. Appendix B lists several resources that provide additional information about these and other research-validated and promising programs for universal social and emotional interventions in schools.

BULLY PREVENTION IN POSITIVE BEHAVIOR SUPPORT

Bullying, like other behaviors that negatively affect school climate, safety, and other conditions for learning, requires a proactive, schoolwide approach that is both effective and efficient. The Bully Prevention in Positive Behavior Support program (BP-PBS; Ross, Horner, & Stiller, 2008; available at http://www.pbis .org) was designed to fit naturally within an established system of SWPBS, thereby enhancing its potential for efficiency, acceptability, and sustainability. The program is designed as a universal, proactive effort to decrease incidents of bullying behavior and teach appropriate, nonreinforcing responses to bullying for potential victims, bystanders, and school personnel. BP-PBS has an emerging research base of experimental and quasi-experimental studies that suggest it can be both effective and efficient in reducing problem behavior when used in schools that are already using SWPBS (Good et al., 2011; Ross & Horner, 2009, 2013). In addition to being part of a schoolwide PBS effort, key

features of the BP-PBS program include the following:

- The term *bullying* is not used in either students' skill lessons or adult responses. Instead, students learn to identify and use skills to deal with behavior that is disrespectful or inappropriate. Ross and Horner (2009) pointed out that bully prevention efforts have been hindered by the difficulty of teaching about and measuring bullying when its definition includes (as it often does) descriptors such as *intentional, repeated acts of unprovoked aggression,* and *behavior against victims who are weaker.* The BP-PBS program is behaviorally oriented: Implementers are not required to interpret whether a power differential existed between the peers involved, and the observable behavior is labeled rather than the person.

- BP-PBS addresses the functional relationship between bullying behavior, the antecedents or context that set the stage for the problem (e.g., availability of peers as victims and onlookers, unstructured areas of the school), and the maintaining consequences (e.g., attention from peers, whether positive or negative).

- All students learn specific skills to use when confronted by disrespectful peer behavior, and all adults learn to ensure that those skills are generalized to settings where problem behavior is likely to occur.

Bully Prevention in Positive Behavior Support Curriculum

The BP-PBS curriculum includes a six-lesson student component and a supervisor component (Ross et al., 2008). The methodology used for the student lessons is essentially the same as for teaching the behavioral expectations in the schoolwide discipline system. That is, teachers use direct instruction: 1) describe and demonstrate targeted skills, 2) check students' understanding and have them practice the steps first in the classroom and then in criterion environments (e.g., cafeteria, playground, bus area), and 3) give corrective feedback for inaccurate skill performance or praise for accurate skill performance. Following initial instruction, teachers continue to prompt or precorrect for use of the skills before students enter predictable challenging settings, and all adults continue to provide corrections and reinforcement when needed.

Lesson Sequence for Bully Prevention in Positive Behavior Support

The first lesson teaches the core of the curriculum, which is the "stop/walk/talk" response to disrespectful behavior. The "stop" signal is the verbal and physical action that students use when problem behavior is directed toward them or when they observe problem behavior directed toward another student. Before implementing the program, the school community either adopts the "stop/walk/talk" language or decides on other words or phrases they will use, as well as a physical action (e.g., the time-out sign) that will be used to communicate "stop." It is important for the words and action to be easily remembered, socially acceptable to the students, and used by all students and staff (Ross et al., 2008). For example, students at a middle school in Canada that implemented BP-PBS decided to say "too far" and cross their hands in front of them as their "stop" signal (Good et al., 2011). The first BP-PBS lesson, which constitutes the social responsibility skills component of the curriculum, teaches the "stop/walk/talk" skill sequence (Ross et al., 2008):

1. Decide if someone is being disrespectful toward you or toward another student (e.g., calling someone a derogatory name or purposefully

tripping them is disrespectful; disagreeing with someone about which game to play at recess or stealing a base while playing softball is not disrespectful).

2. If someone is not respectful toward you, then use the "stop" signal (i.e., the words and physical action the school community has agreed on).

3. As a bystander, if you see someone being treated disrespectfully, then use the "stop" signal.

4. If you use the "stop" signal and disrespectful behavior continues toward you or another student, then walk away and encourage others to walk away.

5. If you walk away and disrespectful behavior continues, then talk with an adult.

6. If someone says "stop" to you, stop, then take a deep breath and go about your day.

Students learn the difference between talking and tattling in the "talk" step of the response. Talking with an adult occurs when the student has tried to solve the problem by using the "stop" and "walk" steps, but the problem behavior did not end. Tattling is not taking responsibility for stopping the problem and instead trying to get someone in trouble.

The social responsibility skills lesson includes multiple opportunities for role playing so that each student is able to describe and demonstrate the "stop/walk/talk" response. The initial lesson, which requires about 50 minutes, is followed by a 30-minute review lesson and more group practice. The next four lessons in the curriculum, which are delivered in 10- to 15-minute lessons over the following 2 weeks, provide instruction and practice in using the "stop/walk/talk" skills in response to specific types of disrespectful behavior—gossip, inappropriate remarks, cyberbullying, and any other specific behaviors of concern at a school.

Supervision Component of Bully Prevention in Positive Behavior Support

The supervision curriculum, which is designed to ensure that all school staff members in all school settings consistently carry out the BP-PBS program, includes the following topics and sessions:

1. Teaching the social responsibility skills ("stop/walk/talk" response) and reinforcing students' use of the skills. Faculty members practice generating examples of when and when not to use the skills, modeling the skills, and teaching students how to respond when someone uses the "stop/walk/talk" system with them.

2. Applying supervision strategies for unstructured settings, which takes place in those settings and includes

   • Checking in with chronic victims before they enter unstructured settings to remind them how to respond to problems

   • Checking in with chronic perpetrators before they enter unstructured settings to remind them how to respond if another student tells them to stop

   • Praising students who use, or attempt to appropriately use, the "stop/walk/talk" response

3. Using the "review and resolve" routine when responding to reports of problem behavior:

   • Ask who, what, when, and where.

   • Ask, "Did you say 'stop'?" "Did you walk away?"

     If the student did not use "stop" and/or "walk," then practice the response and encourage them to use it next time.

     If the student did say "stop" and walked away, then praise the student.

   • If the reporting student used the three-step response appropriately, then resolve the issue with the perpetrator of the problem behavior. Ask, "Were you asked to stop? Did the student walk away?" Practice the three steps with the perpetrator until his or her performance is fluent.

4. At a follow-up session, faculty complete a survey about their perceptions of the extent to which students use the "stop/walk/talk" system, faculty use the BP-PBS supervision strategies, and the effects of the program on school safety. Based on survey results, faculty decide whether students need reteaching because they are not fluent in using the three-step system, faculty need review in order to implement the program with greater fidelity, or there are students at risk for chronic aggression who need more intensive interventions.

Benefits of Bully Prevention in Positive Behavior Support

BP-PBS was designed to mesh with a school's existing SWPBS methods and delivery systems in order to add another support to reduce problem behavior, enhance students' resiliency, and improve school climate. It is a simple approach that can be implemented within a short period of time yet yield noticeable and valued results. Ross and Horner (2009) initially developed, field-tested, and experimentally validated BP-PBS in three elementary schools during lunch recess. The researchers found the use of BP-PBS was functionally related to a 72% reduction in observed incidents of problem behavior for six of the most challenging students in the three schools, along with increases in appropriate responses by victims and bystanders. A middle school study showed a 41% reduction in ODRs for bullying after implementing the BP-PBS program (Good et al., 2011). In addition, teachers involved in this research reported that the program was easy to implement and they would recommend it to others (Ross & Horner, 2009, 2013).

SYSTEMS-CHANGE PROCESS FOR ESTABLISHING AND SUSTAINING SCHOOLWIDE POSITIVE BEHAVIOR SUPPORT

The change from a reactive, punitive, and disjointed approach to school discipline to a proactive, preventive, unified approach can require from relatively minor to dramatic major changes in a school's culture and climate, in the attitudes and skills of teachers and staff, and in administrative practices. The success of both schoolwide and individual student-focused efforts will be limited without a systems-change process for establishing and sustaining a SWPBS initiative. A systems approach is based on an articulated and vital mission statement and incorporates committees or work groups to coordinate and guide the program, administrative support (e.g., involvement, decision-making guidance, resources), operating routines for action planning and communications, and professional development (Sugai & Horner, 2002).

First and foremost, schools must decide that SWPBS will be a priority initiative and identify the meaningful outcomes they hope to achieve (e.g., reduction in ODRs by percentage of students receiving over a certain number, improved attendance, meeting criteria on state assessments and student and teacher assessments of school climate). Baseline data must be obtained on any goal.

Sugai and Horner, directors of the Center on Positive Behavioral Interventions and Supports at the University of Oregon, have articulated five major steps in a process for initiating and sustaining SWPBS.

Step 1. Establish a Schoolwide Positive Behavior Support Leadership Team

To avoid the problems of inefficiency and frustration that can occur when a school

has too many committees and teams, the SWPBS leadership team should play a leadership role in the school regarding student behavior. (Please refer to the section on PBS teams in Chapter 1 for the composition of the schoolwide PBS team and the student-centered PBS teams, which focus on selected and individualized PBS.) Those who are experienced with large-scale and sustained implementation of SWPBS maintain that success rests heavily on having a SWPBS team whose members are viewed as credible and influential by their colleagues (Handler et al., 2007; Simonsen, Sugai, & Negron, 2008). Although the members of the schoolwide team should come to their task ready to promote SWPBS and willing to commit time and effort (the team typically meets monthly and may spend 40–50 hours in planning and preparation in the first year alone [Handler et al., 2007]), they will likely need training and technical assistance in the content of SWPBS and the processes and structures necessary to implement it.

The team's responsibilities include 1) developing ways to communicate with school personnel, including ways to inform others about the team's work and recruit input about the school's behavior support practices; 2) ensuring that the school has an efficient and accurate system for collecting and reporting data on student behavior (e.g., ODRs, suspensions, absences, tardies); 3) conducting needs assessments; 4) establishing measurable progress indicators; 5) developing action plans; and 6) planning in-service professional development activities for faculty and staff.

Step 2. Secure Schoolwide Agreements and Supports

The staff as a whole must (largely) agree on the following for the initiative to be successful: 1) it is a priority for staff development (it needs to be one of the top three school improvement goals [Horner et al., 2004]); 2) it is a long-term (5 years) commitment of staff time, energy, and fiscal resources; and 3) the approach will be preventive and instructional. Sugai and Horner (2002) recommended that schools not attempt full implementation of SWPBS until more than 80% of the staff support the initiative, although other implementers report that this level of buy-in is more crucial for sustainability than for initial implementation (Handler et al., 2007; McIntosh et al., 2013). In addition to the needs assessment and information-sharing activities that must occur at this step, resources must be garnered to secure the in-service professional development activities and materials that will be needed.

Step 3. Develop Data-Based Action Plan

Next, the SWPBS team reviews data to assess the school's discipline system and other universal behavior support practices and make decisions regarding which practices should be improved, maintained, deleted, or added. The types of data required include attendance and tardy patterns; ODRs; detention, suspension, and expulsion data; and behavior incidence data. ODR data are most useful in developing action plans if they include not only the number of referrals per school year but also the average number of referrals per day, the annual referral rate per student attending, the referral rates by problem behaviors and location, and the proportions of students with 1 or more, 5 or more, and 10 or more referrals (Sugai, Sprague, et al., 2000). It is not possible to analyze the functional relationships among antecedents, student behaviors, and consequences or to judge the effectiveness of interventions without specific behavioral data—times, settings, observable behaviors, students, or groups. It is important that the data being gathered are accurate, which requires having

efficient ways to process data (Sugai & Horner, 2002). The Schoolwide Information System (SWIS), a web-based software system for recording, organizing, and reporting ODRs, can summarize data for individual students, groups of students who share particular characteristics (e.g., gender, special education status, grade level), or the entire student body (May et al., 2002). The SWIS was specifically designed to facilitate data collection that is required to measure the effects of SWPBS and problem-solve adjustments to action plans.

These reactive data help determine needed interventions for identified and emerging behavior problems. The team also should consider using more proactive data sources to detect potential problems before they result in referral. For example, universal screening using an instrument such as the Systematic Screening for Behavior Disorders (SSBD; Walker & Severson, 1992) can help identify specific adaptive behaviors in which large numbers of students are deficient so that those behaviors can be targeted by universal interventions (Marchant et al., 2009). The SSBD is described in Chapter 3 (see Figure 3.2) as a tool for identifying students with at-risk profiles who may later require intensive intervention if Tier 1 and 2 prevention strategies are not in place to support them. Marchant and her colleagues (2009) noted, however, that use of the SSBD for universal screening may detect overlapping impairments exhibited by students who are at risk for internalizing and externalizing behavior problems as well as those who merely have some specific adaptive skill impairments (e.g., knowing how to gain peers' attention in appropriate ways, being considerate of others' feelings). Skills needed by large numbers of both typical students and those with at-risk profiles can be incorporated into the school's behavioral expectations or other efforts to increase social and emotional competencies.

Schoolwide Positive Behavior Support Assessment Instruments

An action plan also should reflect baseline assessments (e.g., surveys, checklists) of the extent to which behavior support practices are in place. The following tools have been tested and found to be valid and reliable assessments of the extent to which primary or universal PBS practices and systems are in place:

- The School-Wide Evaluation Tool (SET; Sugai, Lewis-Palmer, Todd, & Horner, 2005) was originally developed as a research instrument and was used for purposes such as assessing the extent to which SWPBS practices are in place before and after school staff receive in-service professional development and technical assistance. They found the SET to be a reliable way to measure the implementation of SWPBS practices and recommended that the SET be used by school districts in which schools are implementing universal supports within SWPBS. The SET can be used first as a baseline assessment of SWPBS features and then to plan annual goals for the schoolwide effort. A reevaluation in each subsequent school year will inform the SWPBS team about the extent to which annual goals have been met and what revisions to the school action plan are needed. The SET is administered by a trained evaluator (e.g., a member of the state's PBS coordinating team, a school district's SWPBS coach) and requires a review of permanent products (e.g., discipline handbook, SWPBS action plan, ODR forms), observations, and interviews with 10 or more staff and 15 or more students. The data collection takes 2–3 hours on average (Sugai et al., 2005).

- The Effective Behavior Support (EBS) Self-Assessment Survey (Sugai, Horner, & Todd, 2003) can be used by schools to guide initial development of SWPBS and to evaluate year-to-year progress on implementation quality and effectiveness. The EBS Survey addresses the schoolwide discipline system as well as classroom behavior management systems and the school's systems for supporting individual students with chronic problem behaviors. The survey's developers recommend that the entire school staff complete the EBS Survey initially but note that schools may elect to have a smaller representative group of school personnel complete the survey in subsequent years.

- The School-wide Benchmarks of Quality (BoQ; Kincaid, Childs, & George, 2010) is administered by a trained evaluator such as a school district's SWPBS coach; however, the coach's independent ratings of the critical elements of SWPBS are reconciled with self-evaluations by the school's PBS team. The BoQ's creators report that in addition to being valid and reliable, the instrument is efficient to use. Their validation research indicated that scorers can use the tool accurately with as little as 30 minutes of training and that completing the BoQ requires as little as 10 minutes from team members and 60–90 minutes from coaches. The BoQ correlates moderately with the SET but measures some critical elements with more specificity and also includes areas not measured by the SET (Cohen, Kincaid, & Childs, 2007).

- The Self-Assessment and Program Review for Positive Behavior Interventions and Supports (SAPR-PBIS™; Walker & Cheney, 2012) is similar to the SET, the EBS Survey, and the BoQ in that it is used to assess implementation of evidence-based practices across the three-tier SWPBS model. The SAPR-PBIS, however, is completed through participatory evaluation by the school's PBS leadership team. Rather than comparing and contrasting the school leadership team's scores on the 10 best practices indicators and their associated benchmarks, team members complete individual SAPR-PBIS forms and then meet to summarize the team's perceptions of the extent to which each indicator is in place. The participatory evaluation process involves team members in structured discussion and reflection as they seek consensual decisions that are based on data and also acknowledge team members' varying experiences. The SAPR-PBIS individual forms can be completed in 30 minutes; the team form requires a 60- to 90-minute team meeting (Walker & Cheney, 2012). An administrator, other leadership team member, or the district PBS coach may facilitate the assessment, conducted twice per year.

- The California School Climate Survey (California Department of Education, 2013b) is an assessment measure that may be helpful to schools that seek data useful not only for measuring their implementation of SWPBS practices but also for fostering a healthy teaching and learning environment. The survey assesses school personnel's perceptions of school practices and issues such as discipline, safety, professionalism, diversity, parent involvement, and community relations. The survey is required annually of all schools in California and is designed to be a companion to the California Healthy Kids Survey (California Department of Education, 2013a), which asks students to report their direct experiences with violent and antisocial behavior, their feelings about school and themselves as students, and their beliefs about the school discipline system. The California School Climate Survey can be used outside of California via the Internet and is free when users pay a small per-student fee to conduct the California Healthy Kids Survey.

Action Plan Components

The SWPBS team examines the discipline data and other needs assessment information to develop an action plan to guide the implementation of the schoolwide unified discipline system; any programs adopted to teach problem solving, social interaction, or conflict resolution skills; any bully prevention programming; and the associated data collection system. An effective action plan typically includes the following components: 1) measurable outcomes, goals, and objectives; 2) specific activities that lead to the accomplishment of objectives; 3) activities to address staff professional development needs; and 4) activities to garner resources and supports.

Teachers and other team members must find the SWPBS plan feasible; that is, strategies must be reasonable and doable (Scott & Martinek, 2006). The total action plan for the school should reflect the simplest and least intrusive set of planning, implementation, and evaluation strategies that will achieve the desired improvements in student behavior, academic achievement, and school climate. School teams are cautioned to implement one intervention step of the action plan at a time rather than trying to do everything at once.

Step 4. Arrange for Accurate and Sustained Implementation

An SWPBS action plan may fall short of achieving the desired effect on school behavior problems, students' social-emotional development, and the learning climate for various reasons. For example, inaccurate or uncommitted implementation of the plan can result in disappointing outcomes, even if intervention components with proven effectiveness are incorporated. Implementing the plan as designed requires ongoing administrative and team leadership, professional development and training to build and maintain faculty and staff skills, continued staff commitment, and recognition and appreciation for implementation efforts and successes (Sugai & Horner, 2002).

Teams can employ strategies to help keep their system of SWPBS on track with respect to implementation steps, fidelity of implementation (i.e., whether interventions are being accurately implemented), and whether implementation is related to valued changes in school climate and student behavior. The SET (Horner et al., 2004), BoQ (Kincaid et al., 2005), and SAPR-PBIS (Walker & Cheney, 2012) are reliable, valid tools for measuring the fidelity of implementation of universal supports within SWPBS in individual schools. Using one of these tools as an annual or semi-annual assessment of a SWPBS effort can help teams stay focused on moving forward. Schools that score higher on these instruments see greater improvements in student outcomes (Bradshaw et al., 2010; Horner et al., 2009; McIntosh, Bennett, & Price, 2011). Research has repeatedly shown that sustaining effective SWPBS requires implementing critical features with fidelity (McIntosh, Filter, Bennett, Ryan, & Sugai, 2009; McIntosh, Horner, & Sugai, 2009).

Although more research is needed to inform our understanding of factors that sustain implementation of SWPBS, crucial factors appear to include making SWPBS a priority, ensuring contextual fit, ensuring that research-based practices are effectively implemented, increasing the efficiency of systems and practices, and using data for continuous regeneration (McIntosh, Filter, et al., 2009). Figure 2.9 summarizes the field's understanding of key sustainability features for SWPBS.

Step 5. Conduct Formative Data-Based Monitoring

Data on student attendance, tardiness, behavior incidents resulting in ODRs, suspensions, and expulsions should be analyzed to determine overall rates of success in improving student behavior as well as success for any subgroups of particular concern. Data on ODRs and suspensions have been shown to provide a valid measure of overall progress toward improving student behavior and school climate (Irvin et al., 2004). Patterns and rates of ODRs and disciplinary exclusions should be analyzed for possible disparities between genders and across different racial and cultural groups. Vincent and Tobin's (2010) examination of disciplinary exclusion data showed that SWPBS implementation in nonclassroom settings appeared to be associated with reductions of exclusions in high schools. The decrease applied only to white students, however; African American students continued to be overrepresented in exclusions. Although the factors that contribute to disproportionalities such as this are still not fully understood, monitoring by groups can alert SWPBS teams if a problem exists, and teams can then begin to further evaluate potential contributing factors (Skiba et al., 2011).

Patterns detected by analyzing discipline referrals also can assist the SWPBS team in judging the extent to which the action plan should emphasize universal, schoolwide, or targeted interventions for smaller groups of students, as well as interventions for individual students with extreme social-behavioral needs (Sugai, Horner, et al., 2000). In general, the need to establish or reform universal SWPBS is indicated if the total number of referrals per year per student is high, the average number of referrals per day is high, or the proportion of students with at least one referral is high. Reform of selected Tier 2 support systems (see Chapter 3) for students at risk for more serious behavior problems may be indicated if the percentage of students with at least 1 referral is low but the percentage of students with 2–10 referrals is relatively high. Individualized, targeted student behavior supports (see Chapters 4 and 5)

What the Research Says

Creating Sustainable Systems of Schoolwide Positive Behavior Support

If schoolwide positive behavior support (SWPBS; or any research-based practice or program) is not implemented skillfully, efficiently, with commitment, and in a way that can be sustained over time, the potential benefits for students and schools will not be realized, regardless of the strength of the evidence base (Fixsen, Naoom, Blase, Friedman, & Wallace, 2005).

Numerous studies have suggested the following key features predict sustained implementation of SWPBS: 1) administrator support, 2) staff buy-in, 3) fidelity of implementation, 4) data-based decision making, 5) effective functioning of the school leadership team, 6) adequacy of resources (e.g., for professional development and data systems), 7) stakeholder involvement, 8) access to ongoing training and coaching, 9) SWPBS philosophy, and 10) school district support (Bambara, Nonnemacher, & Kern, 2009; Coffey & Horner, 2012; Kincaid, Childs, Blase, & Wallace, 2007; Lohrmann, Forman, Martin, & Palmieri, 2008).

Several research teams have made an effort to better understand the relative importance of these features. For example, Coffey and Horner (2012) examined sustainability features in 117 schools that had implemented SWPBS at a high level of fidelity for at least 2 years. Their analysis suggested the three most critical sustainability features were administrative support, effective communication about the core features of SWPBS, and the use of data-based decision making. McIntosh and his colleagues (2013) found that the 257 school team members from whom they gathered quantitative and qualitative data judged certain features as equally important for implementation and sustainability and other features as more important for sustainability. Their results indicated that administrator support and school team functioning were the most important factors for both initial implementation and sustainability. Staff buy-in, integration into typical practice, and parent involvement, however, were viewed as significantly more important to sustainability than to initial implementation.

Additional research will help to further parse the relative contribution of various features of SWPBS to durable and sustained change. Effective SWPBS is suited to its context and achieves outcomes valued by members of local school communities. Therefore, ongoing use of data, including stakeholder feedback, systems process data, and student academic and behavioral performance data, will help schools renew and reinvigorate their SWPBS initiatives as they implement critical features with fidelity (McIntosh, Filter, Bennett, Ryan, & Sugai, 2009; McIntosh, Horner, & Sugai, 2009) and implement the support system more efficiently over time (Gersten, Chard, & Baker, 2000).

Figure 2.9.   Research evidence for creating sustainable systems of schoolwide positive behavior support.

are indicated if there are students who received 10 or more referrals during the year or if the 5% of students with the most office referrals account for a high proportion of all referrals (Sugai, Horner, et al., 2000).

SWPBS leadership teams should celebrate quantitative successes with their colleagues and the broader school community, but they may want to gather and share evidence of other measures of effectiveness as well. A key principle of the PBS approach is that supports and outcomes are personally and socially valued.

Although behavior improvements are one goal of SWPBS, a safe and responsive school climate, improved teaching and learning, and lifestyle improvements such as increased social acceptance and personal responsibility are other aims. Evaluation of SWPBS must consider "meaningful lifestyle and cultural changes that are stable and enduring" (Carr et al., 2002, p. 7). Teams can challenge themselves to answer questions such as, "Have our efforts to decrease ODRs and suspensions, make hallways quieter, and increase cooperative playground behaviors improved the quality of the educational experience in our school as a whole?"

Scott and Barrett (2004) assisted a SWPBS team at an elementary school to measure other benefits that accrued to the school and school system as a result of achieving targeted changes in students' behavior. For instance, they determined that a typical ODR used an average of 10 minutes of administrator time and a typical suspension used 45 minutes of administrator time. Given the rates of reduction in ODRs and suspensions during the first 2 years of the school's SWPBS implementation, administrators saved a total of 31.4 workdays over baseline. For students, the average discipline referral cost 20 minutes of time outside the classroom, whereas suspensions resulted in a loss of approximately 6 hours of instruction per day. Given the improvements in behavior that resulted in decreases in office referrals and suspensions, students in this school gained 158.9 school days across the 2 PBS years.

Teams should not forget the accrued benefits that balance out or even outweigh the costs incurred when implementing SWPBS. Reductions in ODRs and suspensions translate into time that administrators can invest in proactively preventing problem behavior and facilitating improvements to the instructional program. For students, time spent at school rather than out of school can increase opportunities to learn and result in improved academic achievement and life outcomes.

CONCLUSION

SWPBS systems do not fully meet the social, behavioral, or mental health needs of all students. They have been proven effective, however, in preventing the development or worsening of behavior problems in the vast majority of students in a school. Like any significant school improvement effort, effective SWPBS requires accurate, durable implementation of doable practices (Sugai & Horner, 2002). The following elements of effective school change efforts must be in place:

- Teams that create a common vision and keep that vision in focus throughout the process
- Strong administrative leaders
- Staff buy-in and understanding of, and support for, school improvement
- A long-term perspective that provides for unanticipated challenges and delayed dividends
- Capacity-building efforts that include extensive training and support
- The efficient use of human and material resources and a culture and a structure that help all members of the school community succeed. (Osher et al., 2004, p. 7)

3

Classwide and Selected Interventions

FOCUSING QUESTIONS

- What are the characteristics of secondary-tier interventions?
- What instructional and classroom management practices support positive student behavior?
- How do schools identify students in need of secondary-tier support and match them with suitable interventions?
- How do teams monitor, evaluate, and sustain secondary-tier intervention systems?

The secondary tier of SWPBS includes both classroom interventions designed to reinforce schoolwide behavior expectations and enhance achievement for entire classroom groups and selected interventions targeted to students whose needs do not match the intensity of support provided at the universal level. Universal support and interventions such as those described in Chapter 2 can prevent behavior problems and facilitate academic success for the majority of students in schools. Some students, however, will continue to display patterns of difficult behavior. A subset of these students have behavior problems that, although troubling for parents and teachers, do not warrant the specialized, intensive level of intervention required by students with the most severe, chronic behavior problems. Nevertheless, students who demonstrate emerging behavior problems or who experience other risk factors that make more serious behavior problems likely in the future clearly need additional supports to achieve successful social-behavioral and academic outcomes. Schools augment universal interventions with selected interventions for these students (estimated at 5%–15% of a school population) when they establish integrated, comprehensive systems of PBS. This is the secondary level of prevention in the three-tiered model of prevention of behavior problems; it is designed to remediate students' behavior problems or prevent them from worsening to the point in which more intensive, individualized interventions are required. The behaviors most often targeted in research examining Tier 2 group interventions included disruption, noncompliance, getting out of seat, talking out, being off task, and negative physical or verbal interaction (Mitchell, Stormont, & Gage, 2011).

Students who are candidates for selected, often group-based, interventions (other terms used to describe this type of intervention include targeted supports [Freeman et al., 2006] and strategic interventions [Simmons, Kuykendall, King, Cornachione, & Kame'enui, 2000]) may have emerging conduct or psychoemotional disorders or experience family, community, or school factors that place them at risk for more serious behavior and academic difficulties. Research has shown that students who exhibit risk behaviors at an early age, including poor school adjustment, noncompliance, and antisocial behavior, are highly likely to progress to more serious disruptive and aggressive behavior (Loeber, Green, Lahey, Frick, & McBurnett, 2000). Antisocial behavior patterns in young children can be quite durable and resistant to intervention and can place children at severe risk for many negative outcomes, including delinquency, school dropout, drug and alcohol abuse, and relationship difficulties (Walker et al., 2004). In fact, children who are still using immature, coercive behavioral strategies to achieve their social goals by the end of third grade are highly likely to display some degree of antisocial behavior throughout their lives (Walker et al., 2004). Therefore, it is imperative that interventions for these students be provided early, be targeted to students' specific areas of need, and utilize practices with proven effectiveness.

The needs of students who experience risk indicators can be pressing and immediate at times—for example, when the student experiences an event at home or school such as an argument with a peer, failure to make the track team, or the extended absence of a parent. Their needs are more moderate on average, however, so selected interventions can be designed for small groups of students with similar targeted needs. Selected interventions must be easily obtained through a flexible but systematic process, implemented with low effort by teachers and other relevant personnel, and consistent with schoolwide interventions and supports in order to be successful. Tier 2 interventions are developed and applied using data-based decision making and with the benefit of systems to support implementation. In addition, Tier 2 interventions are defined by 1) continuous availability and rapid access, 2) low effort implementation by typical school personnel (e.g., teachers, counselors, social workers, school psychologists), and 3) consistent implementation by all staff across students identified as having similar needs (Anderson & Borgmeier, 2010; Hawken, Adolphson, Macleod, & Schumann, 2009). Selected interventions may include

- Adult or peer mentorship programs

- Homework clubs

- Study skills programs

- Reteaching and more frequently monitoring and reinforcing the schoolwide behavioral expectations

- Social skills interventions, including reinforcement of schoolwide programs or additional small-group instruction

This middle level of PBS is less researched than the primary and tertiary levels (Mitchell et al., 2011; Snell, 2006), although some of the specific intervention practices (e.g., social skills instruction, academic interventions such as peer tutoring, daily behavior report cards, the use of self-management strategies) are well tested. Summaries of the research on the use of evidence-based interventions with targeted groups of students within a tiered PBS framework are woven into each section of this chapter.

Students continue to receive universal, primary tier supports when they receive selected supports. Tier 2 is neither a service location nor a permanent grouping of students. When we refer to "students receiving Tier 2 supports," we do not mean to suggest that this is a static group of students. Secondary-tier interventions are implemented in similar ways for all students, and students move in and out of the targeted group based on careful monitoring of whether the aimed-for improvements are occurring in their behavior, social skills, and academic performance.

The remainder of this chapter first addresses classroom-level academic and behavior support, which can be conceived as another layer of prevention or as a prerequisite for using more particularized interventions. Next, the chapter touches on the team process for developing and coordinating selected interventions and explores ways to identify and provide supports for these students in the middle ground between students with no unusual social or behavioral needs and those with significant needs for behavior support.

CLASSWIDE INTERVENTIONS

Effective instructional and classroom discipline practices can be considered universal classwide supports for students' academic and behavioral success. In a sense, these practices are prerequisites to considering whether a student needs selected or individualized interventions. It can never hurt to begin a behavior intervention process for students who are struggling by examining the match between the student's present level of academic and behavioral performance and the instructional and behavioral demands of the classroom. This section provides brief summaries of key features of classwide PBS: 1) effective instructional

practices, 2) supportive classroom organization and behavior management, and 3) social-behavioral interventions that can be used on a classwide basis rather than being targeted only toward students identified as candidates for selected interventions. These interventions are purely preventative support for some students but are selected interventions for other students.

Teachers or instructional teams can use the Classroom Organization and Management Inventory (see Figure 3.1) to self-assess their use of generally effective practices. The inventory includes four categories of indicators: 1) physical space is well organized and accessible; 2) classroom procedures and instructional routines are clear, consistent, taught, cued, and reinforced; 3) active supervision and monitoring are consistently used; 4) a classwide system of PBS is in place; and 5) effective time management and instructional strategies are used to achieve high rates of used, engaged, and active responding time. Some key points about these indicators and research evidence for their use are provided in the following sections.

Effective Instructional Practices

Educators have long known that effective teaching is associated not only with academic success but also with reduced rates of disruption and other problem behavior (Lee et al., 1999; Sulzer-Azaroff & Mayer, 1991). The instructional practices that enhance students' academic success are well documented and include well-organized classrooms where teachers have established consistent routines and procedures; engaging lessons at appropriate levels of difficulty (e.g., initial practice activities yield a 70% success rate, and independent practice activities are set at a 90% rate of success [Ysseldyke & Christenson, 1987]); a high rate

Classroom Organization and Management Inventory

Classroom: _____ Date: _____

Inventory completed by: _____

Directions: Use the rating scale to assess each evidence-based classroom organization and management feature. Individual teachers may use the inventory to self-assess, or team members may conduct observations of one another. Discuss strengths and shortcomings. Target several weaker indicators for improvement each semester or marking period.

Rating scale:
1 = feature is missing and/or seldom used
2 = feature is partially in place and/or used inconsistently
3 = feature is well established and used consistently

Physical space is well organized and accessible.			
1. All work areas are easily identified, accessible to all students and adults, and suited to the number of students and type of instruction.	1	2	3
2. Teacher(s) can see all students from any position in the room.	1	2	3
3. Traffic flow minimizes student physical contact and maximizes teacher mobility.	1	2	3
4. Room arrangement facilitates organizing students into dyads, triads, and small groups.	1	2	3
5. Frequently used materials are easily accessible.	1	2	3
Classroom procedures and instructional routines are clear, consistent, taught, cued, and reinforced. Consider each of the following:			
6. Beginning of the day/start of class period (personal belongings, needed materials, getting started)	1	2	3
7. End of the day/end of class period (homework, cleaning up, belongings)	1	2	3
8. Transitions within the classroom	1	2	3
9. Transitions exiting and entering the classroom, including using bathroom	1	2	3
10. Using materials (distributing, collecting, storing) and equipment (using sink/fountain, computers)	1	2	3
11. Teacher-led whole-class activities	1	2	3
12. Group work	1	2	3
13. Independent work	1	2	3
14. Special events (assemblies, class visitors, field trips, celebrations)	1	2	3
Active supervision and monitoring are consistently used.			
15. Clear and consistent signals for attention	1	2	3
16. Active, frequent, and regular interaction with all students	1	2	3
17. Using scanning, movement, and proximity to signify awareness of student behavior	1	2	3
18. Predicting/forecasting problems and using strategies such as interruption and redirection to prevent problems	1	2	3

Figure 3.1. Classroom Organization and Management Inventory. (*Sources:* Conroy, Sutherland, Snyder, & Marsh, 2008; Marzano, Marzano, & Pickering, 2003; Newcomer, 2010; Simonsen, Fairbanks, Briesch, Myers, & Sugai, 2008.)

A classwide system of positive behavior support is in place.			
19. Rules/expectations are clear and positively stated, posted, taught, and monitored.	1	2	3
20. Rules are reviewed and cued at appropriate times.	1	2	3
21. Students receive contingent, descriptive praise for meeting expectations (4:1 praise to correction).	1	2	3
22. Students receive contingent, specific error correction (teacher restates the rule/expectation and states the approved behavior) followed by an opportunity to respond correctly.	1	2	3
23. A continuum of consequences is used to respond to incorrect behavior (e.g., communication with parents/guardians, office referral).	1	2	3
Effective time management and instructional strategies are used to achieve high rates of used, engaged, and active responding time.			
24. The class schedule is posted and followed.	1	2	3
25. Appropriate time limits are set for each instructional episode and practice activity.	1	2	3
26. Materials are prepared and ready to go.	1	2	3
27. Directions for each task or activity are clear, monitored, and reinforced.	1	2	3
28. Curriculum content is presented at levels suited to each student, with individualized education program accommodations and modifications used as needed.	1	2	3
29. High rates of engagement (on-task behaviors) are achieved during all learning formats.	1	2	3
30. All students display high rates of active responding (teacher frequently checks for understanding using a variety of techniques; e.g., choral responding, response cards or signals, individual white boards, partner checks).	1	2	3
31. Precorrects are given before transitions.	1	2	3
32. Down time is minimal; students have cushion activities or options for quiet independent work time.	1	2	3
33. Intrusions are handled quickly, with an emphasis on returning to instruction.	1	2	3
Total score: _____/99 points possible = _____%			

of active participation by all students, which is facilitated by the use of small groups and hands-on learning activities; and strategic use of visuals and conceptual organizers (Conroy, Sutherland, Snyder, & Marsh, 2008; Ellis & Worthington, 1994; Good & Brophy, 2008; Kounin, 1970; Marzano, Marzano, & Pickering, 2003; Marzano, Pickering, & Pollock, 2001; Rosenshine, 1983).

Peer tutoring and cooperative learning are two peer-mediated instructional models that are noteworthy for having been used successfully in inclusive classrooms, including those with students having intellectual disabilities and emotional or behavior problems (e.g., Hunt, Staub, Alwell, & Goetz, 1994; McDonnell, Mathot-Buckner, Thorson, & Fister, 2001). Cooperative learning has been linked to a number of positive social and academic outcomes for students with and without disabilities, including enhanced academic achievement and expanded and improved affective skills (e.g., Johnson & Johnson, 1989; Johnson, Johnson, & Stanne, 2000; Slavin, 1991). Chapter 2 in the companion book *Modifying Schoolwork* (Janney &

Snell, 2013) provides information about using cooperative learning groups and peer tutoring as strategies for including students with diverse learning and behavioral needs within shared learning activities.

Some of these generally effective instructional practices and processes may need to be strengthened or made more strategic for students with emerging learning and behavior problems. When concerns first arise about a student's academic performance, teachers can take intermediary steps to remediate problems before requesting the added support of formal secondary interventions. Depending, of course, on the student's learning profile, this response to intervention (RTI) approach might include using the following strategies:

- Increase the use of small-group instruction, both teacher directed and peer mediated.

- Use interest inventories to gain a better understanding of students' motivations.

- Give students choices between two or three options instead of no choices or open-ended choices; for example, if math worksheets are predictive of disruptive behavior, then give a choice of three different worksheets, all of which address the same skills but use varying formats or visual organization.

- Provide more structure when using cooperative learning and peer tutoring (e.g., make sure the student is assigned a role in which she or he will be successful, avoid peer interaction difficulties by carefully choosing the group members).

- Provide brief but strategic and intensive one-to-one instruction (e.g., two 5-minute sessions per day) that focuses on remediation of specific skills.

Effective Classroom Organization and Behavior Management

Effective classroom discipline is prevention oriented, considers environmental influences on students' behavior, emphasizes self-discipline over external control of behavior, and incorporates hierarchies of reinforcement for desired behavior and corrections for negative behavior. Students at risk for behavior problems, however, may need more support in learning how to self-regulate, participate in group processes, and make good choices. Before requesting a secondary-tier intervention for a student, teachers should assess the alignment of their classroom discipline system with the schoolwide discipline system to ensure that they are teaching the behavioral expectations and consistently following through on positive and negative consequences. Students spend the majority of their school day in classrooms, so classrooms are where they have the greatest opportunity to learn schoolwide expectations and effective social behavior.

Teachers also may need to reflect on their relationships with students with problem behavior. Strong evidence exists to support the importance of teachers' rapport with students as a necessary setting event for social and academic growth. Ideal teachers are often described as evidencing two complementary dispositions—warmth and leadership in their relationships with students (Marzano et al., 2003). Yet students whose behavior is disruptive or disrespectful can be trying for teachers and even lead them to respond impulsively or sarcastically. A school's universal PBS efforts should include professional development to ensure educators are able to incorporate culturally responsive teaching methods and management strategies and to apply all elements of behavior support in culturally equitable ways (Sugai et al., 2012; Vincent, Randall, Cartledge, Tobin, & Swain-Bradway, 2011). Teaching teams and individual teachers may need more intensive and individualized support via consultation and coaching to build their fluency in the use of these and other effective classroom management practices (MacSuga & Simonsen, 2011).

Teachers must bear in mind that some students' behavior difficulties will not be prevented or remediated by even the most effective universal or classwide behavior supports. Therefore, teachers may need to adapt certain features of the schoolwide strategies and arrangements, including classroom or school routines, reward systems, and the amount of modeling, cuing, and supervision provided.

Student Snapshot

Observations of second-grader Mariah's disruptive behaviors—which included taunting classmates and talking out during large- and small-group lessons—revealed that the behaviors tended to occur most at times when other students received recognition for doing their classroom jobs but much less on days when Mariah was assigned a classroom job and received positive attention for doing her job. Mr. Jarvis, Mariah's teacher, hypothesized that Mariah was finding ways to receive attention from the teacher and her peers. Although the classroom job routines had already been established, Mr. Jarvis made some adjustments that gave Mariah and several other students more opportunities to fill small roles in the classroom. He made sure to give these students positive attention for completing their jobs. Even a job as small as handing out materials, reading aloud the name of tomorrow's line leader, or carrying something for a teacher had a positive impact on Mariah's and the other students' behavior.

The following is a list of supports that can make classroom systems of behavior support more effective for students, whether used as an additional RTI effort prior to a request for secondary-tier intervention or as a supplement to selected interventions in which students are already participating.

- Provide environmental supports such as careful seating or additional active supervision in situations that predict problems.

- Reteach school and classroom rules for behavior, provide more frequent modeling and cuing, and increase the frequency of reinforcement for meeting expectations.

- Reteach, remind, and reinforce classroom routines and procedures for transitions, group and individual work, homework, signaling for teacher attention, use of the restroom, and so forth. In addition, analyze whether there are aspects of these routines and procedures that should be adjusted—either for the entire class or for one or more particular students.

- Remember to cue positive behavior by reminding the students of what to do rather than what not to do (e.g., "You can throw that paper in the trash" rather than "Do not throw that paper on the floor").

- Use effective praise. Immediately call attention to the specific behavior that was displayed, emphasize the student's own effort and pride, and make it genuine (e.g., "You worked hard to solve that math problem, and it paid off. You should be proud of yourself").

- If reward tickets are given on a random or intermittent basis when a teacher catches a student demonstrating a school expectation, then give the students extra social recognition and enthusiasm as the ticket is bestowed (e.g., "You showed respect for our school when you picked up the trash on the ball field. I appreciate your good citizenship").

- Provide additional supervision—in positive ways. Use "with-it-ness," proximity control, and other surface management techniques to prevent slight disruptions from escalating (Kounin, 1970; Long & Newman, 1996).

- Give the students additional ways to make contributions or fill valued roles (e.g., taking notes to the office, reading to a younger student, researching an answer to a student's question you could not answer, taking down bulletin board displays).

- Provide additional prompting and reinforcement of the social skills being taught in a universal classroom program.

- Have the students assist teachers with role playing during social skills lessons for younger students to give them additional practice in performing social skills, along with valued roles and responsibilities.

- Send home positive notes to parents.

Classwide Social-Behavioral Interventions

Teachers or teams may want to enhance their classwide PBS system with additional social-behavioral interventions when effective instructional practices and a sound classwide discipline system are firmly in place. Teachers can provide preventative, universal support for some students and also provide secondary prevention for other students by using certain evidence-based social-behavioral interventions on a classwide basis.

Mounting evidence supports the effectiveness of classroom-level intervention packages that incorporate multilevel behavior management and academic support elements that can be applied classwide yet increased in intensity for students with disruptive, off-task behavior that puts them at risk for emotional/behavior disorders (Kamps, Kravits, Stolze, & Swaggart, 1999; Kamps et al., 2011). These intervention packages contain explicit instruction and frequent reinforcement of targeted

social skills, group contingencies for meeting behavioral expectations (e.g., use of a game format to award frequent praise and reinforcement tickets to teams of students), classwide peer tutoring, and use of self-management strategies for targeted students (e.g., a desk chart on which to record instances of appropriate behavior). These interventions have been associated with decreased disruptive behavior and increased on-task behavior for classroom groups and the majority of individual students with behavioral risks when they are consistently implemented and there is ongoing guidance from an instructional coach (Kamps et al., 2011; Thorne & Kamps, 2008). However, in spite of being satisfied with the effects on student behavior, participating teachers reported that the interventions took time and effort to implement (Kamps et al., 2011).

Positive peer "tootling," which is designed to take advantage of the positive power of peer influence on social interactions among a classroom group, is one promising intervention that is less comprehensive and requires less teacher time and effort. Tootling is the opposite of tattling: Instead of trying to get a classmate in trouble by reporting a misdeed, students report positive behaviors (the term was constructed by combining "tattling" with the expression "tooting your own horn" [Skinner, Cashwell, & Skinner, 2000]). The classroom teacher or teaching team initiates a tootling intervention by instructing students how to use small cards to report their peers' positive behaviors (e.g., sharing, offering help, complimenting, praising). Students practice writing examples of tootles, which include the student's name, what he or she did, and the name of the recipient of the positive behavior. Tootling begins when students demonstrate success. The teacher provides students with cards to keep on their desks and encourages them to write tootles, which are collected at several predetermined intervals throughout the day and placed in a jar or box on the teacher's desk. The tootles are counted and read aloud at the end of the day. In addition to praising accurate tootling, the class receives a group reward for reaching a certain number of tootles.

Tootling has been successfully taught in Grades 2, 3, and 4 (Cashwell, Skinner, & Smith, 2001; Cihak, Kirk, & Boon, 2009; Skinner et al., 2000). Cihak and colleagues (2009) improved the rate and duration of the improvements in prosocial behavior seen in the two previous studies by ensuring that the group contingency was set just high enough so that the students were able to earn the reward (e.g., more time at recess) but were not assured of earning it every single day. Cihak and colleagues also enhanced previous research designs by measuring not only increases in tootling but also decreases in disruptive behavior (e.g., talking out, out of seat without permission, interfering with another student) and added a reversal phase to the research design. Results showed that disruptive behavior decreased along with the increases in tootling and were functionally related to the tootling intervention. The teacher judged the intervention as highly socially valid and acceptable (Cihak et al., 2009).

TEAM FACILITATION OF SELECTED INTERVENTIONS

Teams need to provide more targeted interventions when students are at risk and displaying emerging or low-level behavior problems in spite of universal school and classroom practices that are in place. If students still struggle even with benefit of universal supports, good teaching, and effective classroom behavior management, then additional, focused interventions are justified. Secondary-tier interventions require data-based decision making and operating systems to ensure that interventions are delivered efficiently, accurately, and sustainably. Features that

support effective and durable implementation include 1) teaming; 2) ongoing training in the selected interventions being implemented; 3) time to plan, problem-solve, and assess; 4) resources for professional development, consultants, program manuals, and other materials; and 5) administrative support (Hawken et al., 2009).

Many schools implementing SWPBS identify a team, sometimes called the student support team, to provide coordination for the planning, implementing, and following up on selected interventions (see Chapter 1). This team may have evolved from an existing child study team, teacher assistance team, or other prereferral intervention team. The student support team (as we shall refer to it here) establishes a regular meeting schedule (often biweekly); teachers or other personnel who work directly with the focal students attend specific team meetings. Secondary-tier PBS requires less expertise in applied behavioral analysis and behavior intervention than specialized, individualized PBS, which is the topic of Chapter 5. At least one member of the team overseeing selected interventions should have expertise in PBS and FBA, however.

The ongoing functions of the student support team are 1) to identify students in need of secondary support, 2) to match students with interventions, 3) to monitor student progress, 4) to communicate with teachers of students participating in interventions, and 5) to communicate with the larger faculty and staff about the school's secondary-tier efforts. Because the team needs to identify students who are not adequately benefiting from the school's universal supports, it is beneficial to have some crossover membership with the SWPBS leadership team, whose members are familiar with administrative behavioral data (Newcomer, Freeman, & Barrett, 2013). If this is not possible, creating a system for ongoing communication between the two teams is essential. Identifying a team member as an implementation coordinator is crucial to the success of selected interventions (Anderson & Borgmeier, 2010). Although it is recommended that selected interventions take no longer than 10 minutes of faculty or staff time daily, if 30 students participate in the intervention, then coordination would require approximately 10 hours per week (Crone, Horner, & Hawkin, 2003).

If a new group intervention program or package is to be adopted, then consultants with expertise in that program may be needed to train school personnel and assist with initial implementation of the intervention. Although all school staff members do not need to have the skill level to implement each selected intervention, all staff should be familiar enough with the interventions to know their purposes, general features, and who they are designed for (Anderson & Borgmeier, 2010).

IDENTIFYING STUDENTS FOR SELECTED INTERVENTIONS

Students must be promptly identified for selected interventions because the purpose of secondary-tier interventions is to prevent academic and behavior problems from worsening or becoming chronic. Identification of students for selected interventions requires consideration of multiple factors—administrative disciplinary data, students' social-behavioral and academic profiles, and the risk and protective factors that students experience. The following is a list of guidelines for appropriate screening and identification of students with antisocial behavior patterns who may be candidates for Tier 2 intervention.

- Use a proactive rather than a reactive process to screen and identify students at risk for behavior problems.

- Use a multiagent (e.g., teacher, parent, observer) and multisetting (e.g., classroom, playground, home setting)

screening and identification approach whenever possible to gain the broadest possible perspective on the dimensions of target students' at-risk status.

- Screen and identify students experiencing risk factors as early as possible in their school careers—ideally at the preschool and kindergarten levels.

- Use teacher nominations and rankings or ratings in the early stages of screening and supplement them later in the process, if possible, by direct observations, school records, peer or parent ratings, and other sources as appropriate (Walker et al., 2004).

- Systematically integrate the screening process into the SWPBS initiative.

The following sections provide descriptions of the three primary methods to identify students who evidence risk factors: 1) administrative data, including ODRs, attendance, and tardies; 2) schoolwide screening for students at risk; and 3) teacher requests for assistance.

Administrative Data

One way to identify students for secondary-tier interventions is to examine schoolwide disciplinary data that have been used to guide primary prevention efforts. Data on ODRs can reveal students who may require selected supports in addition to the universal supports provided for all students. Research revealed strong correlations between ODRs and norm-referenced ratings of certain types of problem behavior (Walker, Cheney, Stage, & Blum, 2005). In addition, obtaining certain levels of ODRs has been found to be a good predictor of chronic school behavior problems, particularly when those referrals were made for particular behaviors. For example, Tobin and Sugai (1999) found that receiving one or more ODRs at the start of middle school was significantly predictive of chronic middle school behavior problems and academic failure; this was especially true if the ODRs were for fighting or harassment. Based on these and similar findings, schools implementing SWPBS often consider students with two to five ODRs as potential candidates for selected interventions, whereas students with six or more referrals would be considered candidates for more specialized, intensive interventions (Horner, Sugai, Todd, & Lewis-Palmer, 2005). If a student receives two or more referrals before the end of December, however, then close monitoring is in order because that rate is a moderately accurate predictor of an annual total of six or more ODRs (McIntosh, Frank, & Spaulding, 2010). Following this initial screening using ODRs, students should be further assessed to determine the student factors (e.g., missing or weak self-control, peer group modeling of antisocial behavior) and the school factors (e.g., poor instructional match, failure of adults to teach and consistently follow through on the schoolwide discipline system) that may have influenced these poor outcomes.

ODRs should not serve as the only measure used to screen for students at risk for greater behavior difficulties. One reason is that although noncompliance and antisocial behavior patterns are among the best predictors of later behavior problems (Loeber et al., 2000), school disciplinary referrals typically do not detect students with "quiet" problem behavior. Disciplinary referrals typically are issued for disruptive, externalizing behavior, not for internalizing behavior difficulties (McIntosh, Campbell, Carter, & Zumbo, 2009). Conditions such as depression, phobias, or social avoidance can be seriously debilitating and deserve an early response (Walker & Severson, 1992).

A second reason to use other data sources in addition to ODRs for at-risk screening relates to the racial and ethnic disproportionality in the administration of school discipline practices. Based on their analysis of school discipline data

reported by more than 350 K–6 and 6–9 schools, Skiba and his colleagues (2011) found that African American students were twice as likely as white students to be referred to the office at the K–6 grade level and nearly four times as likely to receive ODRs at the 6–9 grade level. Hispanic/Latino students were significantly overrepresented at the 6–9 grade level but significantly underrepresented at the K–6 grade level. Furthermore, analysis of the types of infractions leading to ODRs at the middle school level revealed that

> The most likely types of ODR leading to disparate African American discipline are disruption and noncompliance . . . suggesting that the types of referrals in which disproportionality is evident are most likely to be in categories that are more interactive and subjectively interpreted. (Skiba et al., 2011, p. 101)

Other PBS experts who have examined the role of cultural bias in discipline decisions have noted the potential for educators to misconstrue the behavior of students whose culturally specific communication styles differ from their own (Sugai et al., 2012; Vincent et al., 2011).

Thus, using ODR data alone to make decisions about students' participation in selected interventions could lead to false positives and hence disproportionate racial/ethnic representation in those interventions for African American and Hispanic/Latino students, along with the possibility of false negatives for white students and students with internalizing problems. The results of this research point to the need to augment ODR data with more systematic schoolwide screening for behavior problems so that both externalizing and internalizing behavior difficulties are detected (Walker, Cheney, et al., 2005).

Schoolwide Screening

More proactive efforts should be made to identify students who need more support, rather than waiting for them to establish the trajectory of difficulties indicated by ODRs. Antisocial behavior patterns and conduct disorders are likely to be difficult to change and are stable over time; the longer the behavior problem has existed, the more resistant it will be to intervention (Walker, Cheney, et al., 2005). Therefore, it is important for teachers to be aware of risk factors and indicators of emotional and behavior problems and to advocate for the use of preventive support strategies. Risk factors include family and child factors as well as community and school context factors (Henley, 2006; Walker et al., 2004). Community-based risk factors include lack of support services, social or cultural discrimination, socioeconomic disadvantage, and urban areas. Family risk factors include poverty, substance abuse, single parents, long-term parental unemployment, harsh or inconsistent discipline style, social isolation, and family violence. Risk factors within the child can be academic, social, and emotional and include chronic illness, poor problem-solving skills, lack of friends, frequent absences, gang attachments, physical aggressiveness, lack of empathy, and shyness or alienation. These are just some of the at-risk indicators for antisocial behavior and emotional/behavior problems. Positive school climate, requiring responsibility and helpfulness, sense of belonging, access to support services, and opportunities for success and recognition of achievement are among the protective factors that schools can provide.

The following student snapshot illustrates the case of a student who has experienced a number of significant risk factors but also has the benefit of protective factors that make future academic and psychosocial success more probable.

Student Snapshot

Josh, who just entered the sixth grade, has been evaluated twice and found ineligible for special education services based on either his learning difficulties or his obsessive-compulsive tendencies. In addition to his academic and psychological risk factors, Josh had lived in a series of foster homes until he was adopted at age 8; he had experienced a history of inconsistent discipline practice, and, in one case, emotional abuse. Josh had been subjected to social discontinuity in elementary school due to changing schools several times. Josh's adoptive parents, however, are supportive and caring and have a stable family life. Josh has one adoptive brother in high school who willingly helps Josh with his homework and takes Josh to sporting events. Josh attends religious services with his adoptive parents and brother and has received some counseling for his obsessive-compulsive tendencies. Josh's new middle school prides itself on its positive school climate and high rate of parent and community involvement. The school has a well-established, effective schoolwide discipline program, a peer mentoring program that connects sixth graders with an older peer mentor, and an active conflict resolution program.

Many experts in the field of PBS and behavior disorders recommend that schools (especially prekindergarten settings and elementary schools) implement systematic, schoolwide screening for early identification of risk profiles and emerging emotional and behavior problems (e.g., Forness, 1990; O'Shaughnessy, Lane, Gresham, & Beebe-Frankenberger, 2003; Walker, 2010; Walker, Severson, & Feil, 1995).

Figure 3.2 provides descriptions of three systematic screening programs with excellent psychometric properties. These programs are relatively easy to administer (with modest amounts of training), reliably predict behavior disorders in children, and aid in targeting specific social-behavioral goals for instruction. Results from these well-tested schoolwide screening programs provide important information about the type and degree of social skill impairments that students display. The information gleaned should be used in concert with teachers' knowledge of students' classroom

The Social Skills Improvement System (SSIS) Rating Scales (Gresham & Elliott, 2007) are designed to provide targeted assessment of individuals and small groups ages 3–18. Teachers, parents, and students complete separate forms to create a comprehensive evaluation of social skills, problem behaviors (both internalizing and externalizing, as well as bullying, hyperactivity/inattention, and autism spectrum disorders), and achievement in reading and math. The SSIS Rating Scales, which are valid and highly reliable, were standardized on a nationwide sample to create norms by age and gender. Items on the scale are rated on frequency and importance to aid in determining behaviors that may require intervention.

  The Student Risk Screening Scale (SRSS; Drummond, 1993), originally validated for screening of elementary students for early antisocial behavior, now has been validated for screening of middle school students as well (Lane, Kalberg, Parks, & Carter, 2008). The SRSS is easily used and highly reliable in identifying behavioral indicators that lead to conduct disorders and later delinquency if students do not receive appropriate intervention (Loeber, 1991). The easy-to-administer and cost-effective instrument uses a seven-item scale that gives both the frequency and importance of problem behaviors and therefore aids in targeting specific instructional goals. The seven items are stealing; lying, cheating, and sneaking; behavior problems; peer rejection; low academic achievement; negative attitude; and aggressive behavior. Teachers rate students on a scale of 0–3 (0 = never, 1 = occasionally, 2 = sometimes, and 3 = frequently) for each item. The total of the seven ratings is used as an indicator of the student's level of risk: high risk (9–21), moderate risk (4–8), or low risk (0–3). Students who are at high risk should then be evaluated more thoroughly to determine if intervention is warranted.

  The Systematic Screening for Behavior Disorders (SSBD; Walker & Severson, 1992) was originally used with children in first through sixth grades but was later validated for use through ninth grade (Caldarella, Young, Richardson, Young, & Young, 2008). The SSBD, which is cost effective, group administered, and highly valid and reliable, detects both externalizing and internalizing behaviors. The device uses three sequential assessments known as gates: Gate 1 uses teacher nominations, Gate 2 uses a teacher rating scale, and Gate 3 employs direct observation of children in the classroom and on the playground. A trained professional (e.g., school psychologist, social worker, behavior specialist) should conduct the direct observations in Gate 3; the observations yield measures of the student's academic engaged time during independent seat work periods in the classroom and the student's social behavior during recess. Walker and Severson recommended that children who are above normative criteria at Gate 3 be referred for a more comprehensive diagnostic assessment. Researchers have found, however, that students who pass through Gate 2 can be considered at least at moderate risk for developing further emotional or behavior problems (McKinney, Montague, & Hocutt, 1998); their academic and behavioral performance should be carefully monitored if group supports are not immediately provided.

Figure 3.2.   Valid and reliable instruments for screening of behavior problems/disorders.

behavior; evidence of students' risk or protective factors; and administrative data about ODRs, tardies, and absences. And, of course, families' knowledge of the student and his or her behavior at home also gives important input for decision making about intervention.

  In spite of its potential benefits, schoolwide screening for behavior problems warrants careful use and cautious interpretation of the results. Schoolwide behavioral screening tools are mostly designed to serve as curriculum-based or criterion-referenced assessments to guide the choice of social skill goals for intervention (Walker et al., 2004). It is critical to avoid the potential for stereotyping, ability grouping, and labeling that can be suggested by the identification of groups of students sharing family and socioeconomic risk factors (e.g., Oakes, 1985).

School Snapshot

The first-grade team at Hometown Elementary School—four first-grade classroom teachers and a special education teacher—were concerned about the number of students who had not reached their age- and grade-level benchmarks on the statewide assessment of children's phonological awareness and language skills. A number of these same children were having difficulty following school and classroom rules and were not successfully interacting with their peers either in the classroom or on the playground. The first-grade team consulted the school's student support team about the possibility of using a systematic screening process to more specifically determine the social and behavioral needs of their students. The PBS team researched some screening programs and suggested the Student Risk Screening Scale (SRSS; see Figure 3.2). The first-grade team nominated approximately 22 students (about 25% of the school's first graders) for screening based on their knowledge of the students' behavior, social skills, and academic performance. The SRSS scores placed 10 of those students in the moderate-risk range and four in the high-risk range. Eight of the students nominated for screening received scores in the low-risk range. The first-grade team then met with the individual student PBS team to discuss selected interventions that might be used with the 10 students whose scores put them in the moderate-risk range. Observations of the four students in the high-risk range were scheduled by a member of the student support team in preparation for a discussion about whether their problem behaviors warranted a complete FBA.

Teacher Requests for Assistance

In addition to proactive use of administrative disciplinary data and schoolwide screening to identify students in need of secondary-tier interventions, the student support team should establish a process for teachers to request assistance on behalf of a student who is not being adequately supported by universal measures. All school personnel should be aware of the steps and time lines for this process. Requests for assistance should involve a cumulative review of student academic records, administrative discipline records, and other risk indicators.

MATCHING IDENTIFIED STUDENTS WITH SELECTED INTERVENTIONS: SIMPLE FUNCTIONAL BEHAVIOR ASSESSMENT

The student support team and the student's teacher(s) must target the specific problem(s) of concern and match the student with a suitable intervention when a student is nominated or screened for secondary-tier intervention. This is accomplished by carrying out a brief FBA (Newcomer et al., 2013). FBA at the secondary level of prevention is less specialized and complex than FBA conducted for students with the most serious behavior problems (Crone, Horner, & Hawken, 2015). The general consensus in the field of PBS is that a simple or brief FBA to help tailor selected interventions to student needs should 1) be conducted by existing school personnel; 2) be primarily based on indirect data such as school records, administrative disciplinary data, and checklists (completed through interviews or self-report by teachers, staff, and/or parents and by students); and 3) be easy to execute. The complete FBA theory and process is detailed in Chapter 4, and, therefore, only a concise outline of the brief version is presented here.

The purpose of the brief FBA is to identify 1) the approximate frequency of the behavior(s), 2) the antecedents predicting whether the behavior will or will not occur (including both near events or triggers and setting events that may have occurred at a more distant time), and 3) the consequences that follow the behavior and somehow make it effective in achieving a particular purpose. For students needing selected interventions, the purpose or function of problem behaviors is likely to be socially mediated (rather than self-regulatory or sensory). Thus, the combination of data about the antecedents and consequences of the problem behavior will be used to hypothesize whether the behavior serves to 1) obtain attention or other forms of social interaction from a peer or an adult, 2) obtain something tangible or participate in an activity, 3) avoid social interaction with a peer or an adult, or 4) avoid something or some activity. The three steps for conducting a brief FBA and a field-tested instrument to guide school teams in the process are described next.

The first step is to identify the specific behavior(s) of concern, which might include using inappropriate language, not participating in class, being frequently tardy, disrupting class by talking out and being out of assigned area, making negative comments about other students' personal characteristics, being socially withdrawn, or not completing work. Also, consider how often the behavior(s) in question occurs. For example, how many tardies or absences occur each week or month? What is the rate of not completing in-class assignments or homework? How many instances of teasing or ridiculing peers occur each week?

The second step is to gather information about the antecedents and consequences of the behavior.

- *Antecedents:* Consider who is present, what activities are occurring, and when and where the problem tends to occur. For example, does the behavior occur more frequently in English class? In the hallways? In the restroom? When a certain group of peers congregates in the cafeteria? In classes that require a lot of reading or writing? After a long weekend? When the student is asked to work independently? At school and at home immediately before report cards are distributed?

- *Consequences:* Consider what happens after the problem behavior occurs. Does the teacher lecture the student(s) about behavior in front of the class? Do peers laugh? Do peers remove themselves from the situation? Does the teacher send the student to the hallway to calm down?

The third step is to use the FBA information to build a summary statement about the predictors of the behavior and the consequences that are maintaining the behavior. This summary statement is used to select interventions that help avoid predictors of the behavior, teach or strengthen desired behaviors, and avoid reinforcing problem behaviors.

The Functional Assessment Checklist for Teachers and Staff (FACTS; Crone et al., 2015) is a fairly simple tool that is designed to guide teams through the simple FBA process (see Figure 3.3). Information is gathered by a brief interview (15–20 minutes) conducted by someone familiar with the FACTS (e.g., a member of the student support team) with teachers, staff, and parents. There is growing research support for the reliability of the FACTS in helping teams design effective, function-based interventions at the secondary tier of support (Campbell & Anderson, 2008; McIntosh, Campbell, Carter, & Dickey, 2009; McIntosh, Kauffman, et al., 2009). An analysis of the use of the FACTS in 10 research studies showed strong evidence of the reliability, usefulness, and social validity of the FACTS, along with moderate to strong evidence that direct observations yield comparable conclusions about the function of behavior (McIntosh et al., 2008). Some of these studies are summarized in the section of this chapter that describes selected intervention programs. The following Student Snapshot describes use of the FACTS to complete a brief FBA for Savannah, a middle school student with emerging social and academic difficulties.

Student Snapshot

Savannah's eighth-grade student advisory and English teacher, Ms. Franco, was concerned about Savannah's social isolation from peers and her increasing difficulties in completing both classwork and homework assignments. After reviewing Savannah's grades and talking with her other teachers, Ms. Franco realized that English and social studies were the classes of greatest concern academically, but Savannah's social isolation was evident to some extent in all of her classes. Ms. Franco contacted Savannah's mother, a single parent, who said that she had recently started a new

Functional Assessment Checklist for Teachers and Staff (FACTS)

Part A

Student/grade: _____   Date: _____

Interviewer: _____   Respondent(s): _____

1. *Student profile:* Identify the student's strengths or contributions to the school.
_____

2. *Problem behavior(s):* Identify problem behaviors.

___ Tardy	___ Fight/physical aggression	___ Disruptive	___ Theft
___ Unresponsive	___ Inappropriate language	___ Insubordination	___ Vandalism
___ Withdrawn	___ Verbal harassment	___ Work not done	___ Other _____
	___ Verbally inappropriate	___ Self-injury	

Describe problem behavior: _____

3. *Identify routines:* Where, when, and with whom are problem behaviors most likely?

Schedule (times)	Activity	Likelihood of problem behavior Low High	Specific problem behavior
		1 2 3 4 (5) 6	
		1 2 3 4 5 6	
		1 2 3 4 5 6	
		1 2 3 4 5 6	

Part B*

Routines/activities/context: Which routine (only one) from the FACTS—Part A is assessed?

Routine/activities/context	Problem behavior(s)

Provide more detail about the problem behavior(s):

- What does the problem behavior(s) look like?
- How often does the problem behavior(s) occur?
- How long does the problem behavior(s) last when it does occur?
- What is the intensity/level of danger of the problem behavior(s)?

What are the events that predict when the problem behavior(s) will occur? (Predictors)

Related issues (setting events)		Environmental features	
___ Illness	___ Other: _____	___ Reprimand/correction	___ Structured activity
___ Drug use	_____	___ Physical demands	___ Unstructured
___ Negative social	_____	___ Socially isolated	activity
___ Conflict at home	_____	___ With peers	___ Tasks too boring
___ Academic failure	_____	___ Other: _____	___ Activity too long
	_____	_____	___ Tasks too difficult

Figure 3.3.   Functional Assessment Checklist for Teachers and Staff. (FACTS; copyright R.H. Horner, 2015). (*In Part A, all daily routines and activities are listed, and the likelihood of problem behavior is rated. Then the team selects one to three routines that have similar conditions, similar problem behaviors, and ratings of 4, 5, or 6 for further assessment using Part B.) (From Crone, D.A., Hawken, L.S., & Horner, R.H. [2015]. *Building positive behavior support systems in schools: Functional behavioral assessment* [2nd ed.]. New York, NY: Guilford Press; adapted by permission of the author.)

Functional Assessment Checklist for Teachers and Staff (FACTS) *(continued)*   *page 2 of 2*

What consequences appear most likely to maintain the problem behavior(s)?

Things that are obtained		Things avoided or escaped	
___ Adult attention	___ Other:_____	___ Hard tasks	___ Other: _____
___ Peer attention	_____	___ Reprimands	_____
___ Preferred activity	_____	___ Peer negatives	_____
___ Money/things	_____	___ Physical effort	_____
	_____	___ Adult attention	_____

Summary of behavior: Identify the summary that will be used to build a plan of behavior support.

Setting event(s) and predictor(s)	Problem behavior(s)	Maintaining consequence(s)

How confident are you that the summary of behavior is accurate?

Not very confident   Very confident

1	2	3	4	5	6

What current strategies are being used to control the problem behavior?

Strategies for preventing problem behavior	Strategies for responding to problem behavior
___ Schedule change	___ Reprimand
___ Seating change	___ Office referral
___ Curriculum change	___ Detention
___ Other: _____	___ Other: _____

---

job and was at work when Savannah came home from school, so she had been spending less time helping Savannah with her homework. Savannah's mother also said that she was moderately concerned about the fact that Savannah was quiet and did not have a lot of friends.

Ms. Franco completed a request for assistance, which she submitted to the student support team. At the next team meeting, the team met after school with Ms. Franco and Mrs. O'Brien, Savannah's social studies teacher, to complete the FACTS. The two teachers reported during the interview that "work not done" had reached a moderately high likelihood of occurring three to four times per week in English and social studies. Predictors of the behavior were classwork and homework assignments that required independent reading and assignments that were not highly structured (e.g., task steps and rubrics were not provided). The current consequences for

incomplete assignments were conferences with Ms. Franco and lunchtime tutoring sessions with Mrs. O'Brien. Both teachers gave Savannah extensions on assignment due dates but with lowered grades. The two teachers believed that their conferences and tutoring sessions with Savannah provided the adult attention she wanted.

The two teachers reported that the second behavior of concern, "withdrawn," also was very likely to occur during teacher advisory, English, and social studies. Savannah's withdrawal was evidenced by her failure to initiate interactions with classmates and her minimal responses to their attempts to interact with her (e.g., a murmured "hi" at best and no eye contact). The teachers were not able to identify any particular setting events or environmental features associated with this behavior and felt they would need to be more observant of those features in the coming week. The behavior certainly appeared to serve the purpose of avoiding peer attention, however.

The summary statement tentatively generated for Savannah was, "When faced with assignments that are challenging for her (e.g., those that require independent reading and/or are unstructured), Savannah does not complete her work, and this results in having one-to-one time with Ms. Franco and Mrs. O'Brien. Therefore, the function of Savannah not completing her work must be to get adult attention." This summary statement pointed the team in the direction of choosing an intervention that would 1) help Savannah to complete her work more independently and 2) provide more opportunities for Savannah to receive attention from a mentoring adult when she completes her work.

ADOPTING AND IMPLEMENTING SELECTED INTERVENTIONS

Secondary-tier interventions provide students with increased structure, more opportunities to learn social-behavioral skills, and additional monitoring and reinforcement to augment universal behavior support. Selected interventions can change behavior through 1) providing prevention strategies to alter triggering antecedents and setting events; 2) teaching new, desirable behaviors; and 3) making sure that students' appropriate behaviors are reinforced and problem behaviors are not. The new skills that students are taught should include specific social and communication skills to replace problem behaviors as well as the academic and self-management skills needed to aid their overall social and personal adjustment and their academic performance. Interventions at this level should

- Be aligned with the schoolwide expectations for behavior

- Be as low cost and low effort as will yield acceptable results

- Be administered in similar fashion for all participating students

- Be no more intrusive, specialized, or adaptive than necessary

- Be proven effective by research and practice

- Be suited to the antecedents and consequences of problem behavior(s)

- Be selected with family and student involvement

- Demonstrate good contextual fit

- Be frequently monitored and assessed for progress

- Be documented by written materials to promote fidelity of implementation and sustainability

Secondary prevention efforts are, by definition, less resource intensive than tertiary prevention systems for the most serious behavior problems. When choosing the set of selected interventions to offer at a school, it is legitimate to evaluate the balance between the costs and benefits of an intervention. A new program should be adopted only if a number of students and their families will benefit, strong administrative support exists, professional development training and other resources are available, and the program will likely be continued in the future.

In addition to evaluating the evidence base and the resources required for possible interventions, teams need to choose interventions designed to address the behavior problems that are of major concern in their school. Teams should examine administrative data (e.g., ODRs, attendance, tardies, academic records) and the results of schoolwide screening to detect common problems in the student population. There is no database recommending a particular number or array of selected interventions, but it makes sense to implement one main program and then to judge its effectiveness and determine what needs are not being met.

Some programs and supports may already be available in the school for use as selected interventions. Existing supports that could be selectively used for individuals or groups of students include homework clubs; after- or before-school social, physical health, or academic programs (e.g., running or walking clubs, intramural sports, computer clubs); counseling programs; adult and peer mentoring programs; and tutoring by volunteers or older students.

Ramping up existing supports in order to use them as selected interventions requires ensuring that they have adequate definition and structure to be implemented in similar ways for all students and that specific behavioral targets can be set for participants. Certain core features of selected interventions are evident, regardless of the cost, formality, or name of the intervention program or support (Anderson & Borgmeier, 2010; Hawken et al., 2009):

- Specific behavioral goals and a target date for meeting them

- Explicit instruction in targeted skills

- Performance feedback

- Acknowledgement of positive behavior

- Prompting or precorrection of positive behavior

- Opportunities to practice positive behaviors in natural settings

- Fading of support

- Ongoing progress monitoring

- Communication with parents

The research base for Tier 2 interventions is sparse in contrast to that for universal and individualized interventions, but it is growing. Research has been conducted on several manualized interventions and on some proprietary or commercial programs designed for use with groups or sets of students having particular social and behavioral needs. The following sections describe four selected interventions that have an evidence base built at least partially on research conducted in schools utilizing a comprehensive, tiered system of PBS and using teachers and other school personnel as intervention agents. The intervention programs are check-in/check-out, social skills training, First Step to Success, and adult mentoring. If a school is seriously intent on preventing new cases of serious behavior difficulties, and if the program fits with the school's overall improvement plans and other contextual factors, then these programs are worth consideration as interventions for students who are at risk.

Check-In/Check-Out

Check-in/check-out (also known as the behavior education program; Crone et al., 2003) is a manualized intervention specifically designed for secondary-tier delivery. Check-in/check-out provides added structure for participating students, provides more frequent instruction and feedback about expected behavior, increases opportunities for adult social recognition, establishes a relationship with an adult mentor, and improves communication between school and home. The program, which is designed for students with nondangerous behavior, has been demonstrated efficient and effective in decreasing the frequency of problem behavior for elementary students (e.g., Campbell & Anderson, 2011; Fairbanks, Sugai, Guardino, & Lathrop, 2007; Filter et al., 2007; Hawken, MacLeod, & Rawlings, 2007; Taylor-Greene, 2002; Todd, Campbell, Meyer, & Horner, 2008) and middle school students (Hawken & Horner, 2003; Simonsen et al., 2011).

To implement check-in/check-out, schools should determine criteria for entering the program (e.g., 2 or more ODRs by the end of December; nomination by a teacher, parent, or the student). It is recommended that a program coordinator be given designated time to manage the program (Crone et al., 2003). The coordinator may be a counselor, social worker, teacher, or paraeducator. A dedicated behavior education program team is created in some schools, whereas the student support team oversees the intervention in other schools. The student and parents meet with the team to develop a written contract for improving the student's behavior. As part of this contract, students are to "check in" with the coordinator each morning to pick up a daily progress report form. The student gives the teacher the progress report form at the start of each lesson (for elementary school) or class period (for middle and high school). At the end of lesson or class period, the teacher evaluates whether the student met, partially met, or did not meet the schoolwide expectations for behavior, along with praise or corrective feedback. At the end of the day, the student "checks out" with the program coordinator or other mentor and obtains social recognition, discusses how the day went, and possibly receives other reinforcement, depending on the student and the school's program guidelines. Students take a daily report home for their parents' signature.

Research on check-in/check-out programs revealed that effectiveness varies according to the function of the students' behavior problems (Campbell & Anderson, 2008; Filter et al., 2007; March & Horner, 2002; McIntosh, Campbell, Carter, & Dickey, 2009). The intervention was far more effective for students whose behavior problems were motivated by adult attention than for students whose behaviors were motivated by escape from academic tasks or other classroom demands. In some cases, the intervention actually increased incidents of problem behavior for students whose behavior was escape motivated (March & Horner, 2002; McIntosh, Campbell, Carter, & Dickey, 2009). These results point once again to the importance of tailoring interventions to assessment information so that reward systems actually reinforce desired behaviors rather than problem behaviors.

Research has demonstrated that check-in/check-out can be effectively implemented by school district personnel (Filter et al., 2007), and the intervention can be made more efficient once students have made acceptable gains, such as removing the teacher feedback sessions yet still maintaining desired results (Campbell & Anderson, 2011).

Social Skills Training

Some schools choose to implement social skills training schoolwide as part of their universal PBS effort (see Chapter 2). Students who do not respond to those universal interventions or who are identified by screening efforts as lacking in interpersonal skills may benefit from small-group social skills interventions. These interventions might be added as a supplement to ongoing classwide social skills instruction, as long as the two interventions are carefully coordinated. Although there is a broad research base for social skills instruction in general, few published studies report interventions conducted as part of a tiered system of behavior support (Mitchell et al., 2011). The broader research base suggests that the challenges of enhancing social skills in natural contexts lie in accurately targeting specific skill and performance impairments, providing training of sufficient duration to achieve fluent use of new skills, and ensuring that skills transfer and generalize to nontraining settings (Gresham, Sugai, & Horner, 2001). There is emerging evidence, however, of the beneficial effects on students' social skills and problem behavior when well-designed social skills training is implemented within a tiered system of PBS (Gresham, Bao, & Cook, 2006; Lane et al., 2003; Marchant et al., 2007).

Social skills include several dimensions, including 1) peer relations skills (e.g., greeting others, sharing), 2) self-management skills (e.g., recognizing feelings, dealing with criticism), 3) classroom survival skills (e.g., listening, following directions), 4) compliance skills (e.g., accepting "no" for an answer), and 5) assertion skills (e.g., negotiating; Calderella & Merrell, 1997). Effective social skills training appears to include the following steps and features (Gresham et al., 2001; Kavale & Mostert, 2004; McGinnis, 2012; Vaughn et al., 2003):

1. Target specific skill impairments using a research-validated curriculum guide (e.g., McGinnis, 2012) or a standardized social skills assessment tool (e.g., Social Skills Improvement System Rating Scales; Gresham & Elliott, 2008).

2. Create social skills groups with students having similar skill needs.

3. Provide instruction in settings that match the participants' everyday social contexts.

4. Use an explicit, structured teaching sequence for skill acquisition: 1) explain and briefly discuss the target skill and why it is important; 2) describe situations when the skill should be used; 3) have adults or competent peers explicitly model the skill steps as they provide overt self-instruction (i.e., verbalizing the thought process of selecting and monitoring the skill steps); 4) have students take turns role-playing while using self-instruction, first with prompting and performance feedback, then more independently; 5) provide reinforcement for accurate skill use and remind students of times and places they might use the skill as homework.

5. Follow initial acquisition with supports provided in natural contexts—prompt use of the skill, give performance feedback, and reinforce the students' efforts and successes.

6. Monitor student progress and evaluate the program based on the same measures used to identify students for the program.

Note that in Step 4, small-group instruction during acquisition, teachers or other trainers are encouraged to add self-instruction to their social skills role-play demonstrations. Self-instruction, or self-talk, is a crucial self-regulation strategy that comes fairly naturally to some students but is weak or missing in others. Self-regulation strategies include skills for thinking hypothetically about the potential results of one's actions, monitoring subsequent actions, and then reflecting on their effects. Students who lack self-regulation strategies are inefficient learners and are prone to impulsive behavior. Typically developing young children progress through a developmental sequence from being controlled by adults' talk, to overtly talking to themselves about rules and prohibitions (e.g., "Don't touch. It's hot!"), to managing their own behavior by thinking (i.e., covert self-talk; Luria, 1961). Therefore, some social skills training programs (e.g., McGinnis, 2012) incorporate self-instruction as a support for developing self-regulation. Self-management strategies, including self-monitoring, self-instruction, and goal setting, also can be incorporated into academic tasks that challenge students with learning and behavior problems (see Menzies & Lane, 2011).

Chapter 5 provides additional guidance regarding the use of self-management systems for students who receive individualized PBS. Additional approaches and programs for social skills training are described in a companion book in this series, *Social Relationships and Peer Support* (Janney & Snell, 2006).

First Step to Success

The First Step to Success program (Walker et al., 1997) consists of three interconnected modules that provide a comprehensive and successful intervention package for preventing antisocial behavior patterns in young children who experience risk factors for poor behavioral and academic outcomes (Diken &

Rutherford, 2005; Golly, Stiller, & Walker, 1998; Walker, Golly, McLane, & Kimmich, 2005; Walker et al., 1998). The three components include universal screening, school intervention, and family support and parent training. Brief descriptions of the three modules follow.

1. *Universal screening and early detection:* The screening component consists of systematic screening of K–3 classrooms to detect students who are at risk for problem behaviors and students with signs of antisocial behavior. There are four different screening options that vary in cost and complexity.

2. *School intervention:* The school component uses the Contingencies for Learning Academic and Social Skills (CLASS) Program for Acting-Out Children, which teaches adaptive behavior for succeeding at school and developing friendships. The intervention involves close monitoring of classroom behavior, a rich schedule of points and praise for academic engagement and following class rules, and home–school communication about the student's performance at school.

3. *Family support and parent training:* This component uses a 6-week in-home parent training program called Homebase, which focuses on showing parents how to teach their children skills such as cooperating, problem solving, and playing well with other children. The lessons complement the CLASS program.

The second component of First Step to Success is based on 5 years of development and testing, and the third component is based on 30 years of research. The program was cited by Joseph and Strain (2003) as having a high level of evidence of success. The large-scale replication of the program in Oregon (Walker, Golly, et al., 2005) yielded results consistent with the initial trials conducted by the program's authors, including significant improvements in rates of adaptive behavior, aggression, and maladaptive behavior by target students and positive consumer satisfaction. A number of limitations, however, resulted from logistical difficulties, problems with data collection, and the need for behavioral coaches to implement and evaluate the project. The fidelity and overall quality of implementation varied from excellent to quite poor in real-world situations (Walker, Golly, et al., 2005). Subsequent research indicated that effectiveness and implementation of First Step to Success (and, potentially, other manualized interventions) can be enhanced by adding individualized function-based supports (Carter & Horner, 2009).

Mentoring

Formal mentoring programs pair a successful student or adult mentor with an individual student with the intent of creating a supportive relationship in which the adult serves as a model for appropriate social and academic behavior. A mentoring program used as a school-based, selected intervention typically targets students who evidence at-risk factors associated with the home environment, low socioeconomic status, or poor academic performance. The purposes of different programs vary, but they often focus on avoiding substance abuse, building confidence, improving peer and family relationships, improving educational performance and attitudes toward schoolwork, and facilitating higher aspirations (DuBois, Holloway, Valentine, & Cooper, 2002).

Mentoring programs operate using models varying in duration, intensity, and integration with other services, so it is difficult to assess their overall effectiveness. The most accurate summary of the research findings appears to be that "mentoring is an effective intervention strategy for some young people" (Rhodes, 2008,

p. 35). A meta-analysis of research on 55 one-to-one youth mentoring programs found generally positive but modest social, academic, and/or behavioral effects across diverse types of programs, and some evidence showed that benefits can extend beyond the end of program participation (DuBois et al., 2002).

Big Brothers/Big Sisters America is the largest formal mentoring program for school-age children and youth; it is listed as an effective program on the Substance Abuse and Mental Health Services Administration (SAMHSA)'s Registry of Evidence-based Programs and Practices (NREPP) and as a promising program on the Center for the Study and Prevention of Violence's Blueprints registry. Big Brothers/Big Sisters incorporates many of the features that appear to lead to positive outcomes for mentored youth (DuBois et al., 2002; Rhodes, 2008):

- Screening and matching of mentors to students

- Structured, ongoing mentor training that addresses the purpose and goals of the program

- Expectations for mentors regarding how often to meet

- An expectation that long-term student involvement is desirable

- Some mechanism for parent involvement

MONITORING, EVALUATING, AND SUSTAINING SELECTED INTERVENTIONS

Monitoring the use of the planned intervention and changes in students' problem behaviors, social skills, and academic performance should be as great a concern to teachers and other members of school PBS teams as any other aspect of the behavior support system. Student support teams should examine student progress toward intervention targets on each

intervention at least monthly to determine whether 1) the student has responded to the intervention as planned, so that support can be faded; or 2) the student has not responded as planned. If the student has not responded as planned, then the issue may be

- Lack of fidelity of implementation (e.g., due to frequent staff absences, substitutes have been providing the intervention without written documentation of the intervention to guide them)

- Poor intervention match (e.g., the student was participating in a check-in/check-out system, but the FBA had indicated the function of the problem behavior was to escape from academic tasks, so the intervention actually functioned as a reward for the problem behavior [March & Horner, 2002])

- Inadequate intervention intensity (e.g., the student requires a stronger dose of the intervention; the student needs a more comprehensive, individualized PBS plan)

The evaluation of selected interventions should address both individual student progress and trends within the school because it is important to evaluate the secondary prevention system and not only its effects on individual students. The evaluation measure used should be the same measure that was used to identify students who should receive selected interventions. If referrals to the student support team are based on the number of ODRs, then the number and reasons for those referrals should be tracked. If ratings on a social-behavioral screening system were used to detect students needing intervention, then the same rating system should be used again after the intervention is in place to evaluate the effects.

The Benchmarks for Advanced Tiers (Anderson et al., 2011) is a self-evaluation tool that schools implementing a comprehensive system of PBS can use to evaluate the implementation of secondary- and tertiary-tier PBS. This self-evaluation instrument assesses systems (e.g., student identification, support team processes), data management, and the level of implementation of selected intervention strategies. The instrument is completed by the student support team members and reflects their consensual opinions about the extent and quality of implementation. The results can be used for further action planning to improve the fidelity of implementation of the Tier 2 PBS system, which in turn enhances sustainability.

CONCLUSION

Students who are at high risk for developing behavior problems and those who show emerging behavior problems need a higher intensity of support than many of their peers. Best practice suggests and intervention research shows that further prevention efforts are imperative to the future mental health and well-being of students whose behavior difficulties cannot be remediated through universal, schoolwide interventions. The elements, strategies, and processes that can be used to identify and deliver selected behavioral interventions for this group of students have been briefly discussed in this chapter. Further research is needed to help us understand how to be more prescriptive in matching students with interventions and to identify the sorts of training and expertise that teachers need to design and deliver this level of PBS.

4

Individualized Positive Behavior Support

Conducting a Functional Behavior Assessment

FOCUSING QUESTIONS

- What is a comprehensive functional assessment, and why is it needed for individualized PBS?
- What critical information is gathered through the functional assessment process?
- What are the strategies or tools for conducting a functional assessment?

Chapters 4 and 5 describe the four steps of a process that educational teams can use to develop a PBS plan for individual students. Chapter 4 presents Steps 1 and 2, which require defining the behavior(s) of concern and conducting a comprehensive FBA. Chapter 5 concentrates on Steps 3 and 4, which entail designing, implementing, and evaluating an individualized PBS plan.

The students considered in Chapters 4 and 5 are those whose problem behaviors are seriously disruptive or destructive. These students—who most often are classified as having emotional or behavioral disorders, intellectual disabilities, autism, or severe disabilities—have behavior problems that do not improve adequately in response to schoolwide universal supports (Tier 1), classroom management systems, or selected interventions created for groups of students. The number of students with behavioral challenges of this magnitude is relatively small (often estimated at 5%). Proper assessment and effective intervention are likely to require in-service professional development for school staff and the ongoing guidance of experienced behavior specialists for the most challenging cases. More people are involved in designing and providing the specialized interventions needed by these students, so the importance of effective communication, coordination, and collaborative teaming also increases.

Research syntheses that evaluated the outcomes of multiple studies strongly supported the value of FBA as the basis for developing effective individualized behavior supports (Carr et al., 1999; Didden et al., 2006; Goh & Bambara, 2012; Horner et al., 2002; Marquis et al., 2000). Significant improvements have resulted from PBS interventions for diverse participants (e.g., adults and children; people with autism, intellectual disability, emotional/behavioral disorders, and other disabilities; people with a variety of targeted behavior problems, including aggression/destruction, disruption/tantrums, self-injury, and stereotypic behavior). Focusing just on schools, PBS interventions also have been shown to be effective across various grade levels (elementary, middle, high school) and classroom settings (general and special education) and with students with and without disability classifications (Goh & Bambara, 2012). Function-based interventions were far more successful in the studies that have directly contrasted function-based and nonfunction-based interventions on rates of problem behavior for individual students (e.g., Ellingston, Miltenberger, Sticker, Galensky, & Garlinghouse, 2000; Ingram et al., 2005; Newcomer & Lewis, 2004). To illustrate further, early elementary school teachers in one study (Stoiber & Gettinger, 2011) participated in in-service professional development focusing on implementing FBAs and PBS interventions for individual students. The participating teachers changed their classroom practices and demonstrated higher competence and feelings of self-efficacy when working with students who exhibited challenging behaviors compared with teachers who did not receive such training. Furthermore, the children of the participating teachers demonstrated more positive behaviors and fewer challenging behaviors than those of teachers who were not taught to implement FBA or PBS interventions.

This chapter details the process of conducting an FBA for individualized student support. The specific examples in this book that illustrate the process involve students with IEPs who exhibit serious behavior problems and who are based in inclusive, general education classes. The examples come from students known to the authors or their colleagues in K–12 schools, although some demographic information, such as age or gender, has been changed and some examples are composite cases.

WHAT IS FUNCTIONAL BEHAVIOR ASSESSMENT?

As discussed in previous chapters, FBA (also called functional assessment) is a process for gathering and analyzing information to uncover the purpose or function of a student's behavior problems and the relationships between those behaviors and the physical and social context. The FBA process at the individual student level of support is used to make behavior support plans more effective and efficient by addressing those variables that contribute to, support, or maintain problem behaviors by students. Two types of methods are used for collecting comprehensive FBA information:

1. Indirect (informant) methods include records reviews, questionnaires, and checklists. Indirect methods rely on existing records and interviews with knowledgeable people.

2. Direct methods require observing the student in relevant places and situations. Direct methods are used to obtain information at the specific time the behavior occurs.

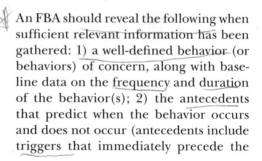 An FBA should reveal the following when sufficient relevant information has been gathered: 1) a well-defined behavior (or behaviors) of concern, along with baseline data on the frequency and duration of the behavior(s); 2) the antecedents that predict when the behavior occurs and does not occur (antecedents include triggers that immediately precede the

behavior and setting events and more distant antecedents that increase the likelihood of problem behavior); 3) the consequences that maintain the problem behavior by enabling the person to obtain something or avoid something; and 4) one or more hypotheses as to why the problem behavior happens based on the information about antecedents and consequences. Functional assessments may also reveal broader quality-of-life variables that can contribute to problem behaviors, such as health and well-being, interpersonal relationships, and choice and control, as well as information needed to personalize interventions, such as student preferences, interests, and skill strengths (see Figure 4.11, the Step 2A worksheet, later in the chapter for more examples). But, at a minimum, functional assessment should focus on the behavior, antecedents, and consequences and function of behavior.

The Behavior

First, the target behavior(s) is defined in observable and measurable terms, and a baseline assessment of the rate or duration of the behavior is conducted. It is crucial to gather baseline data about how frequently or how long a problem behavior occurs so that you can know for certain whether the plan you develop is helping. Sometimes the plan helps you feel like you are doing something to improve the situation, but it has few actual effects on the problem behavior itself. Thus, carefully defining and measuring the target behavior is essential for determining whether your intervention plan is working.

Antecedents

Second, information about what is going on when the behavior occurs—or does not occur—helps reveal how the environment is related to the behavior. For example, if

the behavior tends to occur more often when the student is asked to do paper-and-pencil tasks than when doing hands-on, functional tasks, then the function of the behavior may be to avoid those difficult or nonpreferred tasks. If the behavior occurs more often when the student is left alone than when he or she is working with an adult or with other students, then the purpose of the behavior may be to get attention. If you can discover what antecedent variables (e.g., events, people, places, objects, physical conditions) are triggers for the behavior, then you can change some of those stimuli (at least temporarily) and sometimes prevent problems from occurring. (The specific variables are called *discriminative stimuli* in scientific research; these are the cues that set the stage for the behavior.)

In addition to the effects of specific triggers that often occur just before problem behavior, setting events also can influence behavior. Setting events are biological, social, or physical/environmental incidents or circumstances that are more distant from the occurrence of the behavior but make it more likely that a specific cue will trigger the behavior. This is similar to the phenomenon of "having a bad day" or "getting up on the wrong side of the bed." Once a certain negative event happens, its aftereffects taint the rest of the day. For example, Arlon is eager to please his teachers on most days and happily complies with requests to work. However, requests for work become triggers for refusals and protests ("No, I don't want to do this") on days when he has a scheduled dentist appointment, which makes him very anxious.

When gathering information about antecedents, whether they are immediate triggers or setting events for behavior, look for answers to "who," "what," "when," and "where" questions. The answers to these questions can help uncover patterns of antecedents that predict when the problem behavior will occur.

Consequences and Function of Behavior

The third type of information to gather is about the consequences or what happens after the behavior occurs in order to identify the purpose or function of behavior. Used in this sense, the term *consequences* refers not only to planned rewards or punishments that are being used but also to any event or circumstance that happens following the behavior (e.g., Do other people leave the student alone? Does a crowd of people gather? Does the student immediately or eventually obtain some object that he or she had wanted? Do other students laugh? Is the student reprimanded by an adult?). Learning theory tells us that the student would not continue to use the behavior unless it was effective—at least some of the time—in helping to meet some need or purpose. Information about the consequences that follow the behavior indicates what the person is accomplishing by using the behavior or, in other words, how the environment is reinforcing and, therefore, maintaining the behavior.

When thinking about how consequences maintain a behavior, it is important to realize that our intentions do not necessarily match the way our actions affect another person's behavior. For example, we may think that reprimanding a student for acting out serves as a punishment and that the student will act out less in the future if our reprimands are consistent. If the purpose of the student's acting out is to gain attention, however, then our attention may be rewarding to the student, even if we believe that a reprimand is a negative consequence. There are two primary purposes or functions of behavior (see Chapter 1): to obtain something (e.g., social interaction, tangible) or to avoid something (e.g., social interaction, difficult or disliked tasks, internal stimulation). When conducting a functional

assessment, look for consequences that would suggest one of these functions.

Antecedents, both setting events and triggers, associated with the functions of behavior are likely to be unique and vary across individual students (e.g., some students will seek to avoid crowded environments, whereas others seek them out). To further complicate things, sometimes setting events can function as triggers. Nevertheless, there are some common antecedents known to be problematic for students. Table 4.1 lists typical setting events and common triggers that are associated with functions of behavior.

Hypothesis Statements

Once sufficient information is gathered through functional assessment, hypothesis statements are generated that predict or explain when problem behavior will or will not occur. Hypothesis statements essentially summarize data patterns gathered through the FBA process. They clearly articulate 1) the antecedents that provoke problem behaviors, 2) the behavior(s) of concern, and 3) the perceived function of behavior along with maintaining consequences. For example, an FBA for Alicia might indicate the following:

When Alicia is alone in the cafeteria or in the hallway during class transitions and she sees classmates engaged in socializing (antecedents), she interrupts her peers' conversation, taunts them, and calls them names (target behaviors). The other students tell Alicia to "knock it off" and tease her in return (consequences). If we repeatedly observe this pattern in Alicia's behavior and also observe that Alicia has little interaction of any kind with her peers when she does not interact in these negative ways, then we might hypothesize that the underlying purpose or function of Alicia's taunts is to gain her peers' attention (perceived function).

Self-stimulation is often assumed to occur only for the purposes of obtaining

Table 4.1. Common antecedents to problem behaviors

Setting events	Triggers	Function
Biological Acute illness Allergies Menstrual period General anxiety Mood Disrupted sleep Missed breakfast Missed medication or medication changes Acute pain, fatigue	Absence of social interaction or attention Unengaged for periods of time Someone else gets attention Peers encourage or entice interaction Encounters a problem Peer rejection	To obtain social inter-action, assistance, or attention To obtain (or maintain) a desired object, food, or activity
Social Adult or peer conflict Family stressors (e.g., dying or sick family member, parent divorce) Academic failure Socially isolated Family change (e.g., vacation, business trip, sibling moving)	Sees something wanted Is told "no" or "not now" Transitions (i.e., wants to maintain activity) Schedule or routine change or inter-ruption (i.e., wants to maintain) Desired food, objects, or activities are restricted or denied Teacher demand Correction or confrontation Disliked task or activity	To avoid or escape something disliked or unwanted
Physical/environmental Unstructured activity Too structured activity Schedule changes Too noisy, hot, crowded, or cold	Difficult task or activity Physical effort Tasks too boring or too long Unwanted social interaction Disliked teacher or peer Few opportunities for choice or control Unengaged for periods of time Unpleasant stimuli (e.g., fire alarm, sticky substances, soft or hard foods)	To obtain (internal) or avoid (external) sen-sory stimulation

When antecedent occurs, then target behavior... Consequence
Perceived Function

or avoiding internal stimulation. Self-stimulation can serve other functions, however, as revealed in the FBA for Daniel.

When Daniel's classmates attempt to initiate a conversation with Daniel (antecedent), he often replies with a one-word response but then quickly turns away and watches his fingers as he flicks them (target behaviors). His peers, assuming that he does not want to talk, walk away (consequence). If we find that Daniel's behavior repeatedly follows this pattern and that he rarely engages in self-stimulation during other activities or interactions with adults, then the purpose of Daniel's problem behavior may be to avoid social interaction with his peers (perceived function).

FBA does not require formal testing of the hypothesis statement(s) about the triggering antecedents of the problem behavior and the consequences main-taining the behavior—although simpler verification methods may be used to test hunches. Functional analysis is the process of systematically manipulating the variables (i.e., antecedents, conse-quences) that are believed to be affecting the problem behavior in order to test the accuracy of initial hypotheses (O'Neill, Albin, Storey, Horner, & Sprague, 2014). Functional analysis is primarily used in experimental research about behav-ior problems, but it is seldom used by teachers in school settings for a number of reasons (Horner et al., 2002; Snell et al., 2005). Figure 4.1 provides further description of these differences and advice regarding the use of functional analysis. The FBA described in this book

What is functional behavior assessment (FBA)?

- FBA is a process for gathering and analyzing information to determine the antecedents that predict or set the stage for a behavior problem, the consequences that maintain the behavior, and the purpose the behavior serves for the student.
- FBA does not require testing the hypothesis about the antecedents of the problem behavior and the purpose it serves for the student.

What is functional analysis?

- Functional analysis is a test to confirm or refute the accuracy of a hypothesis about the problem behavior's function and the triggering antecedents when these are not clear, even after a thorough FBA.
- Functional analysis requires intentional and precise presentation of the conditions that provoke the problem behavior, while directly observing and recording the problem behavior.
- Functional analysis can vary in complexity and precision:
  - The most complex versions require experimental manipulation of the antecedent or consequent events believed to be responsible for the behavior; this experiment is usually conducted in controlled, often unnatural settings to tease out only the variables that contribute to problem behavior (e.g., Iwata, Dorsey, Silfer, Baumna, & Richman, 1994; Wacker, Cooper, Peck, Derby, & Berg, 1999).
  - Other versions involve testing hypotheses in natural settings by systematically introducing antecedents or consequences during typical routines (Bambara & Kern, 2005; Carr et al., 1994). This verification process may be less precise because not all variables can be completely controlled, but it verifies whether the problematic variables (e.g., the difficulty of tasks, the availability of social interaction) are valid and relevant to what happens to the person on a day-to-day basis.

What cautions and considerations apply when using functional analysis?

- Functional analysis enables the assessor to learn what the purpose of the problem behavior is and to use that information to develop effective behavior interventions. Its benefits must be weighed against the risks involved, however. Functional analysis requires creating a situation in which the problem behavior occurs and purposefully providing reinforcement for the problem behavior; the risk to the student or others must be minimal.
- Formal, experimental functional analysis artificially isolates the antecedents right before the behavior and the reinforcement right after the behavior and, therefore, is most often conducted in an isolated setting; the process cannot capture the influence of setting events and other variables that occur in the student's real life, such as the possible influence that peers may have on the behavior (Bambara & Kern, 2005; O'Neill et al., 1997).

When is functional analysis used in schools?

Experimental functional analysis conducted in unnatural settings is rarely used in schools and should not be conducted by teachers. If considered at all by a team, then this will require the support of a trained positive behavior support consultant or behavior analyst and permission from parents or care providers (as well as human subjects committees or review boards, as required; Bambara & Kern, 2005; O'Neill et al.,1997).

What alternatives are there to formal, experimental functional analysis?

Conduct simple hypothesis checks by observing the student during typically occurring activities when you have made short-term, nonintrusive alterations to the antecedents (e.g., tasks that are easy or hard) or consequences (e.g., obtaining or not obtaining teacher attention) for the problem behavior. This way, hunches about antecedents or consequences that contribute to problem behavior can be verified informally (see Step 2D in Figure 4.2).

Is hypothesis testing necessary?

No. Research has shown that hypotheses based on descriptive information (e.g., interviews, rating scales) from parents, teachers, and students themselves or on direct observations in natural settings can be highly consistent with those confirmed by more formal functional analysis methods (Arndorfer, Miltenberger, Woster, Rortvedt, & Gaffaney, 1994; Bambara & Goh, 2012; Newcomer & Lewis, 2004).

When is hypothesis testing useful?

Consider using when

- Hypotheses suggested by indirect and direct functional assessment methods are unclear.
- The team is interested in confirming or verifying hunches.
- The team is interested in teasing out instructional variables to better inform the student's support plan.

Never

- Introduce variables that provoke serious destructive behaviors

Figure 4.1. Functional behavior assessment and functional analysis: What is the difference?

utilizes a process for testing hypotheses that seeks a middle ground between formal functional analysis and simply going with a hunch or best guess.

When Is a Functional Behavior Assessment Needed?

IDEA states that in cases in which a behavioral intervention plan is needed, the student's IEP team should consider positive behavioral interventions to address the student's needs. IDEA also states that an FBA is required in cases in which severe disciplinary action is being considered, such as frequent suspensions from school or enrollment in a more restrictive classroom setting, which can result in a change of placement for a student.

Schools should, of course, follow the IDEA requirements for conducting an FBA. It is important, however, to recognize that FBA was a standard of effective practice for addressing the challenging behavior of students with disabilities for a number of years before it was first required by IDEA. In fact, the use of FBA (e.g., the FACTS) is now considered good practice when selecting interventions for implementation at the secondary level of prevention for students who are at risk for developing severe problem behaviors (see Chapter 3).

All students whose behavior remains an impediment to their or their peers' learning, their mental health, or their social relationships, in spite of schoolwide and selected interventions, are candidates for individualized FBA. FBA is best used proactively, however, and should not be reserved only for use in crisis situations (e.g., when considering a change of placement). As a matter of good practice, an FBA should be done during the RTI process or during initial evaluations or reevaluations if a student's behavior inhibits his or her learning or that of others. A simple, common sense guideline to follow is this: If everyone who knows the student is concerned about his or her behavior, then it

is time to take a proactive, systematic, and analytical approach to addressing those problems. FBA is such a process.

The FBA approach—with its emphasis on being analytical and diagnostic rather than reactive or punitive—is useful for all sorts of behavior problems. Once familiar with the process, you may begin to "think" FBA and informally apply what you know about understanding behaviors and preventing problems during your interactions with students. The comprehensive, formal FBA, however, is used only on behalf of students in need of the tertiary level of intervention—those students who have significant, persistent behavior problems.

The schoolwide behavior support system should include delineating the processes and procedures for initiating and conducting an FBA and developing an individualized PBS plan. These processes and procedures should include 1) the composition of the individual student PBS team, 2) the tools and strategies used to conduct an FBA, 3) guidelines for intervention planning, 4) guidelines for data collection to monitor and evaluate interventions, and 5) ways to involve, communicate with, and support families.

Conducting a Functional Behavior Assessment

Figure 4.2 lists the four steps for creating a system of individualized positive behavior supports and the forms and worksheets to be used during the process (blank, photocopiable versions of these forms are available in Appendix A and the forms download). In addition to the forms accompanying each step, use the Team Meeting Agenda and Minutes form (a completed sample is provided in Figure 1.4; a blank, photocopiable version is included in Appendix A and the forms download) to plan each team meeting and maintain written records of all decisions made and actions taken. On the form,

Steps and Tools to Develop
Individualized Positive Behavior Supports

Student: _Anthony Rodriquez_   Date initiated: _October 15, 2014_

School: _Lincoln Elementary_   Grade: _2nd_

Members of positive behavior support team:
Jared Simms (special education teacher)   _Rita Santos (second-grade teacher)_
Marianne Josephs (school district behavior   _Ashley Giles (paraeducator)_
specialist)   _Mara Kellam (school psychologist)_
Angela and Jaime Rodriquez (parents)

Steps and accompanying functional behavior assessment tools (Check box when completed.)

Step 1: Identify the Problem(s) and Decide on Priorities; Make a Safety Plan.

    Step 1A: Identify the Problem(s) and Decide on Priorities.
    ☑ Step 1A Worksheet: Problem Identification and Decisions About Priorities
    ☑ Team Meeting Agenda and Minutes (use at each team meeting)

    Step 1B (if necessary): Make a Safety Plan.
    ☑ Step 1B Worksheet: Safety Plan
    ☑ Incident Record

Step 2: Plan and Conduct the Functional Behavior Assessment.

    Step 2A: Gather Descriptive (Indirect) Information.
    ☑ Step 2A Worksheet: Student-Centered Functional Behavior Assessment Profile
    ☑ Student Schedule Analysis

    Step 2B: Conduct Direct Observations.
    ☑ Interval Recording or Scatter Plot
    ☑ Antecedent-Behavior-Consequence Observation

    Step 2C: Summarize Functional Behavior Assessment and Build Hypothesis Statement(s).
    ☑ Step 2C Worksheet: Summary of Functional Behavior Assessment and Hypothesis Statement(s)

    Step 2D (if necessary): Test Hypotheses.
    ☑ Team Meeting Agenda and Minutes (with plan for verifying hypotheses)
    ☑ Revision of Step 2C Worksheet

Step 3: Design an Individualized Positive Behavior Support Plan.
    ☑ Step 3 Worksheet: Positive Behavior Support Plan

Step 4: Implement, Monitor, and Evaluate the Positive Behavior Support Plan.
    ☑ Step 4 Worksheet: Implementing, Monitoring, and Evaluating the Positive Behavior Support
       Plan (decisions recorded on Team Meeting Agenda and Minutes)

Figure 4.2.   Steps and tools to develop individualized positive behavior supports. (A blank, photocopiable version of this form is available in Appendix A, and blank and filled-in versions are available in the forms download.)

be sure to identify not only the planned actions but also who will carry out these responsibilities and by when. Accountability is crucial to effective PBS teamwork. Other guidelines for making team meetings efficient and genuinely collaborative are described in Chapter 1.

As a general guideline, expect to complete the FBA over the course of 2–3 weeks, with team meetings held weekly or biweekly, and then develop a PBS plan that is initially implemented for about 2 weeks and then reviewed and revised as necessary at follow-up meetings every 2–4 weeks.

 ## Student Snapshot

Anthony is a second grader diagnosed with autism. This is his first year in an inclusive classroom. Prior to this year, he received intensive intervention in an early childhood center for children with autism. He reads slightly below grade level, can write simple sentences, and can communicate through verbal expression. His IEP goals focus on improving his academic competence in math, reading and language arts and include functional goals for expanding social-communication skills and working more independently (see Figure 4.3). Anthony has displayed various behaviors that have concerned his parents and teachers since he was a young child. His educational and therapeutic programs at the center focused on reducing food selectivity, improving his ability to make the transition from activity to activity without tantrums, strengthening expressive language, and preparing him for grade-level academic achievement. His parents are very proud of his accomplishments; however, a different set of problems has emerged in his new classroom. Anthony's problem behaviors and the decisions that his teachers and parents have made about how to support improvements in his behavior are described in the worksheets that accompany each step of the four-step process.

The remainder of this chapter explains the process of conducting an FBA for Anthony and other students with disabilities or serious behavior problems. Examples of the FBA process for students with disabilities are provided, but the same process can be applied to students without IEPs. The accompanying figures illustrate how Anthony's support team used the forms provided in this book to guide their information gathering, problem solving, and decision making.

STEP 1

Identify the Problem(s) and Decide on Priorities; Make a Safety Plan

 Figure 4.4 summarizes the first step in the FBA process. The team defines the behaviors of concern, categorizes their seriousness, and decides which behaviors are intervention priorities in Step 1A. If a student has seriously destructive or dangerous behavior, then the optional Step 1B, developing a safety management plan, also is completed. If a safety management plan is needed, then it should be immediately implemented, even before the FBA is completed.

Step 1A: Identify the Problem(s) and Decide on Priorities

Team members who know the student best use the Step 1A Worksheet: Problem Identification and Decisions About Priorities to describe the problem(s) as precisely as possible, in terms of the observable actions (see Figure 4.5). Make your description as specific as possible so that every member of the team knows exactly which behavior is being considered. For example, instead of describing the behavior in vague terms (e.g., "Leah just won't do anything I tell her to"), describe exactly what Leah does when she is told to do something. Does Leah tear or throw papers when you hand them to her? Does she sit down on the floor and say, "You can't make me" when

Program-at-a-Glance

Student: _Anthony_   Date: _September 2014_

IEP goals (in a few words)	IEP accommodations and modifications
Social/communication • *Use complete sentences to express needs, describe feelings, ask questions, and convey ideas* • *Greetings and good-byes: initiate and respond to peers and adults* • *Join and participate in peer-led instructional (small groups) and social (e.g., recess, board games) activities* *Functional skills* • *Follow classroom schedule with adapted cues* • *Independence in school arrival, departure, restroom, lunch routines* • *Independence in completion of assigned seat work and management of belongings and materials*	• *Receive special education assistance/ instruction with academics, daily routines, transitions, support for communication, peer interactions* • *Weekly curricular adaptations by special education and general education teachers (simplified and reduced content)* • *Assignments modified (e.g., simplified/ reduced content, fewer items per page, word banks)* • *Real coins for counting money* • *Content textbooks not on grade level read orally to him* • *Choice of paper and pencil or computer for writing paragraphs* • *Visual schedule for transitions*

Math
• *Solve problems using addition and subtraction to 20*
• *Time to 30 minutes (face, digit)*
• *Count combinations of coins to $1.00; use money in functional contexts*

	Academic, social, and physical supports
	• *Visual schedules and organizers work well* • *Repeated, direct instructions are sometimes needed during transitions* • *Anecdotal records for IEP progress* • *Core team meetings weekly; whole team monthly*

Language arts
• *Answer inferential comprehension questions, and make predictions based on literature selections*
• *Read novels/stories at 1.5 grade level*
• *Demonstrate understanding of independent stories through summarization and retelling*
• *Compose three-sentence paragraph with capitalization and punctuation (period and question mark)*

Content areas
• *Key concepts for each unit*

Key: IEP, Individualized education program.

Figure 4.3. Program-at-a-Glance for Anthony. (A blank, photocopiable version of this form is available in Appendix A, and blank and filled-in versions are available in the forms download.)

STEP 1

Identify the Problem(s) and
Decide on Priorities; Make a Safety Plan

Ask: What is the specific problem?
Define the problem behavior(s) in observable terms (Step 1A).

Ask: What behavior(s) have priority and warrant a functional behavior assessment and positive behavior support (PBS) plan?
Determine the priority level for each behavior—destructive, disruptive, or distracting—and the rationale for intervention. If there are several problems, then target the most serious for comprehensive PBS and focus on positive programming and improvements in the environment to address those of lesser concern (Step 1A).

Ask: Is a plan for safety management to protect and calm during destructive or seriously disruptive incidents needed immediately?
Develop a written Safety Plan that details when and how to respond to critical incidents, including a procedure for completing Incident Records (Step 1B).

Figure 4.4. Step 1: Identify the Problem(s) and Decide on Priorities; Make a Safety Plan.

it is time to go to music? Instead of defining the behavior as "Gabriel gets upset all the time," try to describe what Gabriel does that tells you he is upset. Does he cry, scream, and hide under the desk? Does he run out of the classroom?

Notice the difference between the two lists of descriptions in Table 4.2. The general labels in the right-hand column do not actually describe what the student does. For example, *aggressive* could mean pushing, hitting, biting, yelling, or many other actions. These general labels tell more about how the behavior is interpreted than about what the behavior itself looks like. In contrast, the observable behaviors listed in the left-hand column

are specific and state exactly what the student did or did not do.

Students often have more than one problem behavior. Several behaviors may happen at once in the same situation, or one behavior may precede another as part of a sequence. (*Response class* is the technical term for a set or group of behaviors that occur together in the same context or serve the same purpose.) If a particular set of behaviors accelerates or decelerates together, then these behaviors should be collectively addressed within the PBS plan. For example, a student may put his or her head down on the desk, cry, and then scream and throw things during the same or similar incident. These four behaviors should

Table 4.2. Differences between observable behavior and general labels

Observable behaviors	General labels
Hitting adults and other students with a fist or open hand	Aggressive
Using profane words in school and on bus	Mean
Crying during instructional time	Self-stimulatory
Rocking upper body back and forth while sitting at desk or table	Frustrated
Throwing books, pencils, papers, and other instructional materials	Uncooperative
Banging head on the floor	Upset
	Angry
	Anxious
	Rude

Step 1A Worksheet: Problem Identification and Decisions About Priorities

Student: _Anthony Rodriquez_   Date: _October 15, 2014_

Describe each problem behavior as specifically as possible—what it looks like and sounds like, how intense it is, and how long each has been a problem. Estimate the frequency and duration of each behavior. Label the behaviors according to their level of priority.

Description of problem behaviors	Level of priority
1. Crying starts off as a low whining with self-talk that gradually progresses to being loud enough to be heard at least 20 feet away and a duration of 60 seconds or more. Rocking back and forth, along with picking at his skin (e.g., arm), occurs simultaneously as the crying escalates. Can occur up to several times a day.	☐ Destructive ☑ Disruptive ☐ Distracting
2. Grabbing objects with one or both hands to obtain a desired item. Occurs several times a week.	☐ Destructive ☑ Disruptive ☐ Distracting
3. Pushing peers with one or both hands on any part of the other person's body. Usually does not result in hurting anyone but is enough to move the person out of his way and could result in injury. Has been a problem in the first grade but has worsened in the past year.	☑ Destructive ☐ Disruptive ☐ Distracting
4. Screaming directed toward a peer with very loud negative comments (e.g., "No!" "That's mine!") that can be heard by everyone in the room. Screaming usually co-occurs with grabbing/pushing if grabbing/pushing did not obtain desired outcome. Usually occurs in a burst of two or three phrases, so each burst will count as one scream. Occurs several times a week.	☐ Destructive ☑ Disruptive ☐ Distracting
5. Occasionally displays refusals to participate in an activity by folding arms and repeating what should happen next. Occurs about once a week but sometimes less.	☐ Destructive ☑ Disruptive ☐ Distracting
6. Frequently observed aligning, organizing, or straightening work tasks in a repetitive sequence before starting independent seat work. Although somewhat odd, this does not interfere with the work of others but can result in a delay in starting and completing an assigned task. If an item becomes out of place during this process, then the entire process needs to be completed again until ordering is done in an exact and seamless manner.	☐ Destructive ☐ Disruptive ☑ Distracting

Decision and rationale: Which behaviors should be priorities for intervention and why?

Crying/rocking and grabbing/pushing or screaming are the most serious because they are disruptive to Anthony's and others' learning and interfere with Anthony's peer relationships. Picking at his arm can result in injury if left unchecked. Screaming often occurs with grabbing and pushing but can sometimes accompany crying and rocking when he is very upset. Refusals, although infrequent, do interfere with his learning. All of these behaviors are interfering with Anthony's relationships in the classroom. Therefore, all these behaviors will be addressed in a behavior support plan. Straightening or organizing materials, although sometimes odd, does not interfere with Anthony's learning or classroom routines.

Is a Safety Plan needed immediately?   (Yes)   No

Figure 4.5.   Step 1A Worksheet: Problem Identification and Decisions About Priorities for Anthony. (A blank, photocopiable version of this form is available in Appendix A, and blank and filled-in versions are available in the forms download.)

be described and worked on together. As you generate hypotheses about the functions of the problem behaviors, you may find that several behaviors that are related to one another are used to achieve the same purpose (e.g., escape difficult tasks). In that case, the support plan should address these behaviors as a set. Yet some problem behaviors may not be closely related and may occur differently in different situations. For example, a student may cry when left alone but puts his or her head down on his or her desk when asked to work on an assignment. These behaviors are probably not closely related. You will generate multiple hypotheses when behaviors serve different functions in different situations. In this case, the support plan will address each behavior somewhat differently.

Although it is important to define all problem behaviors in observable terms, several behavior problems may be grouped into categories such as physical aggression, verbal aggression, nonparticipation, noncompliance, or self-stimulation. In these cases, you would give the set of behaviors a general descriptor, such as aggression, but also list the observable actions that fit under that category, such as hitting or kicking peers, throwing objects at peers, and making threatening gestures.

Also, record an estimate of the frequency and duration of each problem behavior. These estimates should later be verified more systematically (e.g., through direct observation), but this information may be relevant to the team's decisions about priority behaviors.

After defining the behaviors of concern (still using the Step 1A Worksheet: Problem Identification and Decisions About Priorities), the team should rate the seriousness of each problem behavior and decide which behaviors are of greatest concern at the time. Think of three priority levels for problem behaviors in order to decide where to start—destructive, disruptive, and distracting (Janney, Black, & Ferlo, 1989; see Evans & Meyer [1985] for

another way to categorize the seriousness of problem behavior).

Destructive behaviors are health- or life-threatening behaviors to the student or others and should always be top priority. Destructive behaviors include biting or hitting, eye poking, head banging, scratching, cutting, and refusing to eat. These behaviors should be immediately addressed through a plan for safety management until an FBA is conducted and a comprehensive PBS plan is developed.

Disruptive behaviors are next highest in priority. These behaviors prevent teaching and learning from taking place or prevent the student from participating in daily living activities at school, at home, or in the community. Disruptive behaviors include "acting out" behaviors as well as persistent withdrawal from social contact through not speaking, crying, or literally or figuratively pushing away other people to avoid interaction. Stereotypic behaviors (e.g., hand flapping, other repetitive movements) can be disruptive if they prevent the person from engaging in interaction and participation, but this judgment should be based on an FBA. Disruptive behaviors should be addressed through a behavior support plan unless the student has more serious destructive behaviors that should be given higher priority.

Distracting behaviors are given the third and lowest priority. Such behaviors may include echolalia, tics, rocking, hand flapping, fidgeting, lining up materials in the same sequence each day, age-inappropriate interests, and other behaviors that deviate from what is typically expected but do not really cause harm. In general, such behaviors are not part of a formal FBA or intervention plan unless they are either a high priority to the team or in danger of becoming more serious if ignored. For example, persistent scratching may become self-injurious if it is serving to gain attention for the person, echolalia or hand flapping may interfere with social acceptance in public places, and rocking may become disruptive if it increases in intensity as a response to work that is too easy or too difficult. Similarly, age-inappropriate interests may interfere with peer relationships. If distracting behaviors become targets for intervention, then the focus often is primarily on teaching alternative behaviors if such goals are consistent with the student's other IEP goals.

The discussion of intervention priorities may lead the team to decide that lower priority disruptive or distracting behaviors need only to be addressed by improving the environment and preventing the problem behavior. For example, if it is clear that Jeremy displays disruptive behaviors such as throwing and tearing materials only when paper-and-pencil tasks that are not matched to his skill level are assigned to him, then the task requirements could be adapted, or he could be assigned different tasks that are hands on, reflective of his interests, and better matched to his skill level. The formal FBA may be discontinued in such situations, although it is wise to monitor whether the desired changes in the student's behavior problems or academic work occur.

Write the team's decision about which behavior(s) should be targeted for intervention and give the rationale for the decision in the lower portion of the Step 1A Worksheet. Behavior change goals are part of a student's IEP, so decisions regarding priorities should be made in conjunction with the student's IEP team, if it is different from the PBS team.

Step 1B: Make a Safety Plan (If Necessary)

If a student is known to display destructive and dangerous behaviors that can cause serious harm to the student or others or destroy valuable property, then the PBS team should immediately develop a safety plan even before the FBA is conducted. The purpose of a safety plan, known also as a crisis management plan, is to protect the student and others and to deescalate the problem as quickly as possible. A safety plan should also be considered for students whose seriously disruptive behaviors put them at great risk for being placed in a more restrictive classroom or school.

Creating a safety plan requires team problem solving to tailor an individualized plan that will be effective for a particular student's pattern of escalation and recovery and that will have good contextual fit with the particular school and classroom. One way to organize a written safety plan is according to the phases of the crisis cycle of behavior (see Figure 4.6; Colvin, 1993). The Step 1B Worksheet: Safety Plan (see Figure 4.7) assists staff by 1) clarifying who should intervene in a critical incident, 2) giving directions for how to intervene and support the student during the five phases of the crisis cycle, and 3) setting consistent guidelines for reporting on serious incidents and using the safety plan. The safety plan includes the following information:

- The names of the people who will intervene in a serious behavior episode. If only one adult is present, then should someone else be called to assist? How will that other person be made aware of the situation? If there are several adults present, then who is best at helping the student calm down and should, therefore, be the first person to intervene?

- Directions for how to intervene and support the student during the five phases of the crisis cycle:

  1. *Trigger phase:* What physical, verbal, or affective signals does the student send that he or she is feeling threatened and that a serious incident might occur? For example, does the student demonstrate loss of attention, physical agitation, heightened

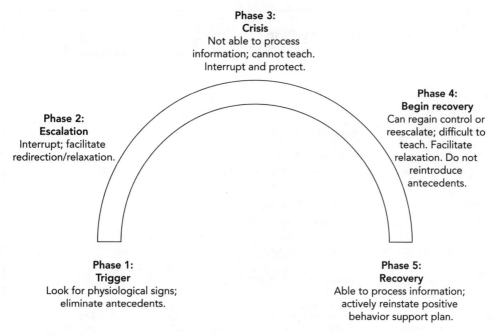

Figure 4.6. Phases of the crisis cycle and corresponding interventions. (From Colvin, B. [1993]. *Managing acting-out behavior.* Eugene, OR: Behavior Associates; reprinted by permission.)

color, excited speech, tears, or sweating? How can antecedents that may have triggered the problem (e.g., a difficult task, waiting for attention, repeated prompts/demands, corrections, teasing) be eliminated? How quickly does the student's behavior tend to accelerate during the trigger phase? (Bambara and Kern [2005] likened the concept of a crisis cycle to an "acting out cycle" and contended that some students have fast versus slow accelerations and slow versus fast deceleration. The student's rates of acceleration and deceleration influence how much time you have to respond and, thus, what strategies you might use in a critical incident.)

2. *Escalation phase:* How will the behavior be interrupted, and how will the student be redirected to more desirable behaviors? Will humor, getting a drink of water, running an errand, or switching gears to move to another place or activity help

interrupt the chain of behaviors? What are some strategies for engaging the student in the new activity? Are there relaxation strategies that the student has been taught, such as deep breathing, visualization, or positive thinking aloud? What posture and tone of voice should the adult maintain?

3. *Crisis phase:* If the problem behavior is not interrupted, then how will you protect the student and everyone present? Will you remove other students? Will you try to move the student to a quiet place? Will aggressive or self-injurious actions be blocked? What position and proximity to the student should the person who is intervening maintain? Will listening to music, deep breathing, taking a walk, or talking to the student about other things in a soothing voice help him or her regain control? (Make sure staff members understand that the student

Step 1B Worksheet: Safety Plan

Student: _Anthony Rodriquez_   Date: _November 5, 2014_

Behavior(s) that call for use of the Safety Plan:

Crying/rocking for over 2 minutes at a level that ceases instruction or pushing/grabbing and screaming at any peer a second time after being reminded of the rules.

Who will intervene in a serious behavior episode?

The special education teacher or paraeducator who is nearest to Anthony at the time

How to intervene and support the student during phases of the crisis cycle:

1. Trigger phase: Describe signals the student sends that indicate feeling threatened or uncomfortable.

    Describe antecedents known to trigger problems and how to eliminate them.

    a. *Any of Anthony's problem behaviors can be signals: crying/rocking, screaming, self-talk, grabbing people or objects, or pushing peers.*

    b. *Triggers include*
        - *Giving Anthony an independent work task. Review the task with Anthony, making sure he knows what to do. Remind him that teachers are here to help him if needed.*
        - *At recess/free time or peer work group activities, when he wants an object that a peer has or wants to engage in the same activity the peer is completing. Before participation during these times, review the rules during recess/free time or peer work group activities, highlighting what it means to share with others.*

2. Escalation phase: Tell how to interrupt, redirect, and facilitate relaxation.

    a. *During independent seat work*
        - *Redirect him to the current task/activity and provide assistance (e.g., "You know how to do this, you did this yesterday. Here's where the next one goes. Let's do this together").*
        - *Provide a break(s) during independent seat work to reduce frustration.*
        - *Model for him how to relax and provide praise. Say, "Let's take two deep breaths."*
        - *Provide structure for the task at hand. Tell him how much longer (e.g., use a timer) or how many more items he will be doing.*

    b. *Pushing/grabbing*
        - *Use eye contact and remind him of the rules in a neutral but firm tone of voice. Be sure to physically position yourself on Anthony's level.*
        - *As soon as Anthony makes any attempt to participate or share, give verbal encouragement and a visual signal such as thumbs up or high five.*

3. Crisis phase: Describe how to interrupt and protect the student and others.

    a. *The paraeducator or special education teacher will immediately move Anthony to the special education office if the behavior does not stop. It is critical to utilize a route that keeps him as far from the other students as possible. Use your body position to guide him, touching him as little as possible.*

    b. *Keep your composure; stay calm and emotionally neutral. Ignore the behavior at this time; just tell Anthony that it is time to go to the office with you so that the class will not be disrupted. This will provide a place for him to calm down and ensure everyone's safety.*

    c. *Have a plan for when you will be in the special education office. Keep a box of items that are effective in helping Anthony calm down in the office (e.g., book about animals). Tell Anthony that he can go back to the classroom once he is calm.*

Figure 4.7.   Step 1B Worksheet: Safety Plan for Anthony. (A blank, photocopiable version of this form is available in Appendix A, and blank and filled-in versions are available in the forms download.)

Step 1B Worksheet: Safety Plan *(continued)*   *page 2 of 2*

4. Begin recovery phase: Describe how to avoid reescalating the behavior and continuing to reach full recovery.
   a. *Preview before going back to the classroom. Explain to Anthony the schedule for the rest of the day, and preview the activity that he will be starting when he returns to the classroom.*
   b. *Review rules before going back to the classroom/activity. This clearly states the expectations for the classroom.*
   c. *Provide the structure needed to successfully complete task when returning back to work (e.g., paraeducator assistance for independent seat work, interact with peers).*
   d. *Provide praise for engaging in work activities and appropriately interacting with peers. Praise should not only happen once. It is important to provide praise frequently and immediately in order for it to be effective.*

5. Recovery phase: Describe any processing/reflecting that should be done with the student and how to reinstitute the positive behavior support plan.
   a. *Remind him of the rules for expected behavior and tell him that you know he can be more successful next time.*
   b. *At this point, we are not doing any processing with Anthony about incidents; later, the PBS plan may include a strategy for Anthony to reflect on his goals and better ways to reach them.*

Directions for reporting and documentation: Give instructions for reporting the incident and completing and filing Incident Records.
   a. *Complete an Incident Record. This needs to be done within 24 hours with as much detail as possible. Be objective in describing the incident, but add your own ideas about why the incident happened and what might prevent it in the future. Anyone who witnessed the behavior should complete an Incident Record. This allows for various points of view to be collected and documented.*

---

essentially is on "automatic pilot" and in a "fight-or-flight" mode at this point. He or she is unable to process complex verbal or rational information, so this is neither a good time to ask the student to process the experience nor an opportune time to try to rationally convince the student that his or her response is inappropriate. Trying to teach during this phase is not productive. Your goal at this point is protection only.)

4. *Begin recovery phase:* Once the student begins to calm down, what antecedents should not be reintroduced because they might reescalate the behavior? What will help to further deescalate the problem? It is still difficult to teach at this point; instead, will listening to music, deep breathing, walking, or talking about other things be used to further calm the student?

5. *Recovery phase:* The student may be ready and able to discuss what happened and what can be learned from the incident. What sort of processing, if any, should be done with the student? Does the student complete a reflection or self-evaluation? How and where is the PBS plan reinstituted? Is the use of alternative behaviors prompted and rewarded? (Carr and colleagues [1994] urged teachers and caregivers to use the window of opportunity that follows the end of a crisis to reinstitute their teaching of alternative behaviors and not to pull back and bask in the return to peace and quiet.) How is the student assisted to reenter the original setting? What participation goal is set, and what prompts are used to engage the student?

• Directions for completing an Incident Record (see Figure 4.8). The

Incident Record

Student: _Anthony_   Completed by: _Jared Simms (special education teacher)_

Day: _Friday_   Date: _November 2, 2014_   Time: _1:00 p.m.–1:30 p.m._

Setting: _Ms. Santos's second-grade classroom_

Class or activity: _Independent group classification and counting activity_

Staff present: _Ms. Santos, Mr. Simms, and Mrs. Giles_

Students present: _18 classmates, working in four groups at different activity centers_

1. Describe what happened earlier in the day or just before the incident that may have led to the incident.

    Anthony was at lunch and was unable to eat his favorite snack because his mother had forgotten to pack it in his lunch. Yesterday, the students also completed group classification and counting activities by rotating through centers. They were split into four groups and were rotated through two, finishing the last two on Friday during math time. The centers were hands on, fun, and preplanned, so I thought Anthony would enjoy them today like he did on Friday.

2. Describe the student's behavior and others' responses during the Trigger and Escalation phases.

    Ms. Santos gave instructions for the center activities and told the groups which centers to go to. Anthony went with his group to their assigned table. The children had to exchange different dinosaurs with one another and had to count and classify the dinosaurs they had during the activity. Anthony's expression seemed to change when he began to collect small plastic dinosaurs to count and graph and realized that another classmate had some of the dinosaurs. I sat down behind him so that I could prompt him to share materials and begin counting another set of dinosaurs. Despite my prompts, he still had a hard time staying focused and would refuse to change animals, however, and I could see him getting more frustrated. He started to push his seat from the table. I reminded him that the materials were there to share with his classmates and were part of the activity. I also reminded him that they were not his dinosaurs. He said, "This is mine" and grabbed all the dinosaurs from his classmate. I tried to ignore the behavior and gently prompted again that part of the game was to share. Anthony kept yelling things such as, "Stupid game" and "Mine, mine, mine."
    Jason, another peer, was sitting beside Anthony and said, "Come on, Anthony, let's play the game. We're going to get in trouble." Anthony pushed his chair back again and grabbed the dinosaurs back from Jason. I reminded Anthony of the rule against pushing and grabbing and tried to position his seat back at the desk, but he still continued to push his seat away several times from the table. Anthony was crying and began rocking back and forth saying, "Mine, I want it." At this point, his group stopped the activity.

3. Describe what the student and others did during the Crisis phase.

    I told Anthony that it was time for us to go to the conference room. I motioned for him to stand up and go to the door. He began to push me away as I grabbed for the animals. I then verbally asked him to put the animals away. He then put them away but continued making noises under his breath and went out the door ahead of me. When we got to the conference room, he laid down on the floor. I said, "Let's take some deep breaths and think about your favorite story; that will help us to calm down." I began to talk about his favorite story from a book he read earlier. He did the deep breathing. He was calm and quiet in about 5 minutes.

4. Describe the Begin Recovery and Recovery phases. Describe how the positive behavior support plan was reintroduced.

    I talked to Anthony about the different dinosaurs in the classroom that were a part of the activity, and I said, "I bet you can pick other dinosaurs if you exchange what you have with the other children. What are some other dinosaurs you could have picked?" He started to say other dinosaurs he could choose to hold. I said a lot of "good jobs" and gave him high fives. We finished talking in the conference room after about 8 minutes.
    Anthony asked, "Do I get computer time now?" I said, "No" and explained that it was time to go back to class to see Ms. Santos and the other boys and girls and that it was almost time for recess. He followed the direction and went to back into the classroom to finish the activity with his group.

5. To what extent was the Safety Plan followed? (Fully) Somewhat Very little

6. What is your hunch about the setting events or triggers of the behavior?

    Anthony's lunchtime routine was thrown off when he did not get the snack he expected to get. Furthermore, it seemed like Anthony planned to start the activity by counting and graphing dinosaurs, but when he could not get the materials he wanted he took them from Jason, rather than moving on to another dinosaur set. Anthony had his mind fixed on the animal set that he believed was his and did not want the other students to play with them.

7. What is your hunch about the purpose of the behavior or how it is working for the student?

    I think Anthony knows full well that he will often be able to get the things he wants if he grabs or pushes. His classmates often back down when he demands things.

8. What might prevent or interrupt the behavior more effectively in the future? What suggestions do you have to improve the Safety Plan?

    Explain the expectation of sharing materials to him before the activity; practice sharing and counting animals with the teacher beforehand to prepare him for the activity.

Figure 4.8. Incident Record for Anthony. (A blank, photocopiable version of this form is available in Appendix A, and blank and filled-in versions are available in the forms download.)

adult who intervened in the situation should complete the report as soon as possible after the episode; the information should be as detailed and specific as possible. Ask the person completing the report to problem-solve about ways the problem could have been prevented or can be handled more effectively in the future. Include instructions about who should be informed about the incident and where the completed Incident Record should be kept.

A written record of serious incidents and the use of a safety plan are required in most schools and can be helpful to the information-gathering and problem-solving processes used in Step 2: Plan and Conduct the Functional Behavior Assessment. An Incident Record such as that shown in Figure 4.8 serves both of these purposes. For example, the special education teacher who completed the sample Incident Record noted that changes in Anthony's lunch routine and Anthony's expectation for using certain animals to complete the classification activity may have helped trigger the incident, and Anthony attempted to get what he wanted by engaging in the difficult behavior. Furthermore, the teacher suggested that problems might be avoided in the future by making expectations for sharing materials clear at the beginning of the activity. This information will be useful for understanding the reasons for Anthony's problem behavior and for designing a support plan.

It can be tempting to think that the way a serious behavior incident is handled will be a primary factor in improving the student's behavior. It is not. The purpose of a safety plan is not to alter the future occurrence of a behavior but to interrupt a serious behavior when it does occur. Safety plans should be maintained for students with serious behaviors even after a behavior support plan

has been implemented in case a serious incident should occur. It may be more fruitful, however, to view a crisis as an event that can be used for further problem solving by the PBS team. "What did we learn that will help to avoid this situation in the future?" is an important question for teachers and the team to ask after a critical incident. Anthony's team always organized a quick team meeting after any serious incident when the special education teacher had been summoned to intervene. The team realized that, aside from ensuring that the serious incident did not result in harm to the student or others, the most important result would be using information about the incident to prevent future episodes. Once a support plan is in place, the frequency of critical incidents can serve as a measure of how effective the behavior support plan is in reducing problem behaviors. If critical incidents still occur, then it suggests that the support plan is not working and should be modified in some way.

One concern about using a safety plan is that some actions may be interpreted as giving in to or reinforcing the student's problem behavior. For example, removing an instructional task after Eleni screams may be viewed as giving in to the student's inappropriate demands. In part, this may be true, but the goal of a safety plan is to prevent or interrupt a crisis that may result in serious consequences for the students or others if allowed to continue and not to teach at the moment of crisis. If a teacher does not give in to the screaming and it results in Eleni hitting a classmate, which means the student must leave the room, then the student has been reinforced for a behavior that is worse than the original problem behavior, and no one benefits. Safety plans are used only in emergencies. The need to use a safety plan should be eliminated once problem behaviors are understood and a behavior support plan is implemented.

STEP 2

Plan and
Conduct the
Functional Behavior Assessment

 After defining the problem behaviors and making decisions about intervention targets (and addressing issues regarding safety management, if needed), the next step is to plan and conduct the FBA (see Figure 4.9).

The time and effort required to conduct an FBA for individualized interventions can vary greatly depending on the seriousness, intensity, and resistance of the target behavior. As previously indicated, the process described in this book is designed for use by school teams who have some training in PBS, with outside expertise added as needed to conduct a valid FBA and design and evaluate an effective PBS plan. Use the most efficient FBA methods required to create an effective

---

STEP 2

Plan and Conduct
the Functional Behavior Assessment

Step 2A. Gather descriptive (indirect) information from people who know the student well, including the student.

Ask: What do we know about the student's quality of life, needs, strengths, interests, and behavior history? Which classes and activities tend to be successful or unsuccessful?

Ask: How often and for how long do the behaviors targeted for intervention occur?

Ask: What information do we already have about the antecedents (both setting events and immediate triggers) that predict the behavior will occur? What consequences may be maintaining the behavior? What hunches do we have about the purpose or function of the problem behavior?

Decide: Do we have full and accurate answers to these questions? If "yes," then go to Step 2B; if "no," then continue to gather description information from key people in the student's life.

Step 2B. Conduct direct observations.

Ask: When, where, and how should direct observations be conducted so that we can gather the information we need to understand the behavior's antecedents, consequences, and purpose? Collect data for about 5 days or until clear patterns emerge.

Decide: Do we have adequate information to build solid hypotheses that will enable us to create an effective positive behavior support plan? If "yes," then go to Step 2C; if "no," then conduct additional observations for about 5 more days or until patterns emerge.

Step 2C. Summarize functional behavior assessment and build hypothesis statement(s).

Ask: What have we learned about the antecedents (setting events and triggers) that predict the behavior, the consequences that are maintaining the behavior, and the purpose the behavior serves for the student? What alternative behaviors will serve the same purpose for the student that the problem behavior now serves?

Decide: Do we have adequate information to complete the Step 2C worksheet, including valid hypothesis statements about the antecedents and consequences of the behavior and the purpose of the behavior? If "yes," then continue to Step 3; if "no," then go to Step 2D.

Step 2D. Test hypotheses.

Ask: When, where, and how can we informally verify (or disprove) our hypothesis statement(s)? How can naturally occurring routines or activities be altered in nonintrusive ways to allow us to compare the student's behavior under the usual conditions and the altered conditions? How often should we conduct the verification test to be sure the results are accurate?

Decide: Are we confident that we have built valid hypothesis statements based on the FBA? If "yes," then continue to Step 3; if "no," then continue testing.

Figure 4.9. Step 2: Plan and Conduct the Functional Behavior Assessment.

PBS plan. The methods used must be adequate, yet feasible, given the context and the personnel available. A wise tactic is to gather information in stages, beginning with the simplest, most user-friendly methods available and then proceeding to the use of more complex methods, as necessary. In some cases it may be possible to implement interventions around initial hunches about the reasons for a student's problem behavior as information is being gathered. The need for gathering more in-depth information may be reduced or eliminated if the student responds well.

The FBA for some students can primarily rely on indirect assessment methods completed by people who know the student well (and by the student, if possible). Discussions of pooled information from reviews of student records and the use of self-reports and interviews to complete FBA checklists and questionnaires may be adequate to enable the team to see the patterns of predictive antecedents and maintaining consequences and to build valid hypotheses. Direct observation methods would only be required to assess the baseline rate of the behavior and the effects of the PBS plan.

Indirect data collection methods must be augmented by direct observations as the complexity of the student's behavior problem and other needs increases. In addition, a structured observational procedure to test or verify the team's hypotheses about the behavior may be required. Hypothesis testing entails a simple verification process that is conducted in naturally occurring classroom routines (see Figure 4.1).

A combination of indirect methods, more extensive direct observations, and a formal functional analysis may be needed in the most complex cases. This certainly may be the case for students with few conventional means of communication who have self-injurious behaviors that serve several purposes. Such procedures, however, should not be conducted without the guidance of a qualified specialist (Horner, Sugai et al., 2000; Scott & Caron, 2005).

Step 2 may require three or four substeps because of the potential variations in the complexity of FBAs. Step 2A: Gather Descriptive (Indirect) Information, Step 2B: Conduct Direct Observations, and Step 2C: Summarize Functional Behavior Assessment and Build Hypothesis Statement(s) are always required; Step 2D: Test Hypotheses may be required. Whether Step 2D is necessary depends on the amount and types of information gathering that are needed in order for the team to understand the behavior well enough to construct effective interventions.

Step 2A: Gather Descriptive (Indirect) Information

After defining the behavior(s) to be targeted for intervention, the team gathers descriptive information about the student and his or her behavior problems from people who know the student well, from the student if possible, and from school records and documents (e.g., the student's IEP, previous behavior support plans, incident logs). Teams can choose from numerous published checklists and interview forms to gather indirect, descriptive information and formulate initial hunches or hypotheses about the student's behavior. Many of the tools are listed in Appendix B and include the Functional Assessment Interview (FAI; O'Neill et al., 2014), the Prevent-Teach-Reinforce (PTR) Functional Behavior Assessment Checklist (Dunlap et al., 2010), the Motivation Assessment Scale (MAS; Durand & Crimmins, 1988), and the FACTS (see Chapter 3; Crone et al., 2015). The Student-Centered FBA Profile, the Student Schedule Analysis, and the Incident Record are tools for indirect assessments provided in this book. It should be noted that the specific tools provided in this book have not been validated by research; however, the format and content of these tools are similar to instruments that have been research

Strengths/skills/interests
- What kinds of things do you do well?
- What school activities do you do best in?
- Do you have special interests or hobbies?

Behaviors of concern/associated events
- What kinds of behaviors get you into trouble?
- How often does this happen?
- When or in what situations/activities do you have the most problems? Least problems?
- What happens in problem situations? What kinds of things are difficult for you?
- If you could change one thing about situations that cause problems for you, what would that be?

Related context
- On days you have the most problems, what happens before or after school (e.g., stayed up late the night before, missed breakfast, had a fight with my parents, worried about being picked on)?
- What good things make a good day for you (before, during, or after school)?
- What bad things make a bad day for you (before, during, or after school)?

Favorite/disliked activities
- What subjects do you like/dislike (discuss or rate each one)?
- Are these subjects difficult/easy or boring/interesting?
- What types of instruction works best for you (small groups, large groups, tutoring, independent seat work)?

Figure 4.10. Sample questions to ask during a student interview. (*Sources:* Chandler & Dahlquist, 2015; Kern, Delaney, Clarke, Dunlap, & Childs, 2001; O'Neill, Albin, Storey, Horner, & Sprague, 2014.)

validated (e.g., the Functional Behavioral Assessment Interview [FBAI; Crone et al., 2015]). Furthermore, there is some evidence that the FBA data and hypotheses generated through indirect methods such as those provided in this book are substantially consistent with the results of FBAs that employ direct observations and functional analysis (Newcomer & Lewis, 2004).

An important source of information to gather during this first stage of assessment is from the student. The purpose of a student interview is to solicit the student's perspectives about the features of the classroom environment that may be related to his or her behaviors. Several instruments such as the Student-Assisted Functional Interview (Kern, Dunlap, Clarke, & Childs, 1994) and the Student-Guided Functional Assessment Interview (O'Neill et al., 2014) are in the resource list provided in Appendix B. A student might be asked to describe the following during an interview: 1) his or her strengths, skills, and preferences; 2) behaviors of concern; 3) perspectives about when behaviors occur and associated

events (i.e., why is it happening); 4) related contextual features or setting events; and 5) favorite and disliked academic tasks. Figure 4.10 lists some of the questions that might be asked during a student interview. These questions, and the instruments themselves, may be adapted for individual students and matched to their age or abilities (Chandler & Dahlquist, 2015). For example, pictures might be used for nonreaders to indicate favorite or disliked academic activities. Or, rather than interviewing students in one session, you can ask students to rate each relevant class activity using icons (e.g., "I liked/disliked this activity." "This worksheet was easy/hard." "This lesson was interesting/boring"). Accumulated information over time can help put the pieces together about the factors that are relevant to the student from his or her perspective.

Student-Centered Functional Behavior Assessment Profile

The Student-Centered FBA Profile (see Figure 4.11) is used to gather information

Step 2A Worksheet: Student-Centered
Functional Behavior Assessment Profile

Student: _Anthony Rodriquez_   Date: _October 30, 2014_

People providing initial information:

Jared Simms/special education teacher   _Rita Santos/second-grade teacher_

Marianne Josephs/school district behavior specialist   _Ashley Giles/paraeducator_

Angela and Jaime Rodriquez/parents   _Mara Kellam/school psychologist_

Directions: At a team meeting, summarize existing information about the student's problem behavior and begin to analyze the possible relationships among the behavior, the student's wants and needs, and the environment.

SECTION I: CLASSROOM CLIMATE

Directions: Review the Classroom Organization and Management Inventory (see Figure 3.1). Rate the extent to which each indicator is in place and the extent to which the target student understands and is responsive to expectations

Ratings:
Good = The indicator is in place satisfactorily.
Fair = The indicator is partially in place but improvement is needed.
Poor = The indicator is in place to an unacceptable degree or not at all.

Indicator	Rating/comments	Improvement needed
Physical space	Good: Classroom space is well organized	None
Classroom procedures/routines	Fair: Procedures are clear; not sure whether Anthony understands all	Individualize for Anthony
Supervision/monitoring	Good: Not sure whether forecasting of problems is clear for Anthony	Make sure Anthony can anticipate problems
Classwide positive behavior support (PBS) system (clear expectations, contingent feedback)	Good: Systems in place	None
Active engagement	Good: Strong systems in place	Perhaps strengthen directions for Anthony

Figure 4.11. Step 2A Worksheet: Student-Centered Functional Behavior Assessment Profile for Anthony. (A blank, photocopiable version of this form is available in Appendix A, and blank and filled-in versions are available in the forms download.)

(continued)

Figure 4.11. *(continued)*

<table>
<tr><td>Step 2A Worksheet (continued)</td><td align="right">page 2 of 5</td></tr>
</table>

SECTION II: QUALITY OF LIFE

Ratings:
Good = The indicator is in place satisfactorily.
Fair = The indicator is partially in place but improvement is needed.
Poor = The indicator is in place to an unacceptable degree or not at all.

Indicator	How is indicator in place?	Rating
Supportive people a. Family b. Adults at school c. Peers at school d. Peers outside of school	a. *Lives with parents, has an older sister, and is close to maternal grandparents* b. *Has positive relationships with special education teacher and classroom teacher; poor relationships with substitute teachers or paraeducators with whom he is unfamiliar. Anthony would benefit from increasing relationships with new teachers (paraeducators and substitutes) in order to be more successful in the classroom when they are present.* c. *Anthony is new to the second-grade classroom, and many of the students do not know him. Classmates are nervous around him and avoid him, especially when he engages in disruptive behaviors. Anthony could benefit from increasing positive friendships with peers in the classroom.* d. *Two classmates live in the neighborhood and know Anthony from hanging around outside of their homes. He also has two cousins, one older and one younger, with whom he visits and plays. Anthony would benefit by increasing peer relationships outside of the classroom as well.*	a. *Good* b. *Fair* c. *Fair to poor* d. *Fair*
Successful places and activities at school	*Participates in regularly scheduled routines and activities at school and participates most successfully during structured, routine, or teacher-led activities such as morning meetings and group instruction. Anthony struggles with independent seat work and unstructured and peer group activities.*	*Good to fair*
Successful places and activities at home and in the community	*Independent at completing daily home routines such as getting ready for school, cleaning up after dinner, and getting ready for bed.* *He participates in weekly events in the community, including attending church on Sundays and going to dinner at his grandparents' house.*	*Good*
Interests and preferences	• *Loves to read, loves books* • *Loves to listen to stories on the computer* • *Loves video games on the computer and on the television* • *Loves animals, especially cats, dogs, and dinosaurs* *Anthony has very strong interests but would benefit from less isolated and more social activities.*	*Fair*
Opportunities to make age-appropriate choices	*Anthony chooses his clothes, what he is having for lunch, and what he will do during free time activities at home. He chooses reading materials, games, computers, and writing utensils (crayons, markers, pens) for independent activities at school.*	*Good*

Based on the quality-of-life indicators, list shortcomings that might be addressed in a PBS plan.

• *Difficulty with unstructured activities and difficulty with tolerating new places or activities*
• *Limited interests in topics and isolated activities; broaden range of interests and activities*
• *Improvements in peer relationships, both in school and at home; increase social opportunities with same-age peers*

SECTION III: ACADEMICS AND COMMUNICATION

Academic strengths	Academic liabilities
• *Loves to read* • *Very attentive during small- or large-group instruction* • *Very good general knowledge*	• *Easily frustrated* • *Difficulty completing independent tasks* • *Seems dependent on teachers during work tasks* • *Insists on keeping materials or sequence of activities the same*

Step 2A Worksheet *(continued)*   *page 3 of 5*

Summarize the current fit between the student's educational programming and his or her academic strengths and liabilities.

Anthony's learning goals are at a lower level than his classmates, but many of the regular lessons and activities are adapted for him. He struggles with math and writing demands but works hard during individual instruction. Anthony has difficulty with independent seat work and with unstructured activities. He also has difficulty tolerating unplanned, new activities or changes in schedules.

Communication

What is the student's primary mode of communication (e.g., speech, signs, gestures, electronic devices), and how successful is the student in using it?

Anthony has good expressive language abilities and uses complete sentences to express his needs and feelings, ask questions, and convey ideas. Overall, he is very responsive to teacher questions and comments and will talk to his teacher when called on in class. He rarely initiates interactions with his teachers or peers. Anthony will express his emotions mostly through verbal language and disruptive behaviors. Anthony utilizes a visual schedule for making the transition throughout the day from activity to activity.

1. *Get attention/help/interaction:*

   Anthony will communicate what he needs when asked, "Do you need help?" but does not initiate requests on his own. Instead, he seems to gain attention by speaking very softly and repetitively to himself and on occasions by picking at his skin and rocking back and forth.

2. *Get preferred activities or tangible items:*

   Anthony is independent in getting materials himself but will push and grab when a peer has a preferred item, he is denied a preferred item, he is asked to give a preferred item to a peer, or he is told to put the item back where it belongs.
   He sometimes pushes peers aside to get to his favorite seat at group or the computer table. He is able to verbalize what he wants or needs when prompted by a teacher.

3. *Avoid/escape attention/interaction:*

   Anthony interacts with familiar teachers really well; he sometimes will fold his arms or walk away from unfamiliar adults. Anthony generally avoids interactions with peers by keeping to himself.

4. *Avoid/escape activity or item:*

   He will fold his arms and refuse to participate when he is trying to avoid or escape unplanned or unscheduled activities.

5. *Calm self when agitated, stressed, angry, overstimulated:*

   Anthony softly and repetitively self-talks under his breath, and sometimes he rocks his body back and forth.

6. *Get sensory stimulation (e.g., when bored):*

   Anthony sometimes rocks back and forth and picks at his arm, which may serve a sensory function, but this is not clear.

SECTION IV: MEDICAL, HEALTH, AND SENSORY CONCERNS

Describe any health concerns or medication that may be affecting the student's mood or behavior:

None at this time; he has regular checkups.

Describe any sensory difficulties or needs:

It seems like he picks at his arms when he is frustrated; unknown if this could be sensory related.

Other important information about medical and health history:

None

Figure 4.11.   (continued)

Step 2A Worksheet (continued)   page 4 of 5

SECTION V: TARGET BEHAVIORS AND PAST INTERVENTIONS

From Step 1A Worksheet, which behavior(s) will be targeted for intervention? Define the behaviors as clearly and specifically as possible. These are the definitions that will be used to collect any additional information and to develop the PBS plan.

1. *Crying/rocking: Crying starts off as a low whining with self-talk that gradually progresses loud enough to be heard at least 20 feet away and for a duration of 60 seconds or more. Rocking back and forth, along with picking at his skin (e.g., arm), occurs simultaneously as the crying escalates.*

2. *Grabbing/pushing: Grabbing objects with one or both hands to obtain a desired item. Pushing peers with one or both hands on any part of the other person's body. Usually does not result in hurting anyone, but he uses enough force to move the person out of his way, and it could result in injury.*

3. *Screaming: Screaming is directed toward a peer with very loud negative comments (e.g., "No!" "That's mine!") that can be heard by everyone in the room. Screaming usually co-occurs with grabbing/pushing if grabbing/ pushing did not obtain desired outcome.*

4. *Refusals: Occasionally displays refusals to participate in an activity by folding arms and repeating what should or should not happen next.*

Describe any current interventions for the behavior(s) (or attach any behavioral intervention plan that is currently in use).

- *No current behavior support plan*
- *He is reminded of the class rules and verbally redirected to the task when he engages in behaviors such as crying, screaming, grabbing, and pushing.*

What works to prevent or interrupt the behavior(s)?	What does not work to prevent or interrupt the behavior(s)?
• *Give him a break to look at a book.* • *Find a hands-on activity instead of a paper-and-pencil activity, or adapt the written task for him.* • *Let him know the schedule, remind him what is happening now, what is next, and what is later by showing him his visual schedule.*	• *Getting into a tug-of-war, giving a lot of corrections or threats* • *Encouraging him to work independently ("I know you can do this, Anthony")* • *Asking him to use his words when peers have materials that he wants*

SECTION VI: PRELIMINARY HUNCHES

Note: The team may want to complete the Student Schedule Analysis and several Incident Records (if they are being used to record incidents warranting use of a Safety Plan) before completing this section of the FBA Profile.

When this antecedent happens (setting event or trigger)	the student is likely to (target behavior)	and this consequence tends to occur	Therefore, the purpose of the behavior may be
1. Change in schedule/new people/new activities	*Refuses to participate by folding arms and talking to self by repeating what will happen next and/or cries/ rocks*	*Paraeducator attempts to refocus him, redirects him to the task, provides prompting to complete task; Anthony sometimes does not complete activity*	*To avoid or escape from difficult or new tasks/ activities*
2. Independent seat work activities or unstructured/ difficult tasks	*Cries/rocks, picks at arms*	*Paraeducator often sits down and works with him during completion of independent seat work*	*To avoid or escape from independent work/unstructured tasks*
3. At recess/free time, wants an object that a peer has or wants to engage in the same activity peer is completing	*Pushing/grabbing peers or screaming*	*Some peers tell him to stop, most peers tend to avoid him; an adult tells Anthony to apologize and Anthony sometimes obtains access to desired items*	*To gain attention from peers and obtain access to desired item(s)*
4. A lot of prompts or corrections in an authoritarian tone of voice or body language by an adult	*Yells "no"; states "That's mine," "I want that," "I won't do it"; cries or grabs materials; pushes or grabs at peers*	*Adult tells him to stop and uses gestures and verbal prompts to try to redirect him; if he does not stop, then adult takes him into the hall to calm down*	*To escape from adult interaction and from the task; obtain access to desired item(s)*

Step 2A Worksheet *(continued)* *page 5 of 5*

SECTION VII: DECISIONS AND NEXT STEPS

1. Should any other people be interviewed to ensure that the information on this profile is complete and accurate?   No

   If "yes," then list others who should be interviewed:

   Ashley Giles, paraeducator

2. Do quantifiable baseline data on the targeted behaviors need to be collected?   No

   If "yes," then when, where, and how will data be collected?

   We will use the Interval Recording or Scatter Plot form to collect frequency data on behaviors (pushing/grabbing, crying/rocking, and screaming) for 5 days. Jared, Ashley, and Rita will develop a schedule among themselves.

3. Is additional information needed to determine if the current hunches about the antecedents, consequences, and purposes of the behaviors are accurate?   No

   If "yes," then when, where, and how will data be collected?

   The Interval Recording and Scatter Plot will give us information about the antecedents and consequences of the behaviors.
   Antecedent-Behavior-Consequence (A-B-C) analysis will help us to better understand why Anthony is escaping independent work tasks or finds tasks difficult. A-B-C analysis observations will be done during the times of day that are usually the most difficult, during independent seat work and during changes in schedules and/or routines. Each activity will be observed three times for about 30–45 minutes each time.
   A-B-C Checklist will be used to identify potential setting events and triggers for refusals.
   We also will keep Incident Records on use of the Safety Plan. Jared, Rita, and Ashley will develop a schedule for conducting the observations.

---

or synthesize information obtained from other indirect resources about relevant aspects of the student's social, personal, behavioral, physical, and academic history and current status. It is designed to focus the initial stage of the FBA on the student's quality of life and the extent to which the student's strengths, needs, and interests are reflected in his or her current educational programming. It also summarizes target behaviors of concern and pools information to form preliminary hunches or hypotheses about problem behaviors.

The importance of encouraging and valuing family involvement cannot be overstated. It is not enough to simply invite families to participate—their priorities and vision for the future should be the foundation for the PBS plan (Dunlap et al., 2001). Implementing a person-centered planning process that is more comprehensive than the one incorporated

into the Student-Centered FBA Profile is one way to create a broader context for family participation. Such techniques include Making Action Plans (MAPS; Vandercook, York, & Forest, 1989), Planning Alternative Tomorrows with Hope (PATH; Pearpoint, O'Brien, & Forest, 1998), and personal futures planning (Mount, 2000).

Team members should do their homework before meeting to complete the Student-Centered FBA Profile so that they can come to the meeting prepared to share their responses to the items on the profile. Team members may decide to use other checklists or interview forms in conjunction with the Student-Centered FBA Profile to assist with their preparation. This information can then be shared and discussed at the team meeting. If there are other people who know the student well (e.g., family members, previous teachers, paraeducators) but did not attend the team meeting at which the Student-Centered FBA Profile was originally completed, then arrange interviews with them as soon as possible. If firsthand interviews with key people are not possible, then perhaps these people will be willing to respond through telephone calls, e-mail messages, or by completing the form themselves. Moving from broad to more specific influences of problem behavior, the Student-Centered FBA Profile provides space for the team to review, discuss, and record relevant information about the following.

- *Classroom climate:* Problem behavior for many students can be prevented when effective classroom management practices are implemented (see Chapter 3). Thus, it is prudent to first appraise the extent to which effective practices are in place before considering individualized interventions. Review the Classroom Organization and Management Inventory (see Figure 3.1), giving careful consideration to whether the student understands classroom expectations and is responsive to classwide interventions.

- *Quality of life:* How are quality-of-life indicators, such as the presence of supportive people, positive peer relationships, access to objects and activities of interest, and opportunities to make choices and decisions, in place for the student? In contrast, how often is the student expected to participate in contexts that are known to be disliked by or challenging for the student? Be sure to consider the student's perspectives gleaned from student interviews. After recording this information, assign a baseline rating for each indicator: Is the presence of each indicator "good," "fair," or "poor" at this time? If there are shortcomings in the presence of these critical indicators, then consider incorporating ideas for improvement into the student's PBS plan. Indeed, if

any quality-of-life indicators are rated as "poor," then making improvements in these areas should be a priority. Factors related to poor quality of life, such as poor peer interactions and general dissatisfaction with school, can signal inadequate contexts that make problem behaviors much more likely to occur. Others who write and conduct research on PBS have expressed similar sentiments (Bambara & Kern, 2005; Carr & Horner, 2007; Turnbull et al., 2004).

- *Academics:* Appraise the student's general academic strengths and liabilities, including the student's perspectives and preferences for academic tasks. List as much information as you can about the teaching approaches and strategies that have and have not worked for the student in the past. List what works (i.e., strategies that help learning and avoid behavior problems) and does not work (i.e., strategies that hinder learning and incite behavior problems) with the student. Also, consider the fit between the student's educational program and his or her academic strengths and weaknesses. Problem behaviors are often caused by a poor educational fit (e.g., the student finds the work challenging or too easy).

- *Communication:* Catalog the student's ability to communicate various wants and needs because communication is essential to social and behavioral health and competence. Describe how the student requests attention, help, and tangible items and how the student protests or rejects a situation or activity. Many students with developmental disabilities experience shortcomings in their communication abilities—and in the ability of others in their environment to interpret or provide support for their communication. These shortcomings should be addressed in the PBS plan.

- *Medical, health, and sensory:* Make note of any medical, health, or sensory difficulties that may be affecting the student's mood, concentration, physical comfort, or behavior.

- *Behavior:* Summarize the behaviors targeted for intervention. In addition, based on a review of IEP files and the knowledge of team members, describe what has and has not helped the student's behavior in the past. If formal behavior intervention plans have been implemented, then you may want to briefly summarize them and their results and keep copies with the student's other PBS records.

- *School records:* Note relevant information from school records, such as official disciplinary actions and attendance information, in this section of the worksheet.

- *Preliminary hunches about the behavior:* The team may or may not choose at this time to brainstorm some preliminary hunches about the predictive antecedents and maintaining consequences for each target behavior identified in Step 1. These hunches also can be informed by the Student Schedule Analysis and any Incident Records that have been completed. Figure 4.12 provides a list of questions to ask as you generate ideas with your team about possible setting events and triggers and the purposes the problem behavior may be serving for the student.

The Student Schedule Analysis is a simple yet helpful way to start looking for patterns in the student's behavior (see Figure 4.13). The classroom teacher and other team members who are familiar with the student's performance on a typical day enter the student's daily schedule in the first and second columns of the form. In the third column, team members estimate the average success rate or, alternatively,

the relative frequency of the target behavior(s) as well as a brief description of the behavior for each class or activity. The fourth, fifth, and sixth columns provide space to describe the behavior, the grouping arrangement, the task type (i.e., whether the activity involves paper-and-pencil tasks, oral communication, or hands-on learning), and the staff member or members who are with the student at that time. You may find that you want to use the columns on the Student Schedule Analysis for factors other than the ones included in Figure 4.13. For example, if you think there may be a relationship between the behavior and the type of seating arrangement or positioning, then you could use one column to note whether the student is positioned at a desk, in a wheelchair, or on the floor for each activity.

The Student Schedule Analysis may help to detect predictive antecedents by identifying when, where, and under what circumstances problem behaviors are most likely based on team member experiences. It also provides a record of how successful or problematic the classroom teacher and other team members perceive each class or activity to be. The opinions of the teacher and other people about whether the problem behavior improves or worsens are one meaningful indicator of the success of a behavior support plan. It is important to collect more objective data on the behavior, however, so that you can tell whether the behavior does in fact improve as a result of the intervention plan.

The Incident Record described earlier in this chapter and illustrated in Figure 4.8 serves as a way to keep track of the use of the safety plan that is necessary for some students. Completed Incident Records also yield information useful to the FBA because they include a report of the antecedents that led up to the critical behavior, what the student did throughout the incident, and the consequences that followed. Examining this information can assist in determining

Teams can use this list of questions to prompt their thinking about 1) setting events, 2) specific triggers that may predict the problem behavior(s), and 3) consequences that may be maintaining the target behavior(s).

1. **Questions to ask about triggers (or close antecedents):**

Where? The answers to "where" questions help you understand whether places and scheduled activities are related to the problem behavior.

Where or in which activity does the problem behavior most likely occur?
Where or in which activity does the problem behavior seldom or never occur?
Does it occur in certain subjects, classes, or school activities (e.g., math, English, music, physical education)?
Does it occur
  - On the playground?
  - In the classroom?
  - In the gym, library, or cafeteria?
  - In the restroom?
  - In the hallways?
  - On the bus or in the car?

When? The answers to "when" questions help you determine whether time of day, days of the week, and schedules are related to the problem behavior.

When does the problem behavior most often occur?
When does the problem behavior almost never occur?
  - Before school?
  - During the morning? During the afternoon?
  - At the end of the day?
  - Before, during, or after lunch?
  - During transitions?
  - During schedule changes? Change of teachers?

Who? The answers to "who" questions help you to see whether particular people or groups are related to the problem behavior.

Who is present when the problem behavior occurs?
Who is present when the problem behavior seldom or never occurs?
  - Are teachers, parents, staff, peers, older students, or strangers present?
  - How many people?
  - Are specific people associated with the presence or absence of problem behavior?
  - Is the student in a one-to-one, small-group, or large-group lesson?
  - Is someone about to come in or about to leave?
  - Is the student alone, with no interaction?

What? The answers to "what" questions help you discover whether certain tasks or situations within activities are related to the problem behavior.

What is going on when the problem behavior occurs?
What is going on when the problem behavior seldom or never occurs?
  - What kind of task is the student being asked to do? Is it hands on, paper and pencil, reading a textbook, or playing a board game?
  - What type of instruction is occurring? Is it individual seat work, a cooperative group activity, or a lecture?
  - Is the task structured or unstructured? Are the expectations clear or unclear?
  - Is the student being asked to do something too easy/boring or too hard/frustrating?
  - Is the student having to wait for help, attention, or a turn?
  - Is the student being told "no?" Is the student denied a desired object, activity, or food?
  - What type of interaction is the student involved in? Is he or she alone, being prompted or corrected, or being spoken to in a particular tone of voice?

Figure 4.12. Questions to ask about antecedents and consequences of problem behaviors.

2. Questions to ask about setting events (or distant antecedents):
What physical or environmental factors may be relevant? Noise? Crowds? High or low temperature? An uncomfortable body position?
What social factors may be relevant? The presence or absence of particular people? Being isolated when other peers are in groups? A conflict at home? Peer teasing?
What biological factors may be relevant? A lack of sleep? Allergies? Hunger? Constipation? Menstruation? A sore throat, cold, or ear infection?
What event factors may be relevant? Change in routine? Upcoming doctor or dentist appointment? Parent trip or vacation?

3. Questions to ask about consequences:
Does the student obtain attention, either positive or negative? From peers? From adults? From parents?
Does the student obtain a desired object, activity, or food immediately or eventually?
Does the student escape, avoid, or delay participation in an activity, task, or situation?
Do demands stop? Is the student sent to the office or time-out?
Does the student escape or avoid adult or peer interaction? Do people back off?

the predicting antecedents and maintaining functions of the behavior.

Completed Incident Records can be sorted into categories according to the types of antecedents that preceded each incident and the consequences that followed. A functional hypothesis may be revealed if the majority of incidents were preceded by the same or similar triggers and followed by the same consequences (e.g., the student obtained something tangible that he or she wanted, a difficult task was terminated).

The team will need to document decisions about what to do next in the last section of the Student-Centered FBA Profile. Should more descriptive information be gathered through interviews and records reviews, or should team discussions be conducted to shape preliminary hunches? Should the team prepare to move on to direct observations?

At the minimum, direct observations will be needed to assess the baseline rate or duration of the problem behavior before implementing a PBS plan. Even though school-based PBS teams are not conducting research, it is difficult to justify using a behavior intervention plan without having a modicum of objective data to show that the target behavior is improving—and improving at an acceptable rate.

Step 2B: Conduct Direct Observations

The amount of time and effort that the team spends conducting direct observations depends on many factors, including how much the behavior varies from one situation or one day to another, the number of problem behaviors targeted for intervention, how often the behaviors occur, and so forth. This section describes two ways to gather information through direct observation of the focus student in naturally occurring situations. A Scatter Plot form can be used to gather baseline data on the frequency with which the target behavior occurs and also is designed to provide information to aid in building or confirming hypothesis statement(s) (see Figures 4.14 and 4.15). The Antecedent-Behavior-Consequence (A-B-C) Observation form (see Figure 4.16) and the alternative A-B-C Checklist (see Figure 4.17) also give a wealth of information about the antecedents and consequences influencing the behavior and are useful when more information is needed to develop hypotheses.

When Are Direct Observations Conducted and by Whom?

The more time-consuming direct observation methods do not necessarily need to

Student Schedule Analysis

Student: _Anthony_

Date: _October 22, 2014_

Staff who work with student on a regular basis:

Jared Simms, special education teacher (JS)
Ashley Giles, paraeducator (AG)
Rita Santos, second grade (RS)

Specialty teachers:

Barns (physical education); Jones (library); Pena (art); Vanier (music)

Target behavior(s):

1. Crying/rocking: A low whining with self-talk that gradually progresses to crying loud enough to be heard at least 20 feet away and has a duration of 60 seconds or more. Rocking back and forth, along with picking at his skin (e.g., arm), occurs simultaneously as the crying escalates.

2. Grabbing/pushing/screaming: Grabbing objects with one or both hands to obtain a desired item. Pushing peers with one or both hands on any part of the other person's body. Usually does not result in hurting anyone, but it is enough to move the person out of his way and could result in injury. Screaming usually co-occurs with grabbing/pushing if grabbing/pushing did not obtain desired outcome.

Time	Class/activity	Rating and behavior + = mild/rare − = excessive/often v = variable	Grouping i = independent 1:1 = one-to-one sg = small group lg = large group u = unstructured p = peer	Task type Paper/pencil Oral/listening Hands on Activity/routine Computer	Staff
8:30	Arrival; walk from bus to classroom	+	i	Activity/routine	AG
8:40	Morning routine: unpack backpack, order lunch, turn in notes, perform classroom jobs	+	i	Activity/routine	AG
9:00	Morning check-in/ weather review	+	lg	Oral/listening	RS
9:15	Math (group lessons and independent seat work)	− (crying/rocking)	lg or i	Paper/pencil	RS and AG
9:55	Snack/break	− (grabbing/pushing/ screaming)	u	Activity/routine	RS
10:05	Specials: physical education (Wednesday and Friday), art (Monday); music (Tuesday); library (Thursday)	+ (Physical education) + (Music) v (Art and library: grabbing/pushing/ screaming)	peer, i, or sg	Physical education: activity/ routine Art: hands on Music: oral/listening Library: oral/ listening	Specialty teachers
10:35	Reading (small-group instruction and independent seat work)	− (crying/rocking)	sg or i	Paper/pencil, hands on, oral/ listening, or computer	RS and JS
11:15	Lunch	+	u or peer	Activity/routine	Cafeteria aides
11:45	Recess/free time	− (grabbing/pushing/ screaming)	i or peer	Activity/routine	RS and AG
12:15	Language arts/ writing	v (crying/rocking)	sg or i	Oral/listening or computer	JS and AG
1:00	Social studies (Monday, Wednesday, Friday); science (Tuesday and Thursday); small-group and peer-to-peer group activities	v (grabbing/pushing/ screaming)	sg, peer, or i	Hands on, oral/ listening, or paper/pencil	RS and AG
1:45	Topic of the week discussion	+	sg	Oral/listening or hands on	RS and JS
2:30	Pack-up routine for departure; activity of choice, if earned	+	i	Activity/routine, computer, or hands on	AG

Figure 4.13. Student Schedule Analysis for Anthony. (From Meyer, L., & Janney, R. [1989]. User-friendly measures of meaningful outcomes: Evaluating behavioral interventions. *Journal of The Association for Persons with Severe Handicaps*, 14 [4], 267; adapted by permission.) (A blank, photocopiable version of this form is available in Appendix A, and blank and filled-in versions are available in the forms download.)

be used across entire days. Observations can be scheduled for times when the information gathered for Step 2A indicates that the problem behavior is most and least likely to occur. For example, the Student Schedule Analysis might indicate that the student's behavior is predictably more of a problem in certain classes or situations than in others; additional data collection can focus on gathering more specific, objective information about the student's behavior in those situations, rather than continuously throughout the day.

If a PBS specialist or school psychologist is consulting with the team, then he or she will be available to conduct at least some of the direct observations or teach other team members, teaching or administrative interns, other support personnel, or paraeducators how to do them. Although it may not be feasible for a teacher to do A-B-C recording while teaching a lesson, it has been the authors' experience that many teachers are able to maintain frequency counts using the Interval Recording/Scatter Plot form. If a special education teacher and a general education teacher are teaching collaboratively, or if a special education consulting teacher is providing consultative services to the classroom, then using some of that time for data collection can be a legitimate use of the special educator's time. If a paraeducator, student teacher, or intern is available, then he or she can be trained to assist in data collection.

Use the Team Meeting Agenda and Minutes form (see Figure 1.4) to record your decisions about which direct observation methods will be used, the names of the people responsible for completing them, and the dates and times when they will be completed.

Measuring Frequency or Duration

Examples of problem behaviors that have a clear starting and stopping point, which enables the observer to count how often the behavior occurs, are used in the following explanations of direct observation methods. For example, if the problem behavior is hitting other people, then the observer would count the frequency with which this happens. Note, however, that if the problem behavior is one that does not have a clear starting or stopping point or if it occurs for greatly varying periods of time, then the observer would need to measure how long each instance lasts. For example, if the student's crying episodes sometimes last just a few minutes and other times for 10 minutes or more, then simply counting the number of times the student cries would not show whether the amount of time spent crying was changing over time. A student could cry five times in 1 day for a total of 5 minutes, or he or she could cry five times in 1 day for a total of 90 minutes. In this case, the duration of the crying is important information to have in addition to the number of times the student cries.

Scatter Plot

Using the Scatter Plot form involves counting (or estimating) the frequency with which a behavior occurs during predetermined intervals of time (e.g., 1 minute, 10 minutes, 30 minutes). The Scatter Plot form can be used in several different ways. One way is to conduct a frequency count as in Figure 4.14. The observer tallies each time the behavior occurs during each time period. A second way is to estimate the number of times a behavior occurs by doing partial interval recording, as used in the original scatter plot method (Touchette, MacDonald, & Langer, 1985). The observer uses a code to record the relative frequency of the behavior during each time interval. For example, an open circle (○) was used in Figure 4.15 to indicate that the behavior had occurred once during a 30-minute time period. The circle was filled in (●) to show more than one occurrence of the behavior. In other words, the person recording the data drew an open circle the first time the behavior

Interval Recording or Scatter Plot

Student: _Anthony_　　　　　　　　　　　　Dates: _11/9/14 through 11/13/14_

Target behaviors:

1. Crying/rocking: A low whining with self-talk that gradually progresses to crying loud enough to be heard at least 20 feet away and has a duration of 60 seconds or more. Rocking back and forth, along with picking at his skin (e.g., arm), occurs simultaneously as the crying escalates.

2. Grabbing/pushing/screaming: Grabbing objects with one or both hands to obtain a desired item. Pushing peers with one or both hands on any part of the other person's body. Usually does not result in hurting anyone, but it is enough to move the person out of his way and could result in injury. Screaming usually co-occurs with grabbing/pushing if grabbing/pushing did not obtain desired outcome.

Used for:　　　✓ Frequency count (tally each time behavior occurs within each interval)
　　　　　　　___ Scatter plot (Key: ○ = one occurrence; ● = more than one occurrence)
　　　　　　　✓ Critical incident and use of Safety Plan (indicated by X)

Time	Activity	Monday 11/9 Cry/rock	Monday 11/9 Grab/push/scream	Tuesday 11/10 Cry/rock	Tuesday 11/10 Grab/push/scream	Wednesday 11/11 Cry/rock	Wednesday 11/11 Grab/push/scream	Thursday 11/12 Cry/rock	Thursday 11/12 Grab/push/scream	Friday 11/13 Cry/rock	Friday 11/13 Grab/push/scream	Total Cry/rock	Total Grab/push/scream
8:30	Arrival/morning routine											0	0
8:40	↓											0	0
9:00	Morning check-in/weather review											0	0
9:15	Math large-group instruction											0	0
9:30	↓ Math large-group instruction											0	0
9:45	↓ Independent seat work	//		/		/		/		/		6	0
9:55	Snack/break				/		//					0	3
10:05	Specials: physical education (Wednesday and Friday), art (Monday), music (Tuesday), library (Thursday)											0	0
10:20	↓		///						//			0	5
10:35	Reading small-group instruction											0	0
10:50	↓ Independent seat work			//		/				//		5	0
11:05	↓ Small-group instruction											0	0

Figure 4.14. Interval Recording or Scatter Plot used to gather frequency data on Anthony's behavior. (A blank, photocopiable version of this form is available in Appendix A, and blank and filled-in versions are available in the forms download.)

Interval Recording or Scatter Plot *(continued)*

Time	Activity	Monday 11/9 Cry/rock	Monday 11/9 Grab/push/scream	Tuesday 11/10 Cry/rock	Tuesday 11/10 Grab/push/scream	Wednesday 11/11 Cry/rock	Wednesday 11/11 Grab/push/scream	Thursday 11/12 Cry/rock	Thursday 11/12 Grab/push/scream	Friday 11/13 Cry/rock	Friday 11/13 Grab/push/scream	Total Cry/rock	Total Grab/push/scream
11:15	Lunch											0	0
11:30	↓											0	0
11:45	↓											0	0
12:00	↓											0	0
12:15	Language arts/ writing small-group instruction											0	0
12:30	↓ Independent seat work	//		/		///				/		7	0
12:45	Social studies/ science small-group instruction										/	0	1
1:00	↓ Independent	/		//		/		/		/		6	0
1:15	↓ Peer to peer		/				//		/		//	0	6
1:30	Free time		/	/			//					1	3
1:45	↓ Independent or peer	/			//	/			/	/		3	3
2:00	Topic of the week discussion small-group instruction											0	0
2:15	↓ Small-group instruction											0	0
2:30	↓ Small-group instruction											0	0
2:45	Pack-up routine/activity of choice											0	0
Total problem behaviors/day		6	6	7	4	7	4	2	4	6	3		

	Crying/rocking	Grabbing/ pushing/ screaming	Critical incidents/ use of Safety Plan
Total per week	28	21	n/a
Average per day	5.6	4.2	n/a
Average per hour	n/a	n/a	n/a

Interval Recording or Scatter Plot

page 1 of 2

Student: <u>*Anthony*</u>   Dates: <u>*11/9/14 through 11/13/14*</u>

Target behaviors:

1. *Crying/rocking: A low whining with self-talk that gradually progresses to crying loud enough to be heard at least 20 feet away and has a duration of 60 seconds or more. Rocking back and forth, along with picking at his skin (e.g., arm), occurs simultaneously as the crying escalates.*

2. *Grabbing/pushing/screaming: Grabbing objects with one or both hands to obtain a desired item. Pushing peers with one or both hands on any part of the other person's body. Usually does not result in hurting anyone, but it is enough to move the person out of his way and could result in injury. Screaming usually co-occurs with grabbing/pushing if grabbing/pushing did not obtain desired outcome.*

Used for: ___ Frequency count (tally each time behavior occurs within each interval)
  _✓_ Scatter plot (Key: ○ = one occurrence; ● = more than one occurrence)
  _✓_ Critical incident and use of Safety Plan (indicated by X)

Time	Activity	Monday 11/9	Tuesday 11/10	Wednesday 11/11	Thursday 11/12	Friday 11/13	Total
8:30	*Arrival/morning routine*						*0*
8:40	↓						*0*
9:00	*Morning check-in/ weather review*						*0*
9:15	*Math large-group instruction*						*0*
9:30	*↓ Math large-group instruction*						*0*
9:45	*↓ Independent seat work*	●	○	○	○	○	*6*
9:55	*Snack/break*						*0*
10:05	*Specials: physical education (Wednesday and Friday), art (Monday), music (Tuesday), library (Thursday)*						*0*
10:20	↓	*Art*	*Music*	*PE*	*Library*	*PE*	*0*
10:35	*Reading small-group instruction*						*0*
10:50	*↓ Independent seat work*		●	○		●	*5*
11:05	*↓ Small-group instruction*						*0*

Figure 4.15. Interval Recording or Scatter Plot used to create a scatter plot for Anthony's behavior. (A blank, photocopiable version of this form is available in Appendix A, and blank and filled-in versions are available in the forms download.) (*Key:* PE, physical education.)

Interval Recording or Scatter Plot *(continued)*   *page 2 of 2*

Time	Activity	Monday 11/9	Tuesday 11/10	Wednesday 11/11	Thursday 11/12	Friday 11/13	Total
11:15	Lunch						0
11:30	↓						0
11:45	↓						0
12:00	↓						0
12:15	Language arts/ writing small-group instruction						0
12:30	↓ Independent seat work	●	○	●		○	7
12:45	Social studies/ science small-group instruction						0
1:00	↓ Independent	○	●	○	○	○	6
1:15	↓ Peer to peer						0
1:30	Free time		○				1
1:45	↓ Independent or peer	○		○		○	3
2:00	Topic of the week discussion small-group instruction						0
2:15	↓ Small-group instruction						0
2:30	↓ Small-group instruction						0
2:45	Pack-up routine/activity of choice						0
Total intervals per day in which behavior occurred		6	7	7	2	6	
Total intervals per week in which behavior occurred							28

occurred. Then the open circle was filled in if the behavior occurred a second time during that 30-minute interval. Further instances of the behavior were not counted again until the next interval began.

When using the Scatter Plot form for frequency or partial interval recording, it is important to use intervals that are short enough to estimate the behavior's frequency as closely as possible. For instance, if the time intervals are 30 minutes and the behavior sometimes occurs up to 10 times per interval, then a closed circle will not tell whether the behavior occurred two times or 10 times during an interval. This means that the recording method could mask a great deal of change in the student's behavior. If the time intervals are 10 minutes long and the behavior typically occurs between one and three times per interval, then a scatter plot will accurately reflect a change in the behavior. Try to establish a time interval that will reliably show variations in the behavior yet will still be feasible for data collection in a classroom situation.

Use of the Scatter Plot form has a great advantage over simply keeping a running tally of the number of times the behavior occurs daily. Interval recording provides information about the relative frequency of the behavior during different time periods and classroom activities so that hypotheses about antecedents and consequences that may be influencing the behavior can be developed. By examining the intervals/activities when the behavior is most and least likely to occur, you can begin to identify particular people, types of activities, amounts of attention, and types or intensity of demands that tend to trigger the problem behavior. For example, Figure 4.14 reveals clear patterns for Anthony. The Scatter Plot shows that Anthony was more likely to cry and rock during independent seat work activities in any academic subject, but this behavior did not occur at all in any large-group activities. In fact, Anthony was always engaged and highly responsive during

any teacher-led activity. Although the specific triggers for crying and rocking were unclear, the team reasoned that his behaviors had nothing to do with a particular academic subject but rather the nature of independent seat work. Task difficulty did not seem to cause problems for Anthony as the complexity of tasks varied across academic subjects and days, yet problem behaviors continued to occur. The team would have to dig a bit more to uncover specific triggers for independent activities. The Scatter Plot form also revealed that grabbing, pushing, and shoving largely occurred during peer-to-peer or unstructured activities in which the teacher did not lead. All of these activities required Anthony to share materials, wait for his turn, and problem-solve when he could not immediately gain access to materials. His grabbing/pushing clearly functioned for him to gain access to materials. The information gained through the Scatter Plot form helped to confirm the team's hunches about where Anthony's behaviors are most problematic and provided a starting point for conceptualizing interventions. At a minimum, it seemed that more structure and support was needed for Anthony in situations in which the teacher was not immediately present.

Antecedent-Behavior-Consequence Observations

Using an A-B-C Observation form (see Figure 4.16) involves observing the student in a naturally occurring situation and immediately recording 1) the antecedents to the student's problem behavior, 2) the student's problem behavior, 3) the consequences or anything that happens after the student's problem behavior, and 4) the observer's hypothesis about the purpose or function of the problem behavior that was observed. With respect to time and effort, A-B-C observations are the most difficult type of information-gathering discussed in this chapter; however, these

Antecedent-Behavior-Consequence Observation

page 1 of 2

Student: *Anthony*

Date: *November 10, 2014*

Setting: *Ms. Santos's 2nd grade classroom*

Observer: *Mara Kellam (school psychologist)*

Class/subject: Social Studies, small group instruction. Topic: Good citizenship

Mr. Simms, special education teacher, is co-teaching with Ms. Santos. Ms. Giles, paraeducator, is in the classroom assisting as needed.

Target behaviors (see Step 2A Worksheet: Student-Centered Functional Behavior Assessment Profile for observable definitions of behaviors)

1. Crying/rocking
2. Grabbing/pushing
3. Screaming
4. Refusing

Time	Antecedents (What was going on before the behavior? What was being said and done?)	Behavior (What did the student do?)	Consequences (What happened after the behavior? How did people react?)	Hypothesis (About the function of the behavior)
12:45	Mr. Simms begins social studies instruction. Mr. Simms explains that the class will be discussing what it means to be a good citizen. Mr. Simms reads a story about citizenship and explains the attributes of a good citizen. He then explains that the class will take 10 minutes to independently list qualities of a person in their lives who they think is a good citizen and why.	Anthony is sitting quietly at his desk. Anthony is focused on Mr. Simms and seems to be listening to the discussion. His favorite pencil and a notebook are in front of him at his desk. When instructed to write qualities of a good citizen, Anthony picks up his pencil and begins to write on his paper.	None	n/a
12:55	Mr. Simms and Ms. Santos ask the students to write down what they think are qualities of a good citizen and write down a person in their lives who they believe is a good citizen.	Anthony gets started right away. He picks up his pencil and writes one word but then begins to look around the classroom at his peers. He twirls his pencil and says under his breath, "I need help." Anthony looks confused, and he continues to self-talk and begins to cry. It was difficult to hear what he was saying because he was mumbling and whispering.	Ms. Giles asks Anthony if he needs help, and Anthony nods his head. Ms. Giles explains the assignment to Anthony, and he begins to write down his answers on a piece of paper given to him by Ms. Giles.	Anthony did not fully understand the expectation of the assignment and attempted to escape, but his attempt was not successful.
1:15	Mr. Simms explains to the class that they will continue to work independently. He will give them situations, and they will write a paragraph in their notebook telling how they would respond to each situation given.	Anthony begins to fidget at his desk again and seems to be looking for something, but he has his pencil and a piece of paper. Anthony starts to mumble under his breath again, but it is difficult to understand what he is saying.	Ms. Giles tells Anthony to get to work and that he knows what to do.	Anthony may be trying to escape the activity again, but he may be looking for help again.

Figure 4.16. Antecedent-Behavior-Consequence Observation for Anthony. (A blank, photocopiable version of this form is available in Appendix A, and blank and filled-in versions are available in the forms download.)

(continued)

Figure 4.16. *(continued)*

Time	Antecedents (What was going on before the behavior? What was being said and done?)	Behavior (What did the student do?)	Consequences (What happened after the behavior? How did people react?)	Hypothesis (About the function of the behavior)
1:20	*Mr. Simms reads the first scenario and the class begins to write their answers in their notebooks.*	*Anthony is continuing to mumble under his breath, but it continues to be difficult to understand what he is saying. Anthony is still fidgeting with his pencil, and he cries and begins to rock.*	*Ms. Santos approaches Anthony and reiterates what Ms. Giles had stated about staying focused and that he knows what to do.*	*Anthony was trying to escape the task. Again, Anthony's attempt to escape the activity was not successful, but did receive attention from the teacher.*
1:30	*Students are writing down their answers to the situation given.*	*Anthony now begins to cry louder and rock harder.*	*Ms. Giles again approaches Anthony and asks him if he needs help. After talking with Anthony, Ms. Giles realizes that Anthony cannot find his favorite notebook to write in. She searches his desk and finds his notebook under some of the paper given to Anthony to complete his assignment.*	*Anthony misplaced an item. He seemed to settle down once Ms. Giles searched for his book. Perhaps his behavior serves to gain teacher assistance instead of escaping from writing in his notebooks.*
1:35	*Ms. Giles finds Anthony's notebook and says, "Just ask for help next time, Anthony."*	*Anthony grabs his notebook from Ms. Giles and begins to refocus and writes his answer in his notebook.*	*Ms. Giles praises Anthony, "That's the way to go."*	*With the correct materials and a better understanding, Anthony completes his assignment. Crying and rocking seem to get him teacher assistance when needed.*

observations can be extremely helpful for problem solving and uncovering problem variables and event patterns that are not yet clear to the team. Furthermore, you can use information from the Student Schedule Analysis or a completed Interval Recording/Scatter Plot to find the specific periods of time that are the most problematic and then conduct observations only during those times.

Figure 4.16 shows a sample A-B-C observation for Anthony. Anthony's team conducted this observation to better understand the specific triggers for Anthony's crying and rocking during independent seat work. The school psychologist conducted three half-hour observations of Anthony on three different days, focusing specifically on independent seat work activities. Anthony's teachers and other team members examined the A-B-C observations and immediately noticed that Anthony participated appropriately while the teacher led an activity and gave directions to the entire class for their independent work assignments. Anthony often encountered problems or seemingly needed additional reassurance from his teachers, however, once he started to work independently. Although Anthony sometimes mumbled requests for help, these requests were rarely audible to his teachers. His teachers offered assistance when he began to rock and cry. The observations revealed that triggers revolved around Anthony's need for assistance—when he did not fully understand an assignment, when he encountered a problem he could not solve, and when he misplaced his pencil or book. The more time Anthony's teachers took to come to his aid, the more likely crying and rocking would escalate into tantrums. Given that Anthony was rarely observed initiating any interactions with his teachers and peers, crying and rocking clearly functioned to communicate, "I need help." The observations pointed to critical skills that Anthony would need to learn to work more independently and appropriately request teacher assistance.

Use of the A-B-C Observation form requires keen observational skills and narrative recording, which can be time consuming. In addition, sometimes observers do not know what antecedent or consequences to look for and as a result may miss critical events. The A-B-C Checklist provides a more time-efficient alternative to the narrative A-B-C Observation form (a blank, photocopiable version of the checklist is available in Appendix A and the forms download). The observer simply makes a checkmark for each occurrence of problem behavior, observed antecedents, the form of the problem behavior, consequences, or perceived function. Items on the checklist can be individualized to the student and contain suspected problem variables based on the team's hunches. When suspected variables are unclear, the checklist can be constructed to contain some common antecedent and consequences that are problematic for

students in general, such as difficult/easy work tasks, teacher demands, corrections, and peer teasing.

Figure 4.17 shows how the A-B-C Checklist was individualized for Anthony. Anthony's refusals to participate in class activities were rare. Anthony's team collaborated to identify possible setting events, triggers, problem behaviors, and consequences relevant for Anthony. His teachers then used the checklist on days he refused to participate in activities to reveal specific setting events and triggers that may have provoked his refusals.

There are no hard-and-fast rules about how long direct observations should continue to estimate the frequency of problem behavior, but 5 consecutive days are a reasonable start (McConnell, Cox, Thomas, & Hilvitz, 2001). Observations should continue until clear patterns emerge when conducting direct observations for the purposes of identifying or confirming suspected antecedents and consequences. When this occurs, the team is ready to move on to the next step.

Step 2C: Summarize Functional Behavior Assessment and Build Hypothesis Statement(s)

Step 2C consists of summarizing all data that have been gathered to develop hypothesis statement(s) about the behavior. The Step 2C Worksheet: Summary of Functional Behavior Assessment and Hypothesis Statement(s) (see Figure 4.18) asks for a report on the baseline frequency and duration of target behavior(s), hypothesis statements for the problem behavior(s), and suggested alternative behaviors that may replace problem behavior(s).

To generate hypothesis statements, the team considers all information gathered through indirect and direct assessments to identify reliable patterns or A-B-C chains that explain why problem behavior occurs (events that predict it, maintain it, and the function served for

Antecedent-Behavior-Consequence Checklist

Date/ period	Activity/setting	Setting event	Antecedent	Behavior	Consequence
11/16 Start: 10:40 a.m. End: 10:50 a.m.	☐ Arrival ☐ Math ☐ Physical education ☐ Music ☑ Reading ☐ Language arts/writing ☐ Lunch ☐ Science ☐ Recess ☐ Library ☐ Snack ☐ Art ☐ Social studies ☐ Departure	☐ Lack of sleep ☐ Missed breakfast ☐ Teacher absent ☑ Half day ☐ Snow day ☐ Schedule change ☐ Not feeling well ☐ _____ ☐ _____ ☐ _____	☐ Teacher direction ☑ Presentation of task ☐ Peer interactions ☐ Nonpre- ferred activity ☐ _____ ☐ _____ ☐ _____	☐ Crying ☐ Rocking ☐ Grabbing ☐ Pushing ☐ Screaming ☑ Refusing	☐ Verbal redirection ☐ Paraeducator assisted with activity ☐ Escape from activity ☑ Did not complete the activity ☐ Delayed the activity ☐ _____ ☐ _____ ☐ _____
11/16 Start: 1:10 p.m. End: 1:20 p.m.	☐ Arrival ☐ Math ☐ Physical education ☐ Music ☐ Reading ☐ Language arts/writing ☐ Lunch ☑ Science ☐ Recess ☐ Library ☐ Snack ☐ Art ☐ Social studies ☐ Departure	☐ Lack of sleep ☐ Missed breakfast ☐ Teacher absent ☑ Half day ☐ Snow day ☐ Schedule change ☐ Not feeling well ☐ _____ ☐ _____ ☐ _____	☑ Teacher direction ☐ Presentation of task ☐ Peer interactions ☐ Nonpre- ferred activity ☐ _____ ☐ _____ ☐ _____	☐ Crying ☐ Rocking ☐ Grabbing ☐ Pushing ☐ Screaming ☑ Refusing	☐ Verbal redirection ☐ Paraeducator assisted with activity ☐ Escape from activity ☐ Did not complete the activity ☑ Delayed the activity ☐ _____ ☐ _____ ☐ _____
11/24 Start: 9:30 a.m. End: 9:40 a.m.	☐ Arrival ☑ Math ☐ Physical education ☐ Music ☐ Reading ☐ Language arts/writing ☐ Lunch ☐ Science ☐ Recess ☐ Library ☐ Snack ☐ Art ☐ Social studies ☐ Departure	☐ Lack of sleep ☐ Missed breakfast ☐ Teacher absent ☐ Half day ☑ Snow day ☐ Schedule change ☐ Not feeling well ☐ _____ ☐ _____ ☐ _____	☐ Teacher direction ☑ Presentation of task ☐ Peer interactions ☐ Nonpre- ferred activity ☐ _____ ☐ _____ ☐ _____	☐ Crying ☐ Rocking ☐ Grabbing ☐ Pushing ☐ Screaming ☑ Refusing	☐ Verbal redirection ☐ Paraeducator assisted with activity ☑ Escape from activity ☐ Did not complete the activity ☐ Delayed the activity ☐ _____ ☐ _____ ☐ _____

Figure 4.17. Antecedent-Behavior-Consequence Checklist for Anthony. (*Sources:* Kern, O'Neill, & Starosta, 2005; Loman & Borgmeier, 2010.) (A blank, photocopiable version of this form is available in Appendix A, and blank and filled-in versions are available in the forms download.)

the student). Answer the following questions when summarizing the patterns: Under what circumstances is problem behavior most likely to occur? When or under what circumstances is it least likely to occur? What consequences typically follow problem behaviors? Based on this A-B-C chain, what function does problem behavior seem to serve for the student? Revisiting the questions in Figure 4.12 can be useful in summarizing predictable patterns.

Hypothesis statements are important because they will create the link between the assessment information gathered and the behavior support plan. Good hypothesis statements 1) are succinct, 2) identify variables that can be changed, 3) are grounded in the assessment information gathered, and 4) reflect team consensus that the hypothesis provides a reasonable explanation for problem behavior (Bambara & Kern, 2005). More than one hypothesis statement may be needed to explain different patterns.

Hypothesis statements have been written in various ways but always include three important pieces of information: 1) the antecedents, 2) a description of the target behavior, and 3) the consequences following the behavior or the function or outcome the behavior served for the student. We recommend the format illustrated in Figure 4.19 for writing hypothesis statements. Additional examples are shown for Anthony in his summary worksheet (see Figure 4.18). Three hypothesis statements were written for Anthony, one for each pattern of problem behavior.

Decision Point:
Do Hypotheses Need Testing?

Generating a valid hypothesis about the purpose of a problem behavior is one of the most important steps in developing a plan for PBS. It also can be a very difficult step. The information that has been gathered through indirect methods and direct

observations sometimes reveals clear patterns that suggest hypotheses about the behavior's purpose(s), as illustrated by the following Student Snapshots.

 ### Student Snapshot

Sofie's problem behavior was throwing materials and sometimes hitting adults on the arm or hand. The team used a scatter plot to analyze the antecedents of Sofie's throwing and hitting and noticed that the behaviors tended to occur at about the same times each day, during one-to-one instructional sessions with the special education teacher or assistant. The behaviors did not occur during small- or large-group lessons of any kind. Incident Records of the times Sofie hit other people showed that the consequence for hitting was to take Sofie to a time-out chair at the back of the classroom where she had to sit for 10 minutes. Because Sofie's one-to-one instructional sessions were only about 10 minutes long, it usually was time for the next activity when Sofie had completed her time-out, so she never completed the tasks provided during her one-to-one instruction. Sofie's hitting did not decrease during the 2 weeks that the team gathered information. The team hypothesized that the purpose of Sofie's throwing and hitting might be to escape the intensive demands of one-to-one instruction. The time-out, which had been intended as a punishment for hitting, was actually negative reinforcement for Sofie, who was using the hitting to escape from a situation she found difficult.

The patterns between antecedents and consequences were quite obvious, and the function of the problem behavior was clear in Sofie's case. It is not so easy to identify the function of the behavior in other cases, however.

 ### Student Snapshot

When Rob had to work independently on lengthy tasks—even tasks that were at an appropriate skill level—he would make no attempt to do the assignment and would instead tell jokes and talk to his classmates.

Step 2C Worksheet: Summary of Functional
Behavior Assessment and Hypothesis Statement(s)   *page 1 of 2*

Directions: Summarize the functional behavior assessment (FBA) information that has been gathered from all sources to build hypothesis statement(s) about targeted problem behaviors. If the student has appropriate alternative behaviors that serve the same purpose as the problem behavior (alternative behaviors may be nonexistent or very weak), then describe those behaviors. Then determine if any data are missing or team members disagree or are uncertain about their hypotheses. Make a plan for further data collection and verification of hypotheses if necessary.

Student: *Anthony Rodriquez*   Date of initial summary: Revision date, if necessary:
                                     November 16, 2014   *November 30, 2014*

People completing this form:

Jared Simms/special education teacher	Angela and Jaime Rodriquez/parents
Ashley Giles/paraeducator	Mara Kellam/school psychologist
Rita Santos/second-grade teacher	

Duration: On average, how long does the behavior occur?

1. Crying/rocking: *Each incident is on average around 60 seconds long, but incidents can occur longer at times.*
2. Grabbing/pushing: *Most incidents are fairly mild, with grabbing only occurring when wanting access to preferred objects. Pushing is less likely to occur if access to preferred object occurs.*
3. Screaming: *Usually occurs in a burst of two or three phrases, lasting several seconds.*
4. Refusing: *Occurs only about once a week, lasting until engagement in activity begins or ends. Can extend over several activities.*

Frequency: On average, how often does the behavior occur?

1. Crying/rocking: Per hour? *n/a*   Per day? *5.6*   Per week? *28*
2. Kicking/pushing: Per hour? *n/a*   Per day? *4.2*   Per week? *21*
3. Screaming: Per hour? *n/a*   Per day? *1*   Per week? *5*
4. Refusing: Per hour? *n/a*   Per day? *1*   Per week? *1*

1. Describe chains of antecedents (both setting events and triggers) that predict the target behavior will occur, observable definitions of the target behaviors, and consequences that seem to be maintaining the behavior. Then hypothesize about the function or purpose of the target behavior(s).

When this happens (setting events and/or triggers)	the student does or is likely to (describe target behavior[s])	and this results in these maintaining consequences	Therefore, the function of the behavior may be
Setting event: *None* Trigger(s): *Anthony encounters a problem during independent seat work activities (e.g., is confused about an assignment, misplaces materials) or requires adult assistance.*	*Anthony will cry and rock (problem behaviors can escalate into tantrums if left unnoticed).*	*Anthony's teachers ask Anthony what is wrong and offer assistance.*	*Anthony gains teacher assistance or help.*
Setting event: *None* Trigger(s): *Unstructured (transitions, recess, free time) and independent small-group activities (e.g., art projects)*	*Anthony is likely to push his peers away, grab materials from them, or scream, "That's mine."*	*Typically results in peers giving into his requests, or refusing (which then results in screaming.)*	*Anthony obtains materials that he wants or perceives to be his.*
Setting event: *Altered classroom schedule (change in planned activity, delayed starts, half days)* Trigger(s): *Anthony is directed to start an activity that does not follow the typical classroom schedule.*	*Anthony is likely to refuse participation by folding his arms and saying, "We are not supposed to do this."*	*Anthony's teachers redirect him to the activity using verbal prompts.*	*Anthony delays or does not complete assigned tasks and escapes unanticipated activities.*

Figure 4.18. Step 2C Worksheet: Summary of Functional Behavior Assessment and Hypothesis Statement(s) for Anthony. (A blank, photocopiable version of this form is available in Appendix A, and blank and filled-in versions are available in the forms download.)

Step 2C Worksheet *(continued)* *page 2 of 2*

2. Describe alternative behaviors that the student has demonstrated (the behaviors may be very weak) that may serve the same function as the problem behavior(s).

   - *During independent seat work, Anthony has been observed saying to himself, "I need help" or "I can't find my pencil" but does not direct his verbalizations toward anyone or speak loudly enough to gain adult attention (does not initiate).*
   - *Also, Anthony will sometimes attempt to solve a problem by searching for missed materials or rereading his work, but he often gives up easily and quickly resorts to crying. Problem solving should be strengthened so that he persists to find a solution.*
   - *Anthony has been observed to share materials during teacher-structured activities but not during unstructured or peer-to-peer activities. He seems to want to use the same materials or computer that he used the day before*
   - *Anthony has been observed to make the transition to new activities without refusals or incident when following his daily visual schedule. We should use his visual schedule to help him predict change when the classroom schedule has to be altered on shortened school days.*

3. Are additional data needed to build hypothesis statement(s)?   Yes   (No)

   Is Step 2D: Test Hypotheses needed to confirm or refute hypotheses?   Yes   (No)

   If "yes," then use the Team Meeting Agenda and Minutes form to plan how, when, and by whom further FBA data collection or verification tests will be conducted. Decide on a date for the next team meeting, at which this worksheet will be revised.

When Rob engaged in these off-task behaviors, his classmates would laugh and the classroom teacher would come to Rob's desk, remind him of the consequences of not completing his classwork, and assist Rob with his assignment. When Rob was involved in small-group activities directed by the classroom teacher or the special education teacher, however, he did relatively well on his schoolwork. The team was not sure whether the purpose of Rob's problem behaviors was to gain attention from his peers and the teacher or to escape from difficult tasks. They needed a strategy to determine which of these hypotheses could be verified.

Building hypotheses can be especially difficult when a student uses a particular problem behavior for more than one purpose. For example, a student with an intellectual disability and no speech may cry in order to say, "I want more juice," "This is too hard," or "I don't feel well." Some students may use several different problem behaviors for the same purpose. A student may express anger or frustration in several different ways (e.g., tantrums, self-injury, hitting others). At times, it can be tempting to conclude that a behavior happens for no reason or has no pattern at all. In actuality, this is seldom the case. If there truly is no discernable pattern to the behavior and it is equally likely to occur in every situation, then it is possible that the behavior is related to a physiological problem. For example, a student with very limited communication skills might slap the side of his or her face with his or her hand to numb the pain of an unfilled cavity in a tooth.

This information is essential to the development of an individualized plan for PBS because the plan will include strategies for teaching the student new skills that will accomplish the purpose of the problem behavior in more positive, effective, and efficient ways. The team must evaluate its findings after summarizing the results of the FBA on the Step 2C worksheet. If the team has confidence in the validity of the hypotheses, then work on a PBS plan can begin. If there is a lack of consensus among team members and lingering uncertainty about the antecedents or the purpose of the problem behavior, however, then tentative hypotheses may require conducting Step 2D: Test Hypotheses.

When this happens
- Antecedents (setting events or triggers)

➡

Student does this
- Target behavior

➡

And results in
- Consequences
- Presumed function or outcome

Sample Hypothesis Statements

When peers attempt to initiate conversation with Katia during unstructured activities (e.g., lunch) (antecedent), Katia will walk away, turn her back, or put her head down on the table (target behavior). This results in peers turning away (consequence) and Katia avoiding social interaction (function).

After 10 minutes of one-to-one reading instruction (antecedent), Blake will engage in off-task behaviors (e.g., fidget with materials, slouch in his chair, drop materials to the floor, request to go to the bathroom) (target behavior), which results in the teacher delaying or terminating instruction (consequence) and Blake avoiding a difficult and disliked task (function).

During large-group activities (antecedent), Mateo frequently does not follow classroom instruction or teases his peers (target behavior). As a result, Mateo is often removed from the group activity and asked to sit with the paraeducator in back of the class to avoid further classroom disruption (consequence). Mateo gains one-to-one time (attention) with the paraeducator (function).

When Wade's morning routine at home is disrupted and he starts his school day in a bad mood (setting event) and he is given directions to start his schoolwork (antecedent), Wade is likely to curse at his teachers and refuse to work. As a result, teachers avoid giving Wade further instructions (consequence) and Wade avoids work and interaction with his teachers (function).

Figure 4.19. Writing hypothesis statements.

Step 2D: Test Hypotheses

Testing or verifying hypotheses requires observing the student during typical routines that vary in particular conditions (differing sets of antecedents and consequences). This procedure allows greater certainty about the triggers of the behavior, the maintaining consequences, and the function or purpose that it serves for the student. It is not recommended that the sort of extensive, precise functional analyses that are conducted in controlled research environments be conducted in classrooms. Educators can, however, make simple, short-term alterations to typically occurring activities that will enable them to be more accurate in designing intervention plans that are related to the specific function of the target behavior. Brief hypothesis tests that educators conduct depend on their hunch about the antecedents and function(s) of the problem behavior. Manipulating the factors that appear to affect problem behavior helps increase confidence that it is these factors, not others,

that are responsible for the problems, which is extremely important because knowing the variables that contribute to problems for the student is the key to successful behavior change or intervention. The steps of the testing process follow.

1. The team identifies what hypothesis needs testing and decides whether to manipulate antecedents or consequences. We recommended manipulating antecedents associated with the function of behavior wherever possible. Introducing and taking away triggers is easier to do, can reveal how instruction should be changed, and may be less problematic for the student. For example, if we wanted to test the hypothesis that Sofie's throwing and hitting functioned to escape from intensive work demands in one-to-one instruction, then we would manipulate the demands (e.g., introduce demanding and less demanding work and observe the effect). We would never attempt to just manipulate consequences (e.g., not allow Sofie to escape

a demanding task), which would cause serious problems for Sofie.

2. The team decides how to test the hypothesis and schedules a desired manipulation in an activity in which it fits. For example, if the hunch is that the student has tantrums in order to escape from difficult tasks, then the teacher presents a difficult task demand several times during a regular instructional period or presents and removes the task (hard task, easy task, hard task, easy task). The hunch is confirmed if the student does not have a tantrum when an easy task is presented and immediately stops the tantrum when the hard task is taken away. Everything else about the situation should stay the same—the seating arrangement, the teacher, the time of day, and so forth. The tasks should be familiar to the student so that the teacher knows which is easy and which is hard for the student.

3. The team determines how often to do this test. This depends on the size of the effects and how quickly they occur. Seeing large effects right away (e.g., no tantrums when easy tasks are introduced) means that the hypothesis is

Table 4.3. Testing hypotheses

Problem behavior and hypothesis	Hypothesis test and results
Behavior: Candice runs from the cafeteria; a paraeducator brings her lunch to her classroom for her. *Hypothesis:* Candice gets anxious and experiences sensory overload when she is in a very noisy place. She escapes from the situation as a way to self-regulate sensory input.	*Test:* Compare Candice's behavior in the cafeteria at lunch with places where others are present but the noise level is much lower, such as her class's library time or in the cafeteria during study hall. *Result that verifies hypothesis:* Candice runs from the cafeteria during lunch but not from the library or the cafeteria during study hall.
Behavior: Jonah is off task, talks out, and sometimes grabs other students when he has to wait for the teacher's attention (e.g., during a large-group lesson, during seat work); the teacher angrily tells him to stop and then gives Jonah a turn or helps him with his work. *Hypothesis:* Jonah has found a way to obtain attention from the teacher.	*Test:* Compare Jonah's behavior under the typical condition with how he behaves when the teacher (or other adult) regularly provides attention before Jonah does the behavior (e.g., "I'll be with you in just a second." "How are you doing?" "You've got it!"). *Result that verifies hypothesis:* Jonah does the problem behaviors less frequently or not at all when the teacher regularly gives him attention and he does not have to tolerate as much waiting.
Behavior: Molly throws materials and cries when she is asked to write with paper and pencil. Materials are then taken, and she is given a break to calm down. *Hypothesis:* Molly is escaping from a task she dislikes because it is too hard.	*Test:* Compare Molly's behavior in the same situation but with a change in the materials (markers, crayons, adapted scissors with help) and alternate with paper and pencil. *Result that verifies hypothesis:* Molly throws things and cries only with paper-and-pencil tasks.
Behavior: Ashley screams and hits herself when she cannot have more juice at snack. The teacher will sometimes go to the cafeteria to get more juice; Ashley stops screaming. *Hypothesis:* Ashley is trying to obtain something she wants (juice).	*Test:* Compare Ashley's behavior when juice is and is not freely available. Also compare her reaction with the availability and unavailability of other beverages (milk, water) to see if it is juice in particular that she wants or any beverage. *Result that verifies hypothesis:* Ashley screams when juice is not readily available, not when it is available. She stops screaming when she is given juice. She also screams when beverages other than juice are available, so the screaming does not indicate that she is simply thirsty, but it indicates that she prefers juice to other beverages.

likely to be accurate. Seeing small or no effects means that the hypothesis is not likely to be accurate.

During the manipulation, we unconditionally give what the person wants at the first sign of the problem behavior and then see if it eliminates the problem. We never want to create a situation in which we cause the problem behavior to escalate. It is crucial, however, to understand that this is not the solution to the behavior problem. This is a specific context that has been set up in order to quickly demonstrate the controlling factors for the behavior. It usually is necessary to observe these situations several times to be certain that the variables being manipulated are, indeed, the ones influencing the behavior. It also can be helpful to test more than one hunch about the possible function of a behavior (O'Neill et al., 2014).

Table 4.3 gives several other hypotheses and possible verification tests that can be administered by teachers in classrooms and other naturally occurring school settings. After conducting function tests and observing effects on the student's behavior that are convincing enough to verify hypotheses about the behavior's function(s), the student's PBS team meets again to revisit the Step 2C Worksheet: Summary of Functional Behavior Assessment and Hypothesis Statement(s). It is time to begin building a PBS plan once the team reaches consensus that the Step 2C worksheet is complete and accurate.

CONCLUSION

It is often said that problem behaviors occur because something is wrong—a mismatch between environmental circumstances (physical, social, and biological) and the student's skills and preferences. Functional assessment is a process for understanding the reasons for problem behaviors. The process uncovers the events that contribute to and maintain problem behaviors and the purpose(s) served for the student. It may also reveal broader context variables related to classroom management and the student's quality of life and fit with his or her educational program. The effectiveness of a student's individual support plan will hinge on an accurate assessment of problematic variables. This chapter provides a process for uncovering these variables, moving from indirect assessments, to direct observation, to testing hypotheses if needed. It also provides a process for teams to work efficiently. If team members can develop a well-informed hypothesis during any step of the FBA process, then they can begin to work on developing a behavior support plan. This process may begin as early as in Step 2A, as team members share, discuss, and synthesize their observations.

The next chapter shows how functional assessment information is used to develop individualized behavior support plans. The authors suggest that all teachers should be familiar with the essential theory of FBA, the crucial role it plays in designing PBS plans, and the variety of data-collection measures that the team can select from to complete the FBA. Only when we come to appreciate the purposes that problem behavior can serve for a student do we understand the significant role that the environment—which we play a large role in creating—serves in teaching, maintaining, and remediating behavior problems.

5

Designing, Using, and Evaluating Individualized Positive Behavior Supports

FOCUSING QUESTIONS

- What are the components of a comprehensive individualized PBS plan?
- How are the results of the FBA reflected in an individualized PBS plan?
- How is the effectiveness of an individualized PBS plan monitored and evaluated?

This chapter presents Steps 3 and 4 of the process of designing an individualized PBS plan for students who need intensive intervention. Step 3: Design an Individualized Positive Behavior Support Plan entails using assessment information from Step 2 to create and write a comprehensive support plan to improve the student's behavior and enhance his or her participation at school, at home, and in the community. Step 4: Implement, Monitor, and Evaluate the Positive Behavior Support Plan requires the student's PBS team to put the PBS plan into action, monitor its implementation, and evaluate its effects.

A plan for individualized PBS is not a plan to control behavior problems. A PBS plan is a comprehensive, integrated set of interventions and supports designed to promote improvements in behavior, academics, physical well-being, school and community participation, and social relationships. It emphasizes changing the conditions that contribute to problem behaviors and teaching the student critical skills needed to achieve desired outcomes. By definition, an individualized PBS plan is based on assessment information and is directly linked to the hypotheses for a problem behavior(s) generated by the team. The intervention strategies selected address what has been learned about the antecedents that set the occasion for the behavior and the consequences that maintain the behavior. In addition to designing and implementing the elements of the plan, the PBS team also needs to put strategies into place to ensure that the plan is being reliably implemented and that the behaviors of concern are improving. If they are not, then additional problem solving will be needed to generate improved alternatives.

For students with significant emotional/behavioral disorders, individualized PBS is most beneficial when incorporated into a wraparound planning process that includes not only teachers and family members but also representatives from the community agencies that can assist in creating an integrated, comprehensive system of care for the student and his or her family. The scope of this book does not include a full explanation of the wraparound process, but Figure 5.1 gives a more detailed definition of the process

and references some of the key research on its outcomes.

STEP 3

Design an Individualized Positive Behavior Support Plan

 An individualized PBS plan typically includes three general types of intervention strategies: 1) prevention, 2) teaching, and 3) responding (see Figure 5.2). (A safety plan also should be developed and immediately implemented if the student exhibits behaviors that are seriously disruptive or destructive; see Chapter 4.)

What the Research Says

Wraparound Process for Students with Emotional or Behavioral Disorders
Although their numbers are relatively small, students with extreme emotional or behavioral disorders (EBD) can present significant challenges to their teachers and peers in the school setting and are at the greatest risk for removal to more restrictive settings and for poor school and life outcomes, such as school dropout, poverty, incarceration, and unemployment. The school-based positive behavior support (PBS) process can lead to some positive results for these students, but using PBS as a complement to a broader wraparound process for planning comprehensive, integrated systems of care can yield greater benefits for students, their families, and their communities. Like the PBS approach, wraparound is individualized, strength based, and multidisciplinary team based; however, wraparound incorporates more community-based agencies and interagency resources, and it places even greater emphasis on creating a full and active partnership with families.

Emerging from the fields of mental health and child welfare, wraparound is a team-based, collaborative process for developing and implementing individualized care plans for youth with and at risk for EBD and their families. Wraparound is not a single service, but instead a process through which specific school and/or community-based interventions can be designed, implemented, and coordinated. The logic is that by bringing together a team made up of family members, natural supports (e.g., extended family, friends, mentors) and school and community professionals, the wraparound process will produce a plan that (a) is accepted by the family, (b) addresses family priorities, and (c) leads to realistic and practical strategies to support the student in his or her home, school and community. (Eber, Hyde, & Suter, 2011, p. 783)

Research on wraparound planning to create integrated, comprehensive systems of care shows promising results that include decreased out-of-home and restrictive school placements along with improved behavioral, academic, social, and postschool adjustment factors for students with EBD (Burns & Goldman,1999; Burns, Schoenwald, Burchard, Faw, & Santos, 2000; Eber & Nelson, 1997; Malloy, Cheney, & Cormier, 1998; Painter, 2012).

Figure 5.1. Wraparound planning for students with emotional or behavioral disorders.

PBS

F CBA

STEP 3

Design an Individualized
Positive Behavior Support Plan

A good plan for individualized positive behavior support has three parts:

1. **Preventing** the problem behavior through 1) strategies to remove or reduce the impact of setting events, 2) strategies to avoid triggers or immediate antecedents that predict the problem behavior, and 3) strategies to increase the likelihood that alternative behaviors will occur. If the Student-Centered Functional Behavior Assessment Profile indicated the need for improvements in quality-of-life indicators or in the fit between the student's educational programming and academic strengths and needs, then include those strategies here.

2. **Teaching** interventions to demonstrate 1) specific replacement behaviors to serve the same purpose as the problem behaviors and 2) interventions to teach other positive alternative behaviors to achieve desired outcomes (e.g., social skills, self-management strategies, academic skills).

3. **Responding** to the problem behavior when it occurs in ways that do not maintain it and responding to alternative behaviors in ways that ensure they work more efficiently and effectively than the problem behavior. If a safety plan also is in use to manage dangerous or destructive behaviors, then maintain records of its use. Evaluate and revise the plan as needed.

A

B

C

Figure 5.2. Step 3: Design an Individualized Positive Behavior Support Plan.

Each of the three components of a hypothesis statement, which summarizes the information gathered by the FBA, has a counterpart in the behavior-change strategies that compose a PBS plan. Prevention strategies change the antecedents—both the setting events and the triggers—of the problem behavior to create an environment more likely to lead to success. Teaching strategies change the student's behavior by replacing problem behaviors with alternative behaviors serving the same purpose and building other desired social and academic skills. Responding strategies change the consequences of behavior by reinforcing the student's use of desired alternative behaviors while minimizing rewards for the student's use of problem behaviors. Horner and his colleagues (Horner, Sugai, et al., 2000) argued that this combination of interventions and supports is meant to accomplish three outcomes that compete with the problem behavior:

1. Making the problem behavior irrelevant by creating an environment in which it is not necessary to use the problem behavior

2. Making the problem behavior ineffective by removing the consequences that were maintaining the behavior

3. Making the problem behavior inefficient by ensuring that a replacement behavior and other alternative skills work better and more easily than the old behavior

Figure 5.3 illustrates the competing behavior pathways model developed by Horner, Sugai, et al. (2000), which shows how each part of the summary hypothesis statement that was constructed from the FBA relates to the three types of intervention strategies (O'Neill et al., 2014). The purpose of an intervention plan based on the competing behavior model is to make the problem behavior irrelevant, ineffective, and inefficient in serving its function. At the same time, the environment is altered to avoid the need to use the problem behavior, and the new, alternative behavior

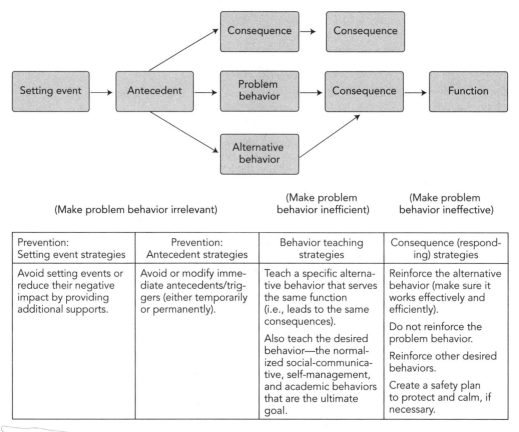

Prevention: Setting event strategies	Prevention: Antecedent strategies	Behavior teaching strategies	Consequence (responding) strategies
Avoid setting events or reduce their negative impact by providing additional supports.	Avoid or modify immediate antecedents/triggers (either temporarily or permanently).	Teach a specific alternative behavior that serves the same function (i.e., leads to the same consequences). Also teach the desired behavior—the normalized social-communicative, self-management, and academic behaviors that are the ultimate goal.	Reinforce the alternative behavior (make sure it works effectively and efficiently). Do not reinforce the problem behavior. Reinforce other desired behaviors. Create a safety plan to protect and calm, if necessary.

Figure 5.3. Competing behavior model. (From O'Neill/Horner/Albin/Sprague/Storey/Newton. *Functional Assessment and Program Development for Problem Behavior, 3E.* © 2015 South-Western, a part of Cengage Learning, Inc. Adapted by permission. www.cengage.com/permissions)

becomes the most effective and efficient way to achieve the purpose that was served by the problem behavior.

Designing a support plan involves team decision making, which is similar to the process for conducting an FBA. First, members of the student's individual PBS team consider interventions that address each of the three components of the hypothesis statement for problem behavior. In addition to the requirement that intervention strategies are linked to the behavior hypothesis, effective behavior support plans need to include strategies specifically chosen to suit the student and family, the context, and the teachers and other personnel who will apply them. The criterion of contextual fit extends to all team members, including family members.

If behavior supports and interventions are to be optimally successful, then they must be logistically doable and take into account student and family preferences and values. Second, once the team agrees that selected interventions are both technically adequate (e.g., address components of the hypothesis) and are acceptable to team members, then a behavior support plan document is written by a designated team member. (Refer to Figure 5.6, which appears later in this chapter, for an example of a completed support plan for Anthony.)

Deciding how to involve the student in developing a behavior support plan can be a difficult task, especially if the student does not talk or have another reliable way to communicate or does not have a trusting relationship with members of the PBS team. There are no rules for the best way to gain the student's involvement. Although student participation in team meetings is encouraged, especially for adolescents, attendance at team meetings may not be feasible or even desirable for some students. All students can provide input through a number of different ways, however, whether or not they attend meetings. Students who have a means to communicate with others can and should fully participate in setting goals, conducting self-assessments, and expressing preferences for the ways they would like help in meeting their goals. These activities can be embedded within everyday classroom routines. Teachers and staff members should offer choices that students with communication difficulties can understand and respond to, and they should carefully observe to understand the student's view and preferences for intervention.

The next sections provide considerations and guidelines for selecting strategies for preventing, teaching, and responding. Understanding how these strategies are linked to hypotheses for problem behavior can help you and your team design effective, individualized PBS plans.

Prevention Strategies: Changing the Antecedents

The first type of behavior support strategy is designed to prevent behavior problems from occurring. Prevention strategies address both specific triggers and setting events and may involve changing the physical environment, the daily schedule, the staff and peers who spend time with the student, or the activities in which the student engages. The changes made to antecedents are sometimes described as stimulus-based interventions because they change the stimuli or the "who-what-when-where" variables that set the stage for the behavior. Teams should ask, "How can triggers or setting events be changed so that problem behaviors are prevented

or made unnecessary?" while reflecting on a behavior hypothesis. Asking, "What antecedent changes can we make that will support the student and encourage desired behaviors?" is an additional way to approach the problem.

A prevention-oriented approach makes sense for several reasons. Removing the antecedents known to induce a problem behavior makes the behavior unnecessary or irrelevant. Therefore, the student is less likely to get more practice using the problem behavior. The more practice one has in using a behavior, the more the old behavior will compete with learning a new behavior. This rule applies both to the student with the problem behavior and to the adults and peers who regularly interact with that student. Teachers do not want to allow students to practice getting into fights, throwing tantrums, hurting themselves, destroying property, or exhibiting other disapproved behaviors. Second, teachers want to avoid a problem behavior while the student has a chance to learn new alternative skills, especially if the behavior is dangerous to the student or others or is seriously disruptive to the classroom. Learning new skills is difficult under conditions that provoke problem behaviors. Third, from a functional perspective, antecedents create problem contexts that the student is seeking to change. Problem behaviors communicate that the student is unhappy or stressed by a situation or that the individual wants something or some action to occur. Thus, from the student's perspective, it makes sense that we seek to modify those conditions that are problematic for the student. Asking a student to endure problem contexts without modification or support neither respects the student's communication nor benefits learning.

The good news is that changing antecedents often results in immediate reductions in problem behaviors because problematic stimuli are avoided or mitigated in some way. Problem behaviors can be prevented in a range of ways. Setting events and triggering antecedents that have been detected through an FBA can be altered to prevent target behaviors from occurring and applied to students individually. At a broader level, and less directly connected with immediate environmental antecedents, teachers can prevent behavior problems in general by providing students with choices and ensuring that educational programming is suited to students' ages, abilities, and interests. The Student-Centered FBA Profile (see Figure 4.11) completed as part of an FBA includes information about the student's relationships with peers and adults, choice-making opportunities, preferences, interests, needs, strengths, and dislikes. If this information indicates shortcomings in the student's quality of life or educational programming, then the PBS plan should incorporate prevention strategies to ameliorate the most dramatic of those shortcomings. Ways to prevent problem behaviors through antecedent changes are discussed in the following section.

Prevention Through Choice Making

Choice making has been well documented as an effective support strategy for challenging behavior (Shogren, Faggella-Luby, Bae, & Wehmeyer, 2004; Tullis et al., 2011). Allowing and enabling students to make choices can be a broad, values-based element of positive educational programming that improves the instructional context in which students are expected to function. Choice making is an integral component of one's quality of life, self-determination, and overall satisfaction with school activities (Wehmeyer & Schalock, 2001). Choice making is also an antecedent intervention for specific problem behaviors. Choice-making interventions have resulted in improved behavior in numerous studies conducted with a wide range of participants (i.e., all ages from preschool students to senior citizens

and participants with diverse intellectual and behavior characteristics) and with a wide array of academic, vocational, domestic, and recreational contexts (Bambara, Koger, Katzer, & Davenport, 1995; Cole & Levinson, 2002; Dunlap et al., 1994; Kern, Mantegna, Vorndran, Bailin, & Hilt, 2001).

Choice making works as an antecedent intervention for two reasons. First, students gain access to preferred materials or activities when asked to make a selection among options. Research on choice making has shown that students' problem behaviors decrease and task engagement increases when they are allowed to choose which assignment or activity they prefer to complete (e.g., Dunlap, Kern-Dunlap, Clarke, & Robbins, 1991) or when they are offered choices about the order in which they want to do a list of required activities (Kern, Mantegna, et al., 2001). Second, choice making provides opportunities for students to direct or co-direct activities with teachers. Having the opportunity to direct or control activities is a powerful motivator for some students. Indeed, providing choice is such a potent support strategy that rates of problem behavior have been shown to decrease when individuals are allowed to choose between two lower preference tasks rather than being assigned those lower preference tasks by their instructor (Bambara, Ager, & Koger, 1994; Vaughn & Horner, 1997).

Providing choice is helpful as an antecedent intervention when students seek to avoid or escape nonpreferred activities, demanding or difficult work tasks, transitions to less preferred activities, or teacher directions or commands. By giving students access to preferred materials or activities and opportunities to self-direct, choice can make these situations better or less problematic for students. Choice can be provided in a number of ways. Teachers can provide options of tasks or activities for students to complete, which is referred to as between-activity or task choices. Even when an activity is required, which makes between-activity choices inappropriate, teachers can offer a number of within-activity choices. These include offering the choice of 1) materials (e.g., pencils, colored markers), 2) location or setting (e.g., desk, back table, library), 3) task sequence (e.g., what to do first, second, or third), 4) specific time work needs to be completed, 5) classmates or teachers with whom to work, and 6) terminating or taking a break from an activity (Brown, Belz, Corsi, & Wenig, 1993; Kern & State, 2009). One study that directly compared between-activity (e.g., working on math or English) and within-activity choices (e.g., writing with a pencil or gel pen) involving students with autism revealed that both choice options were effective in reducing escape-motivated problem behaviors by the students (Rispoli et al., 2013). Thus, when deciding what types of choice options to provide, teams will need to consider what is feasible and appropriate and what options are more likely to motivate the student.

Providing choice opportunities can be applied individually with students or implemented classwide, which may make it more feasible for teachers to deliver choices across students. As teachers plan classroom lessons and activities, they can consider the types of choices that could be made available to all students while also addressing individual student needs (Kern & State, 2009). To illustrate the power of this approach, Kern, Bambara, and Fogt (2002) implemented classwide choice making in a middle school science class for students with emotional and behavioral disorders. As a class, students made choices about unit topics they wanted to learn, and they were offered individual choices about how they wanted to practice or demonstrate mastery of the content during daily lessons (e.g., choice of materials for pollution activity, working with a partner or alone). Compared with traditional lessons in which no choice

was provided, offering classwide choices resulted in improved student engagement and reduced disruptive behaviors for the class overall.

 ## Student Snapshot

Jamal hit and pushed the teacher or assistant as a way to avoid any activity that involved writing. The support team decided to temporarily reduce the amount of writing that Jamal was asked to do in each activity and give him a choice of using a pen, pencil, crayon, or marker. The team members also arranged Jamal's schedule to alternate written activities with other types of activities that Jamal preferred, such as the teacher or assistant reading to him.

Prevention Through Instructional and Curriculum Changes

Behavior problems can be prevented by ensuring that educational programming is well designed, instruction is well matched with students' needs and abilities, and the learning context capitalizes on students' interests and other motivations. All teachers have seen a student's attention and motivation vary along with his or her interest in the subject matter and his or her ability to successfully perform an activity. Even when instructional activities seem well matched to a student's capabilities, further individualization may be necessary, especially for students who have a history of academic failure or who become easily frustrated with new learning tasks. Students may become disruptive when too many demands are placed on them—when they are expected to complete assignments independently that are beyond their independent skill level or when they are asked to maintain effort for long periods of time that extend beyond their endurance. Conversely, some students may become disruptive when assignments are too easy or when asked repeatedly to spend long periods of time practicing known skills. During direct instruction, students can become disruptive when the pace of instruction moves too slowly or when they make too many errors. Some students may seek to avoid instructional tasks that they find uninteresting, irrelevant, or meaningless.

When the function of problem behavior is to escape from academic tasks, teams will need to reexamine the instructional focus. Even when the eventual goal is to improve the skills needed to complete academic tasks, some curricular or instructional revision will be needed at least temporarily to alleviate the desire to escape while increasing the student's motivation to persist and learn new skills. Curricular revisions can be made by changing the content of instruction or the mode of presentation or task completion. When making decisions about what to change, it is important to identify specific aspects of the academic task that challenge students (Kern & Clemens, 2007). For example, problem behavior that is functionally related to task difficulty can be alleviated by better matching instruction to the student's skill level, reducing the number of problems on a worksheet, offering the student short breaks during instruction, and interspersing known or successful tasks among more difficult tasks to keep motivation high by reducing errors or effort. When students seek to escape uninteresting or meaningless tasks, teams will need to consider how to incorporate student preferences or interests in lessons and activities. In addition to providing a choice, student interests may be incorporated by aligning academic tasks with meaningful learning outcomes. For example, writing complete sentences may be made more meaningful when students are asked to write captions for photographs published in the weekly classroom newsletter sent home to parents. Figure 5.4 summarizes some of the research on the positive relationship between appropriate behavior and appropriate curriculum and instructional modifications.

Information gleaned from person-centered planning processes can also assist in designing support plans that create a better fit between students' needs and abilities and their teachers' classroom practices. Kennedy and his colleagues (2001) found that students' behavior and general education participation improved when students were assigned classroom tasks that better reflected their strengths and interests and teachers followed best practice guidelines such as providing predictable schedules, choices, and age-appropriate curriculum. Students' behavior was convincingly linked with the implementation—or lack of implementation—of the behavior support plan.

 ## Student Snapshot

Andrew threw and tore materials at school. The PBS team noticed that Andrew mostly threw items related to assembling or sorting that were used to practice prevocational skills. Andrew did not throw materials when his teacher involved him in more functional activities, such as preparing the snack, setting the table, running errands, and using the computer to write notes to friends. These new activities made sense to Andrew in a way that repetitive, nonfunctional activities did not; therefore, these activities were permanently incorporated into Andrew's educational programming.

Prevention Through Visual and Other Environmental Supports

Some students may engage in problem behaviors because they have difficulty understanding what is expected of them or predicting what will happen next, including when they will be able to gain access to preferred materials or activities. For example, "no," "not now," or "later" may translate into "never" for some students, causing serious disruptions. Other students may have difficulty during transitions, ending one activity and starting another, or may have difficulty with change in routines or activities. For example, much of Anthony's

What the Research Says

Prevention Through Curricular and Instructional Changes

Numerous research studies have shown that altering the curriculum—either its content, mode of presentation, or task completion—can have a positive influence on reducing problem behavior and improving academic performance. Several studies have examined variations in students' academic performance and classroom behavior under two conditions: 1) standard instructional conditions (e.g., performing teacher-selected tasks, engaging in repetitive tasks designed for practicing isolated skills) and 2) instructional conditions that utilized assessment of student preferences and interests, functional activities, academic tasks broken into smaller segments, or shortened instructional sessions. In each case, the researchers found that students' task performance (e.g., productivity, on-task behavior, task completion) and behavior (e.g., leaving the instructional area, hitting materials on the desk, making loud noises) improved when the students were doing tasks that were designed to better match their instructional level, interests and preferences, or stamina or energy level (Clarke et al., 1995; Dunlap, Foster-Johnson, Clarke, Kern, & Childs, 1995; Foster-Johnson, Ferro, & Dunlap, 1994; Kern, Delaney, Clarke, Dunlap, & Childs, 2001; Moore, Anderson, & Kumar, 2005; Umbreit, Lane, & Dejud, 2004).

Kennedy et al. (2001) integrated person-centered planning measures with the other typical direct and indirect methods used to conduct functional behavior assessments for three elementary school students with behavior problems. After obtaining the support team's assessment of focal students' strengths, interests, and dislikes, the researchers assisted the team to construct a matrix showing the degree to which those individual strengths, interests, and dislikes were present in each class period across the day. In addition, they evaluated the quality of instruction in each class period based on the extent to which 14 distinct best practices were present. These sources of information were used to design support plans that created a better fit between the students' needs and abilities and their teachers' classroom practices. The tasks assigned to students better reflected their strengths and interests and best practice guidelines, such as providing predictable schedules, choices, and age-appropriate curriculum. The improvements to students' behavior and general education participation were convincingly linked with the implementation—or lack of implementation—of the behavior support plan.

Figure 5.4. Prevention through curricular and instructional changes.

problem behaviors involving grabbing items, pushing peers, and refusing to work on some days are related to his difficulty with change. He wants the materials he used the day before and will grab or push peers out of the way to get them. He also refuses to work on days where there is a schedule change because he seeks to avoid activities that do not follow the typical sequence.

Teams can consider using visual supports and other environmental adaptations in cases such as these to help students understand, predict, and cope with change. Visual supports can be used in a variety of ways (Meadan, Ostrosky, Triplett, Michna, & Fettig, 2011). First, visual schedules in the form of pictures or text can be used to help illustrate the day's events, what activity will happen next, and changes that may occur. Numerous studies have shown that visual schedules can reduce problem behaviors of children and increase their engagement in activities (Lequia, Machalicek, & Rispoli, 2012). Second, visual supports may be used to structure the environment to increase students' independence and decrease their need for assistance. For example, pictures on cubbies or shelves can help students know where to return classroom materials. Graphic organizers are useful during academic tasks to help students understand tasks and structure their responses. Third, visuals may be used as rule reminder cards (Meadan et al., 2011) to help students understand what are acceptable and unacceptable behaviors and the consequences that will follow these actions. In one study, Brown and Miranda (2006) showed that visual reminders illustrating what a student should do after completing work, and the rewards that could be received, were more effective in decreasing problem behaviors and increasing alternative behaviors than just verbally telling the student about expected behaviors and consequences.

Fourth, visual supports in the form of Social Stories (Gray, 1998) or social narratives can be used to help students adjust to change. Social narratives, now considered an evidence-based practice (Wong, 2013), consist of short, simple sentences often accompanied with pictures or other graphics that describe upcoming situations and give the students options for how to respond. Social narratives are often written from the perspective of the learner and include the thoughts and feelings of the individual and others.

 ### Student Snapshot

Anthony's team combined social narratives with adaptations to his visual schedule to help him anticipate schedule changes and respond appropriately. On the mornings of expected schedule changes, such as school delays, half days for teacher in-service, and when there is a substitute teacher, the paraeducator sits with Anthony to read one of several narratives appropriate for the situation. Excerpts from one story follow: "Today we have a 2-hour delay because of bad weather. Some things will remain the same, but some things will change. We can't fit in everything today. That's okay. If we can't get to (fill in the blank), I know that we will get to it (state when). I will try my best to work at all my lessons and assignments. I know that Ms. Santos will make sure that I can have computer or reading time

sometime today." After discussing the story with Anthony, the paraeducator then makes changes to Anthony's visual schedule. Because Anthony often expresses concern about missing activities, especially his favorite ones, she shows him when activities will take place either the next day or later in the week on his personal calendar if they cannot be scheduled today. She makes sure that Anthony will still have time for independent reading or work at the computer, two activities that he loves and are important to him, regardless of the changes made. She gives him some options of when (either just before lunch or dismissal) and then documents them on his visual schedule.

Not all environmental supports require detailed visuals, text, or graphics. Simple adapted cues such as a vibrating wristwatch or beeps from a tablet computer can be used to help students prepare for transitions. Peers, when properly trained, may also help to convey expectations and support positive behaviors. In one study, teaching peers to provide nonverbal acts of encouragement (e.g., head nods, smiles, thumbs-up) was all that was needed to keep elementary students with autism focused and engaged during independent work (McCurdy & Cole, 2014).

Modifying Schoolwork (Janney & Snell, 2013), another volume in the Teachers' Guides to Inclusive Practices series, provides more examples of visual and other supportive strategies and also details a process teams can use to devise individualized adaptations and supports to address the instructional needs of students who have IEPs.

Prevention Through Alteration of Setting Events

Setting events involve two or more variables linked together that tend to lead to problem behaviors. For example, the absence of breakfast (setting event for Zack) can reduce Zack's tolerance for completing routine paper-and-pencil tasks, whereas allergies (setting event for Sarah) often mean that Sarah reacts negatively to teachers' requests. Setting events that occur prior to the presence of a specific antecedent stimulus (paper-and-pencil tasks or teachers' requests) can make it more likely that a problem behavior will follow, as illustrated in the following example.

 ### Student Snapshot

On some days, Wade starts his school day visibly upset, stomping his feet as he enters the classroom and dropping books on his desk. If corrected or directed to sit down and start working, Wade becomes verbally aggressive and will refuse to do any schoolwork for much of the morning. In a meeting with Wade's parents, the PBS team learned that mornings at home are often difficult for Wade. His mother described Wade as "not a morning person" and reported that the slightest event can cause Wade to become upset (e.g., being rushed in the morning, not having his favorite breakfast cereal, being teased by his brother). Although Wade's parents try their best, they cannot always prevent these and other morning events from happening. They further reasoned that Wade needs to learn how to cope with minor disappointments and disruptions. Wade's teacher sat down with him to come up with a plan to prevent these setting events from influencing Wade's morning at school. They agreed that when he comes to school upset, he should find an isolated area in the classroom, typically in the back of the classroom, to sit and calm down. The teacher agreed that she would not nag, direct, or talk to Wade while he was taking time to gain control. Wade agreed that he would join the class and begin his school day as soon as he was ready. Because Wade was usually eager to start school (on nonsetting event days), taking time lasted no more than 15 minutes. Furthermore, the time Wade needed to regain control lessened each week, until taking time lasted no more than a minute or two. As soon as Wade joined the class, Wade's teacher made it a point of welcoming him and praising his ability to quickly regain self-control.

The negative influence of setting events can be prevented in one of two ways. First, teams may consider whether the event can be avoided in some way. In Zack's case, the team can collaborate with Zack's family to ensure that Zack does not miss breakfast at home, or through daily communication with the family, Zack's teacher can know when he does miss breakfast and can offer him a snack at school. In another example, if making the transition in a noisy and crowded hallway makes it difficult for Elizabeth to tolerate the demands of test taking in the next class, then the noisy environment can be avoided by having Elizabeth make the transition to the next period a few minutes before the bell rings.

Second, if setting events cannot be avoided, then their negative influence can be mitigated if teachers, parents, and others who work with a student recognize these events, communicate about them, and develop strategies that would lessen their impact. In Wade's case, neither Wade's teacher nor his parents could prevent or control all of the events that caused him to become upset. The teacher could control the impact of the events, however, by avoiding directions that would then cause Wade to explode and by giving him the time he needed to regain self-control. Similarly, if a teacher knows that a biological setting event is operative—that the student has not slept well, is ill, has an allergy—then extra care can be taken to make the student feel comfortable. Teams may also consider changing the triggers that set off problem behaviors on difficult setting event days. Perhaps demands can be lessened in some way when the student is not feeling well. If particular adults or peers act as setting events for a student, then those people can work to establish rapport and interact with the student in more positive ways.

Prevention Through Altering Specific Antecedents

We have provided examples of prevention strategies within categories of antecedent interventions commonly used with students (i.e., instructional and curriculum changes, providing visual and other environmental supports, alteration of setting events). These categories provide a good starting place for team consideration. In reality, however, effective antecedent interventions are highly individualized and will require teams to carefully consider how specific triggers and setting events that may be unique to the individual can be changed. The guiding questions posed earlier in this section are useful in this regard. If we know certain antecedents to be problematic, then what can we do to change, avoid, or mitigate their impact? What additional supports can we add antecedently to support learning and desired behaviors? Table 5.1 illustrates the ways to change antecedents.

Antecedent changes are often used as temporary interventions in a behavior support plan. Antecedent changes are made until students learn how to manage things themselves, and then the antecedent interventions are faded or removed. For example, a student might have a disruptive response to virtually any paper-and-pencil academic task. These demands might be temporarily removed but then slowly reintroduced using activities with a high likelihood of success. The student could be provided with a visual schedule showing that the nonpreferred task will be brief and followed by a preferred activity. The teacher also could assign tasks to the student but allow the student to choose the order in which to do them. The temporary removal of the original task demands gives the student and the adults a clean slate and a chance to take small steps toward success.

There are times when antecedent interventions become permanent accommodations for students to provide long-term support for their learning and positive behaviors. For instance, some students may always benefit from using a visual schedule to help them anticipate what happens next. Allowing Elizabeth to make the transition early to her next

class before the bell rings is a reasonable long-term accommodation for avoiding overcrowded hallways that cause her to become upset. The following cases provide additional examples of temporary and permanent antecedent changes.

Student Snapshot

Kent, a kindergarten student classified as having autism, did not have a conventional way to communicate. Kent did not like to sit in a chair at the table to do his work and would often sit or lie down on the floor instead. The support team discovered that this noncompliance probably was because Kent, who was quite large for his age, was not comfortable sitting in a chair designed for a typical kindergarten student. The support team realized that providing Kent with a chair that fit him was a perfectly reasonable accommodation and that no student should be expected to be uncomfortable for significant periods of time.

Student Snapshot

Erica, who had a learning disability in math, would swear and verbally threaten people when she was anxious about whether she could successfully do her math assignments. Erica's teacher decided to demonstrate the first math problem for Erica, coach her through the steps of the second math problem, watch her work on the third math problem, and then ask Erica to raise her hand when she had finished the fourth math problem. After checking Erica's fourth problem, Erica's teacher would ask, "Are you ready to do the rest on your own?" Although Erica's teacher eventually phased out the use of this structured modeling and prompting sequence, she always made sure that Erica had an example of a completed math problem to use as a cue for doing independent math work.

Teaching Strategies

Teaching alternative behaviors is a second type of intervention included in a comprehensive, individualized PBS plan. Indeed, the heart of a behavior support plan is

Table 5.1. Ideas for antecedent changes

Purpose of behavior *If the student seeks to*	Possible strategies *Consider these ideas to prevent*
Avoid academic and instructional tasks	Adjust difficulty or complexity of task; reduce effort • Reduce number of items per page • Intersperse difficult items among easy ones • Preview or preteach sample problems • Shorten activity; schedule in breaks • Divide tasks into smaller chunks and combine with access to preferred activities when completed Provide opportunities for choice and self-direction • Provide alternative options for demonstrating content knowledge • Have the student select and self-manage learning goals • Provide within-activity choices such as choice of materials, location, sequence of tasks or people with whom to work Make instructional tasks more meaningful • Align instruction with student interests or personal goals • Change the mode of learning or the learning context (e.g., computer versus paper-and-pencil tasks, solve math problems for a related art project versus solving worksheet examples)
Avoid teacher directions and corrections	Use behavioral momentum: precede directions with ones the student is likely to follow (e.g., "Pass these papers to all the students," then, "Get your assignment") Use suggestive, rather than directive, language Phrase negative directions into positive ones (e.g., "I'll be over to help you as soon as you try two problems on your own," instead of, "I can't help you unless you try the first two problems by yourself") Intersperse directions among neutral comments and praise statements; pair corrections or criticism with praise Use choice statements to direct, or give students opportunities to set the direction of the activity Use errorless teaching strategies to reduce corrections (e.g., time delay, preteaching)
Avoid social interactions	Create opportunities for positive adult or peer interaction around preferred and meaningful activities (e.g., favorite games, interests) Foster positive relationships/interactions with peers through structured teaching arrangements or activities (e.g., collaborative learning groups) Train peers to support, encourage, and praise social interactions Provide a peer buddy or an adult coach to support and extend interactions with others Improve teacher–student relationships by increasing ratio of positive teacher interactions to negative ones; increase opportunities for praise and positive teacher–student contact
Avoid transitions and escape change	Enhance predictability of transitions and schedule changes through visual schedules, Social Stories, or a preview of upcoming events Provide warnings before transitions; signal with verbal warnings, beeps, or music Provide preferred activity or materials immediately after transition Allow student to make the transition with preferred material
Obtain desired materials, activities, or food	Make desired materials and food easily accessible • Place favorite writing materials in a bin • Put healthy food choices in a cabinet that the individual can reach Pair "no" with "when" (e.g., "You can't use the computer now, but you can after lunch"); show "when" with visual schedule Pair "no" with alternative options that the student prefers (e.g., "No, we don't have time for the computer today, but you can look through your favorite book") Have student schedule desired activities among "must do" activities; when events are cancelled, guide students to understand why and reschedule as soon as possible.

(continued)

Table 5.1.   *(continued)*

Purpose of behavior *If the student seeks to*	Possible strategies *Consider these ideas to prevent*
Obtain social interac- tion or attention	Provide noncontingent attention by scheduling frequent opportunities for teacher or peer attention (e.g., teacher starts school day with special times for student– teacher chats, arranges for the student to serve as teacher helper, checks-in with student every few minutes while doing seat work) Build in opportunities for meaningful and appropriate peer interaction • Schedule cooperative learning groups • Teach peer support, and praise desired social behaviors Provide alternative preferred activity when student has to wait for adult assistance Provide visual cues for appropriately initiating and maintaining social interaction with peers • Conversation books to start topics of conversation • Brag book to share personal experiences and interests • Cue cards to signal what to say during a game Provide precorrections by making expectations for appropriate interactions with others clear
Obtain or avoid sen- sory stimulation	Block or avoid aversive stimuli • Offer ear plugs during fire alarms • Provide gloves for messy art activities • Provide quiet alternative to noisy activity (e.g., go to the library instead of a student assembly) Enrich the environment with preferred materials and activities when the student is understimulated; keep the student engaged

Sources: Bambara and Knoster (2009); Dunlap et al. (2010); Kern and Clemens (2009).

teaching effective, socially appropriate behaviors that help students meet their wants and needs. For most students with serious behavior problems, this means teaching specific replacement skills to achieve the same purpose as the target behavior and also teaching other interpersonal, self-management, and academic skills that will take longer to learn but will lead to the desired long-term outcomes.

Your team developed a hypothesis statement in Step 2 that expresses the purpose or function of the target behavior. The teaching strategies in a PBS plan involve helping the student learn and use alternative ways to accomplish that purpose. In addition, teachers want to show students other more positive ways to meet their needs or desired school, home, and community expectations. This means that teachers have to accept the validity of what the student is trying to do or say. The unspoken message to the student should be, "You do not have to go to this trouble to get what you want or need. If your wants or needs are legitimate, then we will help you to get them met. If they are not legitimate, then we will make an effort to explain why they are not, and we will help you find some suitable alternatives." Teaching alternative skills can be conceptualized around two major intervention approaches: 1) teaching replacement skills that serve the same function as problem behavior and 2) teaching other desired behaviors that address student needs.

Teaching Replacement Skills that Serve a Social-Communicative Function

In this first approach to teaching alternative skills, you will want to replace problem behavior with an equally effective appropriate alternative that will produce the same outcome as the problem behavior. When considering an alternative replacement skill, teams should ask, "What is the purpose or function of the behavior?" and "What alternative skill can we teach that will produce the same outcome for the student?" In other words, how can the student obtain desired results differently?

The most common purposes of problem behavior are social communicative: obtaining attention, nurturance, comfort, or help; obtaining something tangible or a preferred activity; escaping or avoiding tasks or activities; and escaping or avoiding attention or other social interaction (O'Neill et al., 2014). The problem behaviors serving these purposes can be viewed as a form of communication that takes an idiosyncratic or socially inappropriate form. Some students may use conventional forms of communication, but their communication may be difficult to understand. Other students may not have the communication skills needed to convey their messages in socially approved ways; they may have learned that problem behavior, such as hitting, throwing a tantrum, or destroying property, gets them the desired functions. Sometimes a problem behavior works better than a more appropriate behavior. That is, some students may have the skills to communicate appropriately, but problem behavior gets more effective results. Regardless of the reasons, students need to be taught alternative skills that will serve the same social-communication functions but use a more desirable form of behavior (e.g., words, signs, pictures, augmentative and alternative communication devices).

In each example that follows, the student was taught a replacement behavior that communicated the same function as the problem behavior. In each case, the student was first taught a new response that was easy to do and was immediately reinforced so that it was efficient and effective. Later, the student learned more difficult responses that still achieved the same purpose but were more typical and age appropriate in their form.

- Patrick learned to point to a "break" card instead of running from the classroom to seek escape when he was tired of working. At first, he immediately

received a break simply for pointing to the card; later, he learned to pick up the card and wait at the door until the teacher gave him permission to leave the room. (Function: escape disliked tasks)

- Wade learned to say, "I need to take some time" instead of cursing at his teacher and peers when he was in a bad mood or not ready to join the class in the morning. Later, he learned to politely respond to others while gaining self-control. (Function: escape interactions)

- Jade learned to tap a classmate's arm instead of grabbing the arm when she wanted to get the child's attention. Jade eventually learned to use her classmates' names when initiating an interaction. (Function: get peer attention)

- Julia learned to say, "I'm worried" instead of screaming, "I hate you" when she was anxious about something. She later learned how to approach an adult, express her feelings, and ask for help if needed. (Function: get adult assistance)

- Mason learned to point to objects instead of crying and tugging on someone's arm when he wanted something that was out of his reach. He was able to use a picture communication system later in the school year to request items and activities. (Function: get desired item)

Teaching Replacement Skills that Serve an Internal, Automatically Reinforcing Function

The other two purposes served by problem behaviors are quite different from the social-communicative purposes, although they still serve either to obtain something or avoid something. The internally controlled or automatically reinforcing functions of problem behavior are obtaining internal stimulation, such as visual stimulation, endorphin release, or something fun to do, and escaping/avoiding internal stimulation, such as itching, sinus pain, noise, crowding, or hunger (O'Neill et al., 2014).

Problem behaviors that fit this category are not socially motivated but are internally motivated, making them more difficult to address in support plans. Behaviors that serve a self-regulatory purpose are not intended to communicate a message or influence other people. Instead, the individual needs more or less internal stimulation and has found some way to accomplish that purpose. The person does not necessarily care how other people respond to the behavior. The internal stimulation that the behavior provides or alleviates is automatically reinforcing or rewarding for its own sake.

Still, the same logic guides the choice of interventions for both social-communicative and self-regulatory behaviors. Students whose problem behaviors are maintained by the consequences of obtaining or avoiding internal stimulation need to learn a new way to achieve that purpose. For example, students who cover their ears with their hands and scream to avoid loud noises that hurt their ears or frighten them could learn a different way to avoid this aversive sensory input (e.g., using headphones to listen to music, going to a quiet place).

Self-regulatory behaviors often involve repetitive body movement—behaviors that may be described as self-stimulatory or stereotypic. Self-injurious behaviors can serve a self-regulatory function as well, such as eye poking to receive visual stimulation. It is important to understand that the topography of the behavior—the way the behavior looks—does not reveal its function. Flapping one's hands could be a way to relieve too much internal stimulation (e.g., sensory overload, anxiety) or get internal stimulation when one is bored or needs more physical movement. Teachers sometimes assume that all stereotypic behaviors interfere with the student's ability to listen or focus on instruction. Instead, these behaviors may actually help a person to focus by regulating his or her internal state.

The teaching components of a PBS plan may include replacing certain existing self-regulatory behaviors with more normalized—and, in the case of self-destructive behaviors, safer—versions that provide the same result or outcome. For example, eye poking used to obtain visual stimulation might be replaced with opportunities to watch a video game (Kennedy & Souza, 1995), and finger flicking by one's ears might be replaced by listening to music. Rocking used by a student when bored or underaroused might be replaced with opportunities to engage in physical activity, such as working out in the gym. Loud humming used when a student is overstimulated might be replaced by relaxing in a quiet area. Students in all of these examples can be taught to request or independently obtain and engage in replacement activities themselves without teacher mediation. In some cases, interventions are designed not to completely eliminate the behavior but to confine its use to particular times or places. For example, visual cue cards were used in a study involving a young student with autism to signify the times when it was acceptable for him to engage in stereotypic behavior. The student was reminded at the beginning of instructional sessions that it was not time for stereotypy; if he did the target behavior during the session, then the teacher pointed to the "no" card and gave a verbal reminder. The student was shown the "yes" card after the task was completed, and stereotypy was permitted (Conroy, Asmus, Sellers, & Ladwig, 2005). Another example is giving a student with autism a card or other symbol to use to request deep pressure or ask for the weighted vest that provides the sensory input needed to feel comfortable. Most people would consider these alternatives to be more acceptable than running to the library to squeeze oneself between a bookshelf and the wall.

The challenge of teaching replacement skills for problem behaviors that serve a self-regulatory function is to find a replacement that actually works—one that provides the same sensory feedback or outcome or one that the student is willing to accept as an alternative. This is tricky because no replacement can provide the exact same sensory feedback that the student receives through self-stimulation or self-injurious behavior. Alternatives can be found, however, through careful assessment and planning. If the replacement activity cannot serve a similar sensory function and is not acceptable to the student, then it is possible to find an activity that the student might want to do instead. For example, Angel, who likes to keep his hands busy, learned to make loop rugs when unoccupied, rather than pick at threads and shred his clothing. Nicole happily accepted chewing gum as an alternative to constantly picking up and putting small items in her mouth. Doing informal hypothesis testing by introducing various options one at a time is one way to verify whether a replacement activity would work or whether other options should be tried (see Chapter 4).

Other Desired Behaviors that Address Student Needs

In addition to learning specific replacement skills to accomplish their purposes, most students with serious behavior problems also benefit from broader or more general improvements in their academic, social interaction, and self-control skills. Although replacing a single problem behavior with a more appropriate way to communicate or regulate internal stimulation can decrease the incidence of problem behavior, students virtually always need to learn other skills to succeed in school and other settings and to achieve the lasting behavior and lifestyle improvements that are the goal of PBS. Single replacement skills are often insufficient

targets by themselves and sometimes do not produce the most desirable educational or interpersonal learning outcome. Asking for a break is indeed a better alternative to screaming, but permitting a student to continually escape from necessary academic instruction is not educationally beneficial. Thus, when considering what other alternative skills to teach, teams might ask, "What other skills are needed to compete with problem behaviors and achieve desired outcomes?" To identify skills that could be taught, it is sometimes helpful to also ask, "Why does the student need to engage in the problem behavior?" and "What other skills does the student need to learn to be successful and meet classroom and other social expectations?"

 ### Student Snapshot

Anthony's crying and rocking during independent work times functioned to gain access to teacher assistance. To replace this behavior with a functional alternative, Anthony's team decided to teach him to raise his hand instead when he needed help. Hand-raising was an appropriate and useful alternative to crying and rocking. Other critical skills were revealed, however, when the team considered that the long-term goal for Anthony was to improve his overall ability to work independently. First, the team thought about the reasons why Anthony needed such frequent teacher assistance. They recognized that Anthony had poor problem-solving skills and depended on teachers to find solutions rather than figuring out solutions for himself. Thus, a misplaced book, a missing pencil, or initial confusion about an assignment would result in Anthony immediately seeking teacher help. Second, they realized that Anthony rarely initiated interactions with his teachers or peers at any time during the school day. Anthony's needs were often anticipated by adults at his previous placement in a self-contained classroom with a much higher adult-to-student ratio, and, therefore, he had little need to initiate, request assistance, or problem-solve. Therefore, Anthony's support plan addressed teaching him the following in order to help him be successful in school, meet desired outcomes, and prevent long-term problem behaviors: 1) to raise his hand when he needed assistance, 2) to problem-solve during independent work to decrease his need for assistance, and 3) to initiate requests for materials or assistance throughout the school day with both teachers and peers.

When identifying other desired outcomes that address student needs, any number of alternative skills could be targeted for intervention (Dunlap et al., 2010; Halle, Bambara, & Reichle, 2005). These include teaching

- Specific academic skills that will help students maintain active engagement and complete assigned tasks while minimizing frustration

- Problem-solving skills to help students work independently and resolve social conflicts

- Social-communicative skills to help students express their needs and improve their social competence and relationships with others

- School-related social skills to help students to better follow school rules and expectations and receive positive recognition and feedback from teachers

- Self-management skills consisting of goal setting, monitoring and evaluating one's own behaviors, and self-regulating, to self-direct and self-control behaviors

- Coping skills, such as controlling anger, accepting criticism, relaxing or leave-taking during stressful events, to help students deal with disappointments or other unwanted situations

In essence, by teaching students other desired alternatives, we are giving them the power to change the conditions that lead to problem behaviors while also improving their academic and social competence, which will lead to a better quality

of life. In addition, we are giving students the strategies needed to cope with or deal with difficulties in situations that cannot or should not be changed. Achieving this latter outcome through alternative skills may be more difficult for students to learn because we are asking them to tolerate something that they may dislike or find aversive. Learning alternative ways of coping with difficult situations, however, may be made palatable by pairing instruction for coping skills with other alternative skills, antecedent intervention strategies, and a lot of support and encouragement.

 ## Student Snapshot

Anthony's team decided that teaching him to request materials, rather than grabbing or pushing his classmates, was an appropriate replacement skill. Classroom materials were meant to be shared, however, and there would be times that Anthony would have to accept not immediately getting what he wanted without screaming. Ms. Santos placed some of Anthony's favorite materials (e.g., colored markers, pens, glue sticks) in a plastic bin labeled "Anthony" to lessen the frequency that Anthony would be required to share. Next, she gave Anthony a problem-solving self-management card that listed several options for how to respond when he wanted a favorite material. It said, "When my classmate has something I want, I can ask politely, wait my turn, choose something else from my box, or plan to use it another time." Ms. Santos coached Anthony on how to use the card during small-group and unstructured activities and reminded him how to respond and self-monitor his success by checking off one or more options. To make self-control even more motivating, Anthony was rewarded with a few minutes of computer time after each activity when he used one of the options without engaging in problem behaviors.

Methods for Teaching Alternative Skills

Teaching alternative skills, whether replacement skills or other desired behaviors, requires 1) identifying an alternative skill that is effective and relatively easy or motivating to use, 2) teaching the student how and when to use the skill, and 3) ensuring that teachers and others in the environment respond to the skill so that it works better than the problem behavior. In addition, to make replacement skills truly functional for the student, performing the replacement skill needs to take less effort than the problem behavior (efficiency), and using the replacement skill needs to accomplish the desired purpose or same outcome more often and more consistently than the problem behavior (effectiveness). In other words, motivation is enhanced because the student achieves the same outcome through a more efficient and effective alternative. The following case illustrates this point.

Student Snapshot

Sidney, who typically did not talk and communicated using a few words and gestures, would grab teachers' or classmates' arms or clothing when he was left alone at his desk and wanted to gain their attention and interact with them. This was a behavior that was easy to do—he would grab whoever was nearby—and also was extremely effective in getting people to come close, talk with him, and touch him. At first, the PBS team provided Sidney with a photograph album with pictures of his teachers and classmates as a device to assist his communication efforts. They tried to teach Sidney to find and point to a photograph of the person with whom he wanted to interact. It often took Sidney several minutes to retrieve the photograph album and locate the picture of a particular person, however, even when he was provided with adult assistance. Thus, this was not a very efficient replacement behavior. Also, the classmates or teachers that Sidney was pointing to in the photograph album often were not in Sidney's immediate vicinity and did not notice that Sidney was pointing to their pictures. Therefore, the likelihood was not high that Sidney's attempt to gain the desired attention using the photograph album would be successful; the effectiveness of the replacement behavior was not nearly as effective as Sidney's old

behavior. When Sidney was taught to hold out his hand to indicate "give me five" as a way to initiate an interaction, however, he had an easy-to-do replacement skill that was very likely to be immediately reinforced by gaining attention.

The principles of effectiveness and efficiency apply to teaching other desired behaviors but in different ways from teaching a simple one-to-one replacement skill. Desired alternatives compete with, but do not necessarily replace, problem behavior to achieve the same outcome that the student is seeking to achieve. Therefore, teams will need to ensure that the desired alternatives are motivating for the student to use, which may require introducing new outcomes and ensuring they are desirable. For example, in Anthony's case, sharing materials or waiting to use them at some other time does not achieve the same outcome that Anthony achieved through grabbing. His teacher made it easier for Anthony to use alternative skills, however, by giving him several response options and rewarding him for using them with time on the computer, one of his favorite activities. This combination of making the desired alternatives easy and providing competitive outcomes (e.g., access to the computer) makes it more likely that Anthony will use other desired alternatives to replace grabbing. Teaching alternative skills requires developing an instructional plan ensuring that relevant adults and peers

- Know what the alternative skill is

- Know how, when, and by whom the skill will be taught

- Know how generalization and maintenance of the skill will be ensured

A combination of methods is typically used, including 1) rearranging antecedents to prevent problem behaviors from occurring and cue the use of the alternative skill; 2) incidental teaching to model, shape, prompt, and reinforce the use of the alternative skill in natural contexts; and, in some cases, 3) skill-based teaching approaches to provide direct instruction and practice of the alternative skill in instructional environments. If the alternative skill is to become more efficient and effective for the student than the problem behavior, then instruction must take the student beyond the acquisition stage of accurately performing the skill in specific instructional contexts. The student also must learn when to use the skill and learn to use it fluently (i.e., fast enough for the skill to be effective in obtaining the desired results). A further consideration in teaching alternative skills is to ensure that the student's use of the skill generalizes to all of the people, places, and situations where the problem behavior is a concern and that skill use is maintained over time.

Figure 5.5 outlines the instructional methods used to teach alternative skills, including both specific replacement skills and other desired alternative skills. The methods used will vary depending on the student's cognitive and communication abilities. For instance, cognitive strategies that involve self-talk may not always be the most appropriate intervention for students who have an intellectual disability. Many of the methods that require verbal mediation (e.g., role playing, social-cognitive processes) can be adapted for students with intellectual disabilities, however, by using visual cues and simplifying the steps in the process.

Functional communication training (Durand & Merges, 2001) or, more broadly, communication-based intervention (Carr et al., 1994) is a specific approach to teaching replacement communication skills. Communication-based interventions, which are part of an overall PBS plan, are designed to teach people with developmental disabilities (primarily those with intellectual disabilities or autism) and severe problem behavior to use positive forms of communication to achieve their goals.

(It does not address internal stimulation as a function of problem behavior.) The approach is similar to the one described in this book, but it utilizes a more rigorous functional analysis and very intensive instructional programming to accelerate the acquisition of new communication skills, the generalization of new communication skills across people and stimulus conditions, and the maintenance of those skills across time. Functional communication training has been validated through extensive research in both clinical and community settings with people having developmental disabilities and severe behavior problems, including aggression, self-injury, and property destruction (Carr et al., 1994; Durand & Merges, 2001).

Responding Strategies

Responding strategies (also known as consequence strategies) involve making changes to the consequences that follow the student's behaviors with the intent of making the new alternative behaviors work better, or more reinforcing to use, than the problem behavior. The PBS approach requires team members to consider changing the way they react to both positive and negative behaviors—reinforcing alternative behaviors while decreasing or eliminating the reinforcement or outcomes for problem behaviors.

Responding to Alternative Behaviors

Teams should consider asking, "How will we reinforce the student's use of alternative behaviors in ways that make alternatives more efficient and effective than the problem behavior?" to encourage the student to use alternative behaviors instead of problem behaviors. Consider a reinforcement strategy for each alternative skill you intend to teach.

Reinforcement is automatic when teaching a replacement skill because the student receives the same outcome as the problem behavior. For example, when

Modeling: When the student has an opportunity (contrived or naturally occurring) to use the new skill or behavior, an adult or peer demonstrates the skill. In some cases, salient features of the model may be verbally described to the student (i.e., the student may receive visual, verbal, or physical prompts as he or she performs the skill or behavior and may later receive performance feedback).

Prompting and shaping: When the student has an opportunity (contrived or naturally occurring) to use the new skill or behavior, a sequence of prompts is used to elicit the new skill, which then is reinforced by providing the requested object or activity. For example, the prompting sequence might be 1) a natural cue, 2) a gesture, and 3) a partial physical prompt. The new skill is shaped by reinforcing the student's current form of the skill (or the frequency with which it is used) and by slowly working toward the criterion form and frequency.

Behavior rehearsal: The student practices role playing or rehearsing a target skill under controlled conditions (e.g., in the classroom with the teacher right before going to the lunchroom, where the problem often arises). The student also may verbalize what he or she will do or say when an opportunity to use the skill arises. Social Stories (Gray, 1998) and cognitive picture and script rehearsal strategies (Groden & LeVasseur, 1994) are adapted approaches to this category of teaching method. These two techniques, designed for students with Asperger syndrome, autism, or intellectual disabilities, provide the student with a social script, often accompanied by pictures or drawings, that leads him or her through the process of rehearsing for a difficult situation.

Coaching: The student is given verbal directions on how and when to use the skill; skill use is followed by verbal feedback and discussion of the student's performance. Coaching is often used with modeling.

Incidental teaching: Naturally occurring daily activities are used as opportunities for instruction. An adult or peer uses a combination of prompting, shaping, coaching, and modeling to improve skill use. Incidental teaching may make use of teachable moments when the student has missed an opportunity to use a skill, or activities may be arranged to provide teaching opportunities (e.g., a preferred item is purposefully left in sight but out of the student's reach).

Self-management strategies: Students are provided with devices (e.g., checklist, wrist counter, photograph, series of pictures) that are used to cue the new skill or self-evaluate their performance of the skill. This may be combined with self-reinforcement. Self-monitoring strategies (a type of self-management strategy) require teaching students to use a device (e.g., wrist counter, interval recording form, checklist) to count instances of their own behavior.

Social-cognitive processes: Students are taught metacognitive processes that increase awareness of their own and others' behaviors and feelings. These processes, which are taught through direct instruction, include self-talk, problem-solving strategies, relaxation training, anger management, and behavior rehearsal. These processes are especially helpful when teaching the cognitive processes involved in using social and self-management skills such as anger control, problem solving, attribution training, and perspective taking.

Systematic desensitization strategies: Students are taught to tolerate aversive or difficult situations by gradually exposing the student to the aversive situation while teaching coping skills for dealing with the situation. This strategy is typically used to decrease anxiety and phobias around aversive stimuli or events (e.g., crowded rooms, noisy environments, sticky foods, going to the dentist) but can be applied to build tolerance for any disliked activity, such as incrementally having a student work for longer periods of time or wait to obtain access to materials or teacher assistance.

Figure 5.5. Methods for teaching alternative skills and behaviors.

Anthony raises his hand, he will be reinforced by gaining teacher assistance. To ensure that the student consistently uses the replacement skill, however, adults will need to respond consistently and immediately to the student's use of the replacement skill, especially during the early stages of learning. Delays in adult responding (e.g., waiting several minutes after Anthony raises his hand) or inconsistent responding when the student is first learning the skill will teach inconsistent student behaviors—sometimes the student will use the replacement skill, other times not. Delays can be introduced—"I'll be there in a minute, Anthony"—after the student has learned to reliably use the skill for some time.

Strategies for reinforcing other desired alternatives (e.g., social interaction skills, problem-solving strategies) are the same as the strategies used for teaching any other skill. Wherever possible, use consequences that are natural to the skill, such as praise and acknowledgement for a job well done, social interaction, or access to a preferred activity, so that the student will continue to use the skill under natural conditions. Self-monitoring of behaviors is one way to help students see the connection between appropriate responding and positive outcomes. Teams may consider using more extrinsic reward systems, however, such as point cards and extra rewards or privileges for alternative behaviors that may be especially difficult for the student to learn.

Responding to Problem Behaviors

With prevention and teaching strategies in place, the student's use of problem behaviors should diminish. Teams will still need to consider how to respond should they occur by asking, "How will we respond to make problem behavior ineffective?" Some possible ways of responding that fit with this approach are 1) nonreinforcement followed by redirection to the acceptable behavior and 2) natural or logical and educational consequences. (A safety plan also is needed when the behavior is seriously disruptive or destructive.) On the contrary, adults and peers conscientiously or differentially provide reinforcement to the individual 1) when the alternative behavior is used and 2) when the problem behavior does not occur. The following is a brief description of each of these strategies and a discussion of some important rules to follow in deciding which strategies to use for a particular student.

Nonreinforcement and Redirection

Nonreinforcement means not responding to a behavior in a way that enables the behavior to achieve its purpose. It means not allowing the behavior to work for the

student in the way it has worked in the past. Durand (1990) described nonreinforcement as a response-independent consequence that makes the challenging behavior nonfunctional.

Nonreinforcement must be used in conjunction with redirecting the student to an alternative behavior and then reinforcing the alternative behavior (or an attempt by the student to use an alternative behavior) to be effective and educational. In a sense, nonreinforcement means ignoring the problem behavior; it does not mean completely ignoring students and doing nothing to help them alter their behavior. For example, if Rose grabs a peer's shirt as a way to say, "Hi, let's play," then the teacher can prompt Rose to use the replacement behavior of tapping the peer on the shoulder and then praise Rose for using her new behavior. The peer also will then agree to play with Rose, which is where the real reinforcement occurs.

Nonreinforcement and redirection 1) show the student what to do as an alternative to a problem behavior and 2) provide the opportunity for reinforcement of the desired behavior. Teachers are not really teaching a student if their strategy is simply to ignore the student in the hope that he or she will eventually hit on the correct behavior.

Natural, Logical, and Educational Consequences

Certainly, one way that people learn to avoid making social and behavioral mistakes is by experiencing the consequences of their behavior. Sometimes there is a place for using negative consequences in a behavior support plan, but only if the consequences used meet several criteria. Negative consequences should not inflict pain, humiliation, or embarrassment on the student. They should not be chosen arbitrarily but should be in keeping with the hypotheses generated by the FBA.

Negative consequences should be naturally or logically related to the behavior.

Natural consequences occur as a result of the behavior itself. For example, the natural consequence of breaking or losing a toy is that the item is no longer available. Some behaviors do not really have a natural consequence; there is no subsequent event that is naturally contingent on the behavior's occurrence. Logical consequences may be developed in such a case. Logical consequences are consequences that fit the behavior and are reasonably related to it. For example, a logical consequence for failing to finish work is not having free time.

It is extremely important to understand that negative consequences can be natural or logical but inconsistent with a PBS approach if they are used in a manner that is cold, authoritarian, or uninformed by an understanding of the causes and functions of difficult behavior. Certainly, natural and logical consequences, by definition, can be punishing in that they are stimuli or events that are contingent on a behavior and decrease the future occurrence of the behavior. Exposure of students to natural or logical consequences, however, should never be done in a punitive or intemperate way. Theoretically, the natural consequence of running out into a street without looking is getting hit by a car. Yet this is not the way teachers would instruct students in crossing the street. Therefore, it is not enough for consequences to be natural or logical; they also should be educational and respectful. Just as teachers should follow nonreinforcement with redirection to a more appropriate behavior, teachers also should follow natural or logical consequences with a response that is designed to strengthen the student's use of approved behavior. The following are suggestions to consider when using four common negative consequences in ways that are not merely natural or logical but also educational and respectful:

1. *Corrections and restitution:* Corrections, or having a student correct a behavioral mistake, can be a logical, educational consequence. For example, prompting a student to hang his or her coat in his or her cubbyhole or locker after he or she had thrown it on the floor or having a student clean up milk that was spilled are corrections. Restitution is a particular type of correction that involves making things right with another person. Asking a student to apologize for hurting someone or to return a book that was stolen from a classmate are logical consequences that involve restitution and can be educational as well.

There are several things, however, to watch out for when responding in this way. Forcing a correction or restitution may end up in a verbal or physical tug-of-war with the student. It can be difficult to conclude a tug-of-war in a way that is educational and respectful. It is best to often wait until the student is calm and has some perspective on the incident before discussing the correction. Otherwise, you even may lose sight of the original lesson you were hoping to convey, which has to do with being a good citizen and treating other people fairly and with respect.

2. *Verbal reprimands:* It is easy to fall into the habit of scolding students when they do things they should not do, but this often has a negative effect on students with problem behavior. Although at times scolding can be effective in halting a behavior, at other times it has no effect or even the opposite effect of what was intended. For instance, if a student has few positive ways to communicate and has learned that negative behavior is a more certain way to get attention than being quiet and compliant, then verbal comments that teachers think of as being reprimands can actually be reinforcing to the student.

When students understand words and rules and are "just testing" to see whether they can get away with a behavior without consequences, it makes sense to remind them of the rule that has been broken. For example, if a student runs down the hallway jostling other students but understands that this is not allowed and is doing it just to see whether he or she can get away with it, then it is appropriate to give a reminder: "Remember our hallway rule: Walk and stay in line." If a student who does not talk and does not understand rules is throwing art materials on the floor as a way to get attention, however, then talking about the behavior may teach that student that throwing things is the way to say, "Pay attention to me!" A better way to respond in that case might be to interrupt the behavior by removing some of the materials and redirecting the student to the art project at hand.

3. *Response cost: Taking away privileges or things:* Taking away privileges as a consequence to problem behavior can be a logical and educational consequence. It needs to be accomplished, however, with the student's level of cognitive and social development in mind, and it needs to be followed by teaching so that the student learns what to do instead in the future. For example, a student pushes a classmate while the science class is watching a nature movie that everyone has been looking forward to seeing. Simply not allowing the student to watch the movie for a few minutes can be just as effective, if not more so, than banishing him or her from the classroom until the movie is over or taking away movie-watching privileges for the semester. The teacher could pull the student aside after the movie is over to discuss what happened and make a plan for success in the future.

If a behavior support plan includes taking away items or privileges, then it should be done in a neutral way immediately after the problem has occurred, and whatever is taken away should be naturally or logically related to the problem behavior. For example, if a kindergarten student grabs a toy from a classmate, then the toy might be taken away for a few minutes, but not the child's dessert. Taking away items or privileges should be followed by an opportunity to practice an approved behavior in order to be educational. Thus, if a teacher has taken a toy away from a child for a few minutes, then the teacher would let the child try playing with the toy again, spending a few minutes modeling and shaping an acceptable way to play in order to promote successful play.

4. *Taking a break:* Taking a break, or sometimes referred to as taking time, means simply having the student go to another part of the room, take a walk, or do something else to get away from where the problem occurred for as long as it takes to interrupt the problem behavior and the student to calm down. This way of responding is theoretically similar to the idea of time-out, but the use of that term is avoided because there are many different ways to use time-out and most of them are punitive. The purpose of this strategy is to short-circuit the crisis cycle and prevent the student from losing control. It can also help students learn to control themselves. For example, the A-B-C information that Mike's team collected showed that Mike gets anxious and then disruptive when he does one lesson immediately after another with no time in between to reorient himself. In addition to building more breaks into Mike's schedule and providing him with a picture schedule so that he would always know which activity was next, Mike was taught to

perceive his own triggers and ask, "May I take a short break?" when these signals arose. Mike was eventually taught internal self-calming strategies, which are more desirable self-management methods.

Reinforcement for the Absence of Problem Behavior

A plan for differential reinforcement of other behavior (DRO) allows you to provide a selected reinforcer to a student for each specified period of time in which the targeted problem behavior is not displayed. This behavior management strategy does nothing to teach an alternative behavior if used alone. DRO is consistent with a PBS approach, however, if used in conjunction with antecedent strategies and teaching replacement behaviors that match the functions of problem behaviors. A common DRO plan involves rewarding the student for not displaying several off-task behaviors (e.g., talking to classmates, inappropriately using materials, being out of his or her seat). The reward must be easily attainable so that the student will actually receive the reward and not simply be frustrated by an enticement that is beyond reach. For example, if a student engages in some type of disruptive behavior (e.g., making loud noises, getting out of his or her seat, throwing materials) at an average rate of once every 2 minutes and you devise a DRO plan in which the student must refrain from disruptive behavior for 1 hour to receive the reward, then he or she will not be successful in obtaining the reward and may even stop trying.

Contingent reward programs such as DRO are more positive and proactive than contingent punishment programs such as response cost. The two interventions may at first seem to be similar, but there is a considerable difference between taking away something valued by the student as a consequence of demonstrating a negative behavior (as in response cost) and bestowing something valued by the student for demonstrating positive behavior (as in DRO). For example, as part of a response cost intervention, a student might have computer time scheduled after each academic period but have that time taken away if targeted problem behavior occurs during the academic session. A DRO intervention allows the student to earn computer time if the problem behavior does not occur during a specified period of time.

Although an environment that is rich in rewarding activities and interactions is one element of a plan for PBS, you should caution against making extrinsic rewards (e.g., grades, praise, edible treats) the centerpiece of a behavior support plan. A more educational approach asks how the social context and the instructional activities can be altered to make learning and the social context more meaningful, rather than trying to find a treat that will induce short-term compliance in the student. Some students may not have learned that interacting with others and participating in daily activities can be rewarding. In that case, teaching the student the value of interaction and participation should be a top priority.

Writing a Behavior Support Plan: Putting It All Together

The culminating product of the team's decisions for selecting interventions around preventing, teaching, and responding is the behavior support plan document. Figure 5.6 provides a completed example of the Step 3 Worksheet: Positive Behavior Support Plan designed for Anthony and shows how preventing, teaching, and responding strategies fit together to create a comprehensive plan of support.

Major sections of the support plan include 1) hypothesis statements, which summarize the results of the FBA; 2) goal statements, which articulate expected student outcomes as a result of implementing the plan; and 3) selected preventing,

Step 3 Worksheet: Positive Behavior Support Plan

Student: _Anthony Rodriquez_   Date: _November 23, 2014_

Team members designing this plan:

Jared Simms (special education teacher)   Angela and Jaime Rodriquez (parents)
Rita Santos (second-grade teacher)   Mara Kellam (school psychologist)
Marianne Josephs (school district behavior specialist)   Ashley Giles (paraeducator)

Behavior hypotheses (when this happens [antecedents], the student does this [target behavior], and results in [consequences and presumed function of behavior])

1. Anthony will cry and rock when he encounters a problem during independent seat work activities (e.g., is confused about an assignment, misplaces materials) or requires adult assistance. This results in Anthony's teachers responding by offering assistance and Anthony receiving help.

2. Anthony is likely to push his peers away, grab materials from them, or scream, "That's mine" during unstructured (transitions, recess, free time) and independent small-group activities (e.g., art projects). This typically results in peers giving in to his requests and Anthony obtaining desired materials.

3. Anthony is likely to refuse participation by folding his arms and saying, "We are not supposed to do this" on shortened school days and when directed to start an activity that does not follow the typical classroom schedule. This results in Anthony delaying or not completing assigned tasks and functions to escape unanticipated activities.

Goals

Increase	Decrease
1. Working independently using appropriate problem-solving skills and requesting teacher assistance as needed	1. Decrease crying/rocking and grabbing/pushing peers or screaming as a means of expressing his need for assistance or obtaining desired materials
2. Sharing materials with peers and using appropriate problem-solving skills to obtain desired materials	2. Decrease refusals to participate in essential instructional activities
3. Participating in all classroom activities, including those that follow a schedule change	
4. Initiating socially in the form of requests and greetings to adults and peers	

Interventions and support strategies to be implemented

Preventing (antecedent changes)		Teaching replacement and other desired skills	Responding to alternative skills and problem behaviors
Alter setting event	Alter trigger(s)		
Independent seat work	Preview all work expectations; make sure Anthony understands what is expected of him; be sure work is at his independent level of performance.

Remind him to raise his hand if he needs assistance.

Introduce problem-solving self-management card to encourage Anthony to attempt problem solving before asking for help. | Teach Anthony to request teacher assistance by raising his hand.

Teach Anthony to work more independently by using problem-solving strategies for 1) missing or misplaced items (e.g., look in his desk, look under papers/books) and 2) understanding his assignment or working through challenges (e.g., reread directions, try another problem, go back and reread again).

Teach Anthony to self-monitor his use of problem-solving strategies and completion of assignments without teacher assistance by checking off behaviors on his self-management card. | Respond immediately to Anthony's hand raises during early learning; ask him what he needs. Model/prompt hand raising at the first sign of distress (self-talk), and then provide immediate assistance. Praise him!

Once Anthony has learned to raise his hand, respond by directing him to follow the problem-solving steps on his card. Coach him through selecting a solution and praise all attempts.

Later, once he has learned hand-raising and problem solving, praise him when working independently and when solving problems on his own rather than using hand raising as a first resort. Review self-monitoring card after the activity (praise successes or problem-solve how to do better next time). |

Figure 5.6. Step 3 Worksheet: Positive Behavior Support Plan for Anthony. (A blank, photocopiable version of this form is available in Appendix A, and blank and filled-in versions are available in the forms download.)

Step 3 Worksheet: Positive Behavior Support Plan *(continued)*   *page 2 of 2*

Preventing (antecedent changes)		Teaching replacement and other desired skills	Responding to alternative skills and problem behaviors
Alter setting event	**Alter trigger(s)**		
Unstructured, independent, and small-group activities	Provide Anthony with a bin of favorite materials (e.g., markers, pens, glue sticks). Preview expectations and sharing options before each activity (e.g., use his own materials, ask politely, wait for materials). Provide problem-solving self-management card.	Teach Anthony to choose and follow one of the sharing options on his problem-solving card. Start by sitting next to Anthony and coaching him, and then fade support. Teach Anthony to self-monitor his use of one or more sharing options without teacher assistance.	Praise all acts of sharing—prompted and unprompted alternatives to grabbing items or pushing peers. At the first sign of grabbing or pushing, redirect Anthony back to one of the alternatives. Have Anthony choose which option to follow. If Anthony continues to push or grab after being redirected, then prompt Anthony to take time. When he is calm and away from the activity, remind Anthony of the rules for sharing and problem-solve solutions before introducing him back to the activity. Review self-monitoring card with Anthony after the activity (praise successes or problem-solve how to do better next time). If, at any time, problem behaviors escalate to screaming and repeated grabbing, then follow Step C (crisis intervention) of the Safety Plan.
Changes in classroom schedule: Read Social Story and change visual schedule to help Anthony predict changes; have Anthony choose times to schedule independent leisure reading or computer time.	Have Anthony refer to his visual schedule during transitions; remind him of expectations for participation.	Teach Anthony to cope with schedule changes by following his visual schedule; provide coaching as needed.	As soon as Anthony participates in an unscheduled activity, provide immediate praise. If Anthony refuses or delays participation, then redirect him to his visual schedule and wait for him to participate. Praise him as soon as he participates. At the end of the day, review all activities successfully completed. Implement a reward system for successful completion. If Anthony does not complete an assignment, then arrange for him to make it up during recess, independent reading, or computer time.
All activities		Use incidental teaching strategies to teach social initiations throughout the school day.	Praise attempts and independent initiations; provide access to materials.

Is Safety Plan still needed?   Yes   No

If so, attach Safety Plan that has been revised and updated as needed.

teaching, and responding strategies that address the hypotheses for problem behaviors and map out a plan for achieving desired student outcomes. You know you will have a solid plan when these three sections link together.

Goal statements identify specific behaviors to be decreased (problem behaviors) and positive behaviors (alternative skills) to be increased. Goal statements that are clearly defined in observable terms will be used to select measures for evaluating student progress and the overall effects of the support plan. It is important to note that Anthony's plan provides a map or framework for supporting him at this point in time, but the plan will continue to be revised as the PBS team evaluates its impact.

Naturally, the complexity of PBS plans varies widely depending on the complexity of the student's learning and behavioral needs and the support team's ability to implement interventions. No one knows exactly what the minimum requirements are for effective interventions for significant behavior problems, nor does anyone know exactly how much training a typical teacher or support team member needs to successfully implement a comprehensive PBS plan. Many research studies conducted in schools show significant effects on students' behavior when relatively commonplace interventions and supports are faithfully implemented by teachers, student teachers, paraprofessionals, and parents (e.g., Clarke, Worcester, Dunlap, Murray, & Bradley-Klug, 2002; Gann, Ferro, Umbreit, & Liaupsin, 2014; Kern, Gallagher, Starosta, Hickman, & George, 2006; Strain, Wilson, & Dunlap, 2011). Intervention plans in published research rely heavily on prevention of behavior problems through antecedent changes that are mostly low effort (e.g., changing seating arrangements, reducing task length, interspersing easier and more difficult tasks, using proximity control, giving students choices in academic

tasks), on instructional strategies that are almost universally effective (e.g., match task demands with learners' skill levels, use systematic instruction), and on consequence strategies that are based on accepted operant learning principles (e.g., give specific praise and attention for improved behavior, do not reinforce undesirable behavior). Given these and other findings on effective behavior support in schools, the following are some additional suggestions for making a successful plan for PBS that will be reliably implemented:

• Start by implementing broad strategies to improve the educational and social context, including relationship building between the staff and the student, creating peer support in the classroom and school, and ensuring that the educational programming is appropriate and meaningful. (The facilitation of positive relationships among students is examined in depth in the companion book *Social Relationships and Peer Support* [Janney & Snell, 2006].) Broad improvements made in these areas, especially if the Student-Centered FBA Profile (see Figure 4.11) suggests a need, can make implementing the support plan easier and more effective by creating a context that supports learning.

• Consider targeting classroom activities or school settings that are most problematic first. A comprehensive support plan is implemented over time, usually spanning the school year. It is unrealistic to implement all components in all problematic situations at once, which can overwhelm teachers and the student, especially if the plan is complex. Therefore, consider implementing components of the support plan in classroom activities in which problem behavior causes the most trouble for the student or the greatest classroom disruption. Systematically add interventions in other activities as teachers gain confidence and skill and student behaviors improve.

- When implementing components of the plan, start by making antecedent changes first. Putting conditions in place that prevent problem behaviors enhances student motivation for learning alternative skills and makes it easier for teachers to teach.

- Similarly, when teaching alternative skills, consider the value of teaching specific replacement skills first and then teaching other desired alternatives when possible. Replacement skills that produce the same outcome as problem behaviors provide an immediate payoff for students and are generally easier to learn than other alternative skills that may take more time and effort to learn. Build success by building on small successes first.

- Be sure the selected strategies have a good contextual fit. Strategies that are considered time consuming, difficult to implement, or inconsistent with teachers' views about acceptability are not likely to be carried out in the long run, even if the strategies appropriately address student needs (Boardman, Arguelles, Vaughn, Hughes, & Klingner, 2005). Make sure selected strategies are doable, can be realistically carried out under typical classroom conditions, are appropriate to the setting, and are acceptable to teachers, parents, and the student. Never force-fit an intervention that cannot be realistically carried out or is unacceptable to those involved. Instead, modify it until it does fit while still addressing student needs.

- Ask, "What do we (team members) need to implement the behavior support plan?" This question gets at contextual fit in a different way by asking team members to consider what supports are needed for them to support the student. Do teachers feel confident that they can carry out the strategies? Would they benefit from peer coaching or additional professional development? Do teachers need additional resources? Would they benefit from having a behavior specialist visit their classroom regularly for expert consultation or having an assigned paraeducator make additional teaching materials or organize activities while the teacher spends more time with the student? Does the team meet frequently enough to provide ongoing support, feedback, and general camaraderie for teachers as they implement the student's plan? Would teachers benefit from more frequent meetings or informal check-ins from their peers? Figure 5.7 summarizes some questions to evaluate a support plan's contextual fit with the classroom environment and team member needs.

- Design and use intervention fidelity checklists to support implementation. Even when a behavior support plan has a good contextual fit, it will fail if it is not implemented. Good and well-intended behavior support plans all too often end up in some file unimplemented when they are not translated into plans for daily action. The intervention fidelity checklist is a useful tool for translating strategies into actionable steps for daily use. For example, see the fidelity checklist created for Anthony in Figure 5.8. Checklists are developed for the point in time that strategies are to be implemented, then they are updated as strategies are added or modified. Teachers and paraeducators can use the checklist to self-monitor their own implementation or to observe one another to ensure that the support plan strategies are implemented as intended.

- Plan for implementation across settings. One of the greatest challenges

Directions: Review these questions as a team. "No" answers require the team to generate a solution to the problem.

Questions about potential effectiveness
Do all team members
- Agree with the hypothesis(es) for problem behaviors?
- Agree that the elements of the support plan address core components of the behavior hypothesis(es)?
- Agree that the key components of the support plan will be effective in reaching targeted goals or student outcomes?
- Believe that the overall plan is in the best interest of the student?

Questions about implementation feasibility and sustainability
Do all team members
- Agree that the intervention and support strategies can be realistically carried out in their settings?
- Agree that the intervention and support strategies are appropriate to typical classroom routines?
- Believe the strategies will take little effort or time to carry out?
- Agree with the overall plan for implementing components of the student's support plan?

Questions about team member needs
Do all team members
- Feel confident in their skills or abilities to carry out all strategies?
- Believe that they have adequate training, resources, and ongoing supervision or supports to implement the student's support plan?
- Believe that the team is there to address their needs and concerns as well as the student's?
- Believe that the school administration is supportive of their efforts?

Questions concerning family and student values
In addition to the previous questions, do the family and student
- Agree that the support plan is consistent with their beliefs and values?
- Agree that the support plan is respectful of the student and family concerns?

Figure 5.7. Questions for evaluating contextual fit. (*Sources:* Albin, Lucyshyn, Horner, & Flannery, 2006; Bambara & Kern, 2005; Horner, Salentine, & Albin, 2003.)

for promoting positive behavior change is that problem behaviors often occur across settings (e.g., across different classrooms, at home). Generalization and maintenance of positive behaviors are enhanced by implementing components of the PBS plan in different settings at school and at home (Carr et al., 1999). To the extent that problem behaviors serve the same function in different settings, teams should consider how relevant strategies can be applied in each setting, but remember that each setting is a different context. Strategies must be adapted to fit each context or else they will not be carried out. Team members should consider how to adapt strategies to fit each context when teams are comprised of teachers from multiple

classrooms or parents. For example, in Anthony's case, helping him overcome problems associated with independent seat work is not relevant for home, but helping him cope with unanticipated schedule or routine changes at home is relevant. Anthony's team will need to consider how to adapt strategies to help him predict and cope with changes at home. Does it make sense for Anthony's parents to read him Social Stories at home? Is it easier for them to review his schedule for the next day each night before bedtime and preview what will happen in the form of discussions? Multiple effective options that fit the setting can be identified as long as the strategy addresses the hypothesis for the causes of problem behavior.

Intervention Integrity Checklist

Instructor: _____   Date: _____

Observer: _____

Independent seat work: Raise hand

Activities observed: _____

Yes/No/NA   1.   Instructor previews assignment; checks for Anthony's understanding.

Yes/No/NA   2.   Instructor reminds Anthony to raise his hand if he needs help.

Yes/No/NA   3.   Instructor immediately responds when Anthony raises his hand.

Yes/No/NA   4.   Instructor prompts Anthony to raise his hand at the first sign of distress or if Anthony begins to self-talk, cry, or rock.

Unstructured/small group: Sharing materials

Activities observed: _____

Yes/No/NA   1.   Instructor provides Anthony with a bin of his materials.

Yes/No/NA   2.   Instructor ensures Anthony has his self-management card.

Yes/No/NA   3.   Instructor reviews behavioral expectations and options for sharing on his card.

Yes/No/NA   4.   Anthony uses card to appropriately self-monitor.

Yes/No/NA   5.   Instructor stays in close proximity, praising Anthony for good choices.

Yes/No/NA   6.   At the first sign of grabbing/pushing, instructor redirects Anthony to choose an option from his card. After a second reminder, Anthony is prompted to take time.

Yes/No/NA   7.   Instructor follows safety plan if problem behaviors (grabbing, pushing, screaming) disrupt classroom activities or threaten safety of others.

Yes/No/NA   8.   Instructor reviews the self-management card with Anthony at the end of the activity, praising successes and problem-solving how to do better next time if needed.

Change in classroom schedule

Yes/No/NA   1.   Instructor reads social narrative about changes in the school day.

Yes/No/NA   2.   Instructor sits with Anthony to make changes in his visual schedule and reviews expectations for participation in activities.

Yes/No/NA   3.   Instructor ensures that independent reading or computer time is scheduled.

Yes/No/NA   4.   Anthony uses his visual schedule to self-monitor his participation in activities.

Yes/No/NA   5.   Instructor praises Anthony for participating in each activity.

Yes/No/NA   6.   If Anthony delays or refuses participation, then the instructor redirects Anthony back to his schedule and waits for participation.

Yes/No/NA   7.   Instructor reviews the visual schedule with Anthony at the end of the day and schedules in extra computer time for the next day for participating in all activities.

Yes/No/NA   8.   Instructor schedules make-up time for any missed work for the next day during recess, leisure reading, or computer time.

Total number of steps completed (tally total number of "yes" answers) _____
Total number of steps (tally total number of "yes" answers plus "no" answers) _____
Percentage of plan followed (number of "yes" answers ÷ total number of steps × 100) = _____

Figure 5.8.   Sample Intervention Integrity Checklist for Anthony's individualized behavior support plan. (*Key:* NA, not applicable.) (*Source:* Bambara & Kunsch, 2014.)

STEP 4

Implement,
Monitor, and Evaluate the
Positive Behavior Support Plan

 After the behavior support strategies have been developed, the support team must discuss the specifics of putting the plan into action (see Figure 5.9). Materials may need to be gathered, other individuals who work with the student but who have not been part of the planning team may need to be contacted, and responsibilities for monitoring the plan's implementation and effectiveness should be determined. Complete the Step 4 Worksheet: Implementing, Monitoring, and Evaluating the Positive Behavior Support Plan (a blank, photocopiable version of this form is available in Appendix A and the forms download) at a team meeting, and record decisions

made and actions to be taken on a Team Meeting Agenda and Minutes form (see Figure 1.4). The first section of the Step 4 worksheet lists issues that need immediate consideration in order to put the plan into place; the second part lists issues related to ongoing monitoring, evaluation, and revision of the PBS plan.

Evaluation typically requires a variety of formal and informal strategies; it is crucial that the strategies selected be user friendly and efficient—or else they will not be carried out. Support team members should not ignore their subjective evaluation of the results of the plan; after all, if those who directly support the student and have implemented the plan are satisfied with the results, then the behavior change has been noticeable and the plan has been doable. We urge you, however, to conduct some formal, ongoing data collection and analysis as part of any behavior support plan. One reason this is important is that

---

STEP 4

Implement, Monitor, and Evaluate
the Positive Behavior Support Plan

Ask: What steps need to be taken to put the plan into action?
What materials need to be made, purchased, or adapted?
Who else needs to be informed about the plan?
What in-service training, modeling, or coaching do team members and other staff members need?
Who will develop teaching plans for replacement skills and other alternative academic or social-communication skills, and how will the plans be shared with others?
When, how, and by whom will behavior-change and skill acquisition data be collected?
When will we put the various intervention strategies of the plan into place?

Ask: How and when will the use and effects of the positive behavior support plan be evaluated and revised as necessary?
What rate of improvement in targeted behaviors and the use of alternative skills is acceptable?
What is the system for monitoring whether the plan is being used as designed?
How will we solicit and consider team members' and other relevant people's judgments about the plan's effectiveness, efficiency, appropriateness for the student, and context and comfort level in implementing the plan?
How will the student's feedback about the acceptability of the interventions and progress toward his or her goals be solicited?
Are there temporary antecedent strategies that can be faded?
Is there new information to suggest the hypothesis about the predictive antecedents, maintaining consequences, or function of the behavior was inaccurate?

Figure 5.9.   Step 4: Implement, Monitor and Evaluate the Positive Behavior Support Plan.

behavior-change and skill acquisition goals associated with the PBS plan may also be goals on the student's IEP, which must be monitored at regular intervals. A second reason is that teachers and staff members can be tempted at times to stop using a support strategy too quickly because they are not able to see the small steps that could add up to important progress or because they are not aware that the strategy has not been consistently implemented. (Teachers and staff members may believe that a strategy is working because it helps them feel like they are doing something to improve the situation, but the strategy may have few actual effects on the problem behavior.) The system for monitoring and evaluating the PBS plan should address two primary questions:

1. What improvements have we perceived and documented in a) target problem behavior(s), b) use of the replacement skill(s), and c) learning other desired alternative skills? Are improvements being made at an acceptable rate?

2. How and when will the PBS plan, its use, and its effects be evaluated and any needed revisions made to the plan?

Evaluating Progress

Progress data, often a continuation of the same data gathered during the FBA, should be examined at each team meeting and formally evaluated at regular intervals. The FBA tools presented in this book can be used on a periodic basis to evaluate the student's PBS plan. Choose a method to measure each goal stated in the PBS plan and determine how often you will measure to evaluate progress.

Student Schedule Analysis

The Student Schedule Analysis, which was used to gather information in Step 2A (see Figure 4.13), can be useful for keeping a record of the changes that are made to the student's schedule to create a more

positive day and to assess changes in staff perceptions of the student's degree of success throughout the day. Complete a new Student Schedule Analysis each time the student's daily schedule is revised to alter the antecedent conditions. After the behavior support plan has been in place for about 2 weeks, and periodically from then on, you can calculate the percentage of the classes or activities on the student's daily schedule that the team has rated as successful or unsuccessful. If the rate of successful activities is not increasing, then you may need to look again at the antecedents of the successful and unsuccessful times of day or at your hypothesis about the function of the problem behavior.

Interval Recording or Scatter Plot

The Interval Recording or Scatter Plot (see Figure 4.14) should be used almost daily during the initial implementation of the support plan, but it can be used less frequently as time passes (e.g., once or twice a week, during the times of day that are the most problematic). Data on the problem behavior's rate of occurrence can be summarized daily or weekly and graphed to give a visual representation of progress (see Figure 5.10). Be sure to record comments that may be relevant to the student's performance on a particular day or week (e.g., Was a new support strategy implemented? Was there a substitute teacher?).

Incident Record

If Incident Records (see Figure 4.8) continue to be needed, then maintain a frequency count of the number of times the safety plan is used. Examine the Incident Records for problems with the Safety Plan or indications of antecedents that triggered the incident. The need to use a safety plan should be virtually eliminated once core components of a support plan are implemented. If use of the safety plan does not decrease, then there is a definite need for more information gathering and

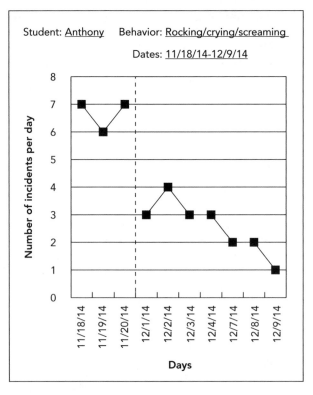

Figure 5.10. Behavior-change graph for Anthony.

analysis. Your observations recorded in the Incident Record can reveal antecedents or consequences that need to be changed.

Progress on the
Use of Alternative Skills

In addition to recording data on the occurrence of problem behavior, data on the use of alternative skills are needed for evaluating IEP goals and for documenting the student's use of replacement and other desired behaviors. Figure 5.11 shows how Anthony's teacher collected data on Anthony's use of hand-raising (replacement skills) to request teacher assistance during independent work times. The special education teacher or the paraeducator observed and recorded Anthony's hand-raising during four opportunities for independent work at least 2 days each week (see Figure 5.11). To estimate the frequency of hand-raising, data were recorded by marking a (P) on

a data-collection notecard the first time Anthony raised his hand when prompted and changing the (P) to an asterisk (*) if he raised his hand independently at any time during work period. A (+) was recorded if hand-raising was not needed by Anthony and he worked independently during the entire period. Anthony's teacher graphed the data weekly on a simple line graph to create a visual representation of Anthony's progress showing the number of periods Anthony successfully raised his hand or worked independently. Later, Anthony's teacher increased the standard for success by assigning an asterisk only when Anthony independently raised his hand without any teacher prompting for that period.

Lifestyle Improvements:
Quality-of-Life Indicators

The quality-of-life indicators that were evaluated and recorded on the Student-Centered

Observation of Alternative Skills

Student: _Anthony_   Observer: _Simms_

Dates: _2/9/15–2/24/15_   Observation schedule: _2–3 days per week_

Behavior: _Raise hand when in need of teacher assistance without crying_

Coding:

P = prompted   * = independently raised hand   + = worked independently
Change P to * at any time during work period that Anthony raises his hand independently.

Activity	Monday 2/9	Wednesday 2/11	Friday 2/13	Monday 2/16	Tuesday 2/17	Monday 2/24
Math	P	*	*	*	+	*
Reading	P	P	+	+	*	+
Language arts	P	P	*	+	*	*
Science/social studies	*	*	*	*	*	*
Totals Hand raises (*) Independent work (+)	1/4 0/4	2/4 0/4	3/4 1/4	2/4 2/4	3/4 1/4	3/4 1/4

Figure 5.11.   Observations of alternative skills for Anthony.

FBA Profile (see Figure 4.11) can be periodically updated to show changes in the student's relationships, autonomy, and participation patterns. The number of new opportunities for participation in school and community activities, relationships, and choice making can be recorded as a way to check support team accountability for putting the planned supports into place.

Monitoring and Revising the Plan

The support team should meet after 2–3 weeks of implementing the initial plan to 1) examine the student's progress data and 2) discuss implementation of the plan. These two topics should be discussed at each team meeting. Although behavior change takes time, a lack of noticeable progress after 2 weeks or so should alert the PBS team to the possible need of revision—revision of key components or strategies within the plan or revision of how team members implement the

plan. Using a positive approach requires a commitment to understanding why problem behaviors are occurring and how improvements can be made. Lack of sufficient progress signals the need for more analysis and decision making, not punitive interventions or placement in restrictive settings.

If some element of the plan is clearly aversive or anxiety producing for the student, impossible to implement, or otherwise disastrous, then consider dropping it right away. Do remember, however, that old habits die hard and the initial stages of a change are the most difficult for everyone involved. Be careful not to drop a promising support strategy too quickly because it has not performed miracles. Supporting a student with difficult behavior requires continuous problem solving and adjustments to the strategies being implemented. If a part of the plan you have implemented is not resulting in improvements after about 2 weeks, however, then the support team may need to brainstorm again or talk to other people (parents or professionals) who may have other ideas. It is also important to ensure that potentially effective strategies are being implemented as intended. Table 5.2 describes steps the team could take if the student is not making adequate progress.

If the student's progress is generally consistent with the goals of the plan, then you can begin to slowly and methodically remove some of the temporary prevention strategies. For instance, if the student's schedule had been adjusted so that short intervals of work time were alternated with short intervals of break time, then those intervals can slowly become more typical, with the goal of eventually enabling the student to function on a schedule expected of a student his or her age. The need for safety management procedures should be decreasing as the student experiences greater success and learns alternative skills, and the student's behavior change may be sustained through more

typical rates of reinforcement. A key assumption behind the PBS approach is that an effective plan is one that can be gradually phased out over time because the student has gained the skills needed to successfully participate in school, home, or community settings and the environment has become more supportive of positive behavior. Although some students may require lifelong accommodations and supports, the teacher's goal is always to help individuals lead a life that is as typical as possible.

CONCLUSION

There still is much to learn about supporting and teaching children and youth with seriously difficult behavior. Evidence of the effectiveness of comprehensive PBS based on FBA, however, is clear and convincing. One of the greatest PBS implementation difficulties occurs when the adults implementing the plan are accustomed to using

Table 5.2. Analyzing poor progress: What to do when the student is not making progress

Questions to ask	Steps to take
Are the strategies being implemented as designed?	Implement and review fidelity checklists. Strengthen contextual fit. Are the strategies doable? Do they fit the context? Are they easily implemented? Address team member needs and concerns. Consider whether additional resources or professional development are needed.
Do the strategies match the hypotheses for problem behaviors?	Revise preventing, teaching, or responding strategies to better align with hypotheses for problem behavior. Select other strategies to address hypotheses if needed.
Are the strategies sufficiently effective? Are they addressing the student's needs?	Consider whether antecedent interventions are powerful enough to prevent problem behaviors. Consider whether alternative skills provide effective outcomes for the student and are easy for the student to use. Consider whether the student is motivated and is happy with the intervention and the outcomes.
Are the hypotheses for problem behavior correct?	Review collected functional behavior assessment (FBA) data; consider whether certain patterns were missed. Collect new FBA data to gather additional information. Consider whether life-altering events (e.g., family stress, illness) could have affected the original hypotheses.
Are we missing the big picture with regard to the student's overall quality of life and satisfaction with school?	Align the student's educational programming with his or her interests and goals. Improve relationships with peers and adults. Coordinate school supports with community services to address multiple aspects of the student's life.

Sources: Bambara and Knoster (2009); Dunlap et al. (2010).

reactive rather than proactive behavioral interventions and are not skilled in the use of collaborative teaming (Bambara et al., 2009; Scott, McIntyre, et al., 2005). Due to a variety of factors (e.g., previous instruction in behavior management that emphasized manipulating consequences over more educative approaches, lack of a school vision of the goal of behavior support, inexperience that makes one fearful or insecure about teaching students with behavior difficulties, burnout and discouragement), team members can tend to conceive of behavior problems as needing management and continue to use punishment-oriented, exclusionary, and other reactive approaches rather than the proactive approaches that define a PBS orientation (Scott, Nelson, & Zabala, 2003).

Behavior support plans for students with the most dangerous or destructive behavior problems may require school-based teams to seek the assistance of expert consultants or work with wrap-around teams. Student-centered PBS teams who have been through relatively modest amounts of in-service professional development in the assessment, planning, and intervention processes—and who have a commitment to the education and well-being of the student—can create and implement supports that efficiently and effectively enable the student to make meaningful improvements. The most important take-away messages from Chapters 4 and 5 are these: First, seek to understand why students do what they do by carefully assessing the students' environment and their skills. Second, develop interventions and supports that address the factors that contribute to problem behavior. Avoid the temptation to use strategies that do not logically connect to your understanding of the reasons for problem behaviors. Third, approach a student's problem behaviors as you would any teaching problem. Your ultimate goal is to shape new skills and motivate the student to use them instead of problem behaviors. When interventions fail, ask why, and seek to revise or strengthen your strategies as you would in any teaching problem. Finally, cultivate and capitalize on team camaraderie for ongoing support. Strong collaboration among team members not only strengthens a plan but also provides the support for team members to persevere during times of difficulty and ultimately achieve success. The satisfaction of students, family members, and teachers with the results is what will determine the ultimate outcomes for the student, which, we all hope, will be a supportive environment in which the student can thrive.

References

Aber, J.L., Brown, J.L., & Jones, S.M. (2003). Developmental trajectories toward violence in middle childhood: Course, demographic differences, and response to school-based intervention. *Developmental Psychology, 39,* 324–348.

Achilles, G.M., McLaughlin, M.J., & Croninger, R.G. (2007). Sociocultural correlates of disciplinary exclusion among students with emotional, behavioral, and learning disabilities in the SEELS national dataset. *Journal of Emotional and Behavioral Disorders, 15,* 33–45.

Albin, R.W., Lucyshyn, J.M., Horner, R.H., & Flannery, K.B. (1996). Contextual fit for behavioral support plans: A model for "goodness of fit." In L.K. Koegel, R.L. Koegel, & G. Dunlap (Eds.), *Positive behavioral support: Including people with difficult behavior in the community* (pp. 81–98). Baltimore, MD: Paul H. Brookes Publishing Co.

Anderson, C.M., & Borgmeier, C. (2010). Tier II interventions within the framework of school-wide positive behavior support: Essential features for design, implementation, and maintenance. *Behavioral and Analytical Practices, 3,* 33–45.

Anderson, C., Childs, K., Kincaid, D., Horner, R., George, H., Todd, A., . . . Spaulding, S. (2011). *Benchmarks for advanced tiers, v. 2.5.* Eugene, OR: Educational and Community Supports, University of Oregon and University of South Florida.

Arndorfer, R., Miltenberger, R., Woster, S., Rortvedt, A., & Gaffaney, T. (1994). Home-based descriptive and experimental analysis of problem behaviors in children. *Topics in Early Childhood Special Education, 14,* 64–87.

Baker, B.L., Blacher, J., Crnic, K.A., & Edelbrock, C. (2002). Behavior problems and parenting stress in families of three-year-old children with and without developmental delays. *American Journal on Mental Retardation, 107,* 433–444.

Bambara, L.M., Ager, C., & Koger, F. (1994). The effects of choice and task preference on the work performance of adults with severe disabilities. *Journal of Applied Behavior Analysis, 27,* 555–556.

Bambara, L.M., Goh, A., Kern, L., & Caskie, G. (2012). Perceived barriers and enablers to implementing individualized positive behavior interventions and supports in school settings. *Journal of Positive Behavior Interventions,* 1–13.

Bambara, L.M., & Kern, L. (2005). *Individualized supports for students with problem behaviors: Designing positive behavior plans.* New York, NY: Guilford Press.

Bambara, L.M., & Knoster, T.P. (2009). *Designing positive behavior support plans* (2nd ed.). Washington, DC: American Association on Intellectual and Developmental Disabilities.

Bambara, L.M., Koger, F., Katzer, T., & Davenport, T.A. (1995). Embedding choice in the context of daily routines: An experimental case study. *Journal of The Association for Persons with Severe Handicaps, 20,* 185–195.

Bambara, L.M., & Kunsch, C. (2014). Effective teaming for positive behavior support. In F. Brown, J.L. Anderson, & R.L. DePry (Eds.), *Individual positive behavior supports: A standards-based guide to practices in school and community settings* (pp. 47–70). Baltimore, MD: Paul H. Brookes Publishing Co.

Bambara, L.M., Nonnemacher, S., & Kern, L. (2009). Sustaining school-based individualized positive behavior support perceived barriers and enablers. *Journal of Positive Behavior Interventions, 11,* 161–176.

Barry, L.M., & Messer, J.J. (2003). A practical application of self-management for students diagnosed with attention-deficit/hyperactivity disorder. *Journal of Positive Behavior Interventions, 5,* 238–248.

Bauer, N.S., Lozano, P., & Rivara, F.P. (2007). The effectiveness of the Olweus Bullying Prevention Program in public middle schools: A controlled trial. *Journal of Adolescent Health, 40,* 266–274.

Berliner, D.C. (1986). In pursuit of the expert pedagogue. *Educational Researcher, 15,* 5–13.

Boardman, A.G., Arguelles, M.E., Vaughn, S., Hughes, M.T., & Klinger, J. (2005). Special education teachers' views of research based practices. *Journal of Special Education, 39*, 168–180.

Bohanon, H., Fenning, P., Carney, K., Minnis-Kim, M., Anderson-Harriss, S., Moroz, K., . . . Pigott, T. (2006). School-wide application of positive behavior support in an urban high school. *Journal of Positive Behavior Interventions, 8*, 131–145.

Bowditch, C. (1993). Getting rid of troublemakers: High school disciplinary procedures and the production of dropouts. *Social Problems, 40*, 493–507.

Boyle, D., & Hassett-Walker, C. (2008). Reducing overt and relational aggression among young children: The results from a two-year outcome evaluation. *Journal of School Violence, 7*, 27–42.

Bradshaw, C.P., Mitchell, M.M., & Leaf, P.J. (2010). Examining the effects of school-wide positive behavioral interventions and supports on student outcomes results from a randomized controlled effectiveness trial in elementary schools. *Journal of Positive Behavior Interventions, 12*, 133–148.

Brooks, A., Todd, A.W., Tofflemoyer, S., & Horner, R.H. (2003). Use of functional assessment and a self-management system to increase academic engagement and work completion. *Journal of Positive Behavior Interventions, 5*, 144–153.

Brophy, J., & Good, T. (1986). Teacher behavior and student achievement. In M. Wittrock (Ed.), *Handbook of research on teaching* (3rd ed., pp. 328–375). New York, NY: Macmillan.

Brown, F., Belz, P., Corsi, L., & Wenig, B. (1993). Choice diversity for people with severe disabilities. *Education and Training in Mental Retardation, 28*, 318–326.

Brown, K.E., & Mirenda, P. (2006). Contingency mapping use of a novel visual support strategy as an adjunct to functional equivalence training. *Journal of Positive Behavior Interventions, 8*, 155–164.

Burns, B.J., & Goldman, S.K. (Eds.). (1999). *Promising practices in wraparound for children with serious emotional disturbance and their families* (1998 Series, Vol. 4). Washington, DC: American Institute for Research, Center for Effective Collaboration and Practice.

Burns, B.J., Schoenwald, S.K., Burchard, J.D., Faw, L., & Santos, A.B. (2000). Comprehensive community-based interventions for youth with severe emotional disorders: Multisystemic therapy and the wraparound process. *Journal of Child and Family Studies, 9*, 283–314.

Calderella, P., & Merrell, K. (1997). Common dimensions of social skills of children and adolescents: A taxonomy of positive behaviors. *School Psychology Review, 26*, 264–278.

Caldarella, P., Young, E., Richardson, M., Young, B., & Young, K. (2008). Validation of the Systematic Screening for Behavior Disorders in middle and junior high school. *Journal of Emotional and Behavioral Disorders, 16*, 105–117.

California Department of Education. (2013a). *California Healthy Kids Survey.* Los Alamitos, CA: Author. Available from cscs.wested.org

California Department of Education. (2013b). *California School Climate Survey.* Los Alamitos, CA: Author. Available from cscs.wested.org

Callahan, K., & Rademacher, J.A. (1999). Using self-management strategies to increase the on-task behavior of a student with autism. *Journal of Positive Behavior Intervention, 1*, 117–122.

Campbell, A., & Anderson, C.M. (2008). Enhancing effects of check-in/check-out with function-based support. *Behavioral Disorders, 33*, 233–245.

Campbell, A., & Anderson, C.M. (2011). Check-in check-out: A systematic evaluation and component analysis. *Journal of Applied Behavior Analysis, 44*, 315–326.

Carr, E.G., & Carlson, J.I. (1993). Reduction of severe behavior problems in the community using a multicomponent treatment approach. *Journal of Applied Behavior Analysis, 26*, 157–172.

Carr, E.G., Dunlap, G., Horner, R.H., Koegel, R.L., Turnbull, A., Sailor, W., . . . Fox, L. (2002). Positive behavior support: Evolution of an applied science. *Journal of Positive Behavior Interventions, 4*, 4–16.

Carr, E.G., & Horner, R.H. (2007). The expanding vision of positive behavior support research perspectives on happiness, helpfulness, hopefulness. *Journal of Positive Behavior Interventions, 9*, 3–14.

Carr, E.G., Horner, R.H., Turnbull, A.P., Marquis, J.G., McLaughlin, D.M., McAtee, D.M., & Doolabh, A. (Eds.). (1999). *Positive behavior support for people with developmental disabilities: A research synthesis.* Washington, DC: American Association on Mental Retardation.

Carr, E.G., Levin, L., McConnachie, G., Carlson, J.I., Kemp, D.C., & Smith, C.E. (1994). *Communication-based intervention for problem behavior: A user's guide for producing positive change.* Baltimore, MD: Paul H. Brookes Publishing Co.

Carr, E.G., Reeve, C.E., & Magito-McLaughlin, D. (1996). Contextual influences on problem behavior in people with developmental disabilities. In L.K. Koegel, R.L. Koegel, & G. Dunlap (Eds.), *Positive behavioral support: Including people with difficult behavior in the community* (pp. 403–423). Baltimore, MD: Paul H. Brookes Publishing Co.

Carr, E.G., Smith, C.E., Giacin, T.A., Whelan, B.M., & Pancari, J. (2003). Menstrual discomfort as a biological setting event for severe problem behavior: Assessment and intervention. *American Journal on Mental Retardation, 108,* 117–133.

Carter, D.R., & Horner, R.H. (2007). Adding functional behavioral assessment to First Step to Success: A case study. *Journal of Positive Behavior Interventions, 9,* 229–238.

Cashwell, T.H., Skinner, C.H., & Smith, E.S. (2001). Increasing second-grade students' reports of peers' prosocial behaviors via direct instruction, group reinforcement, and progress feedback: A replication and extension. *Education and Treatment of Children, 24,* 161–175.

Center for the Study and Prevention of Violence. (2014). *Blueprints for healthy youth development.* Retrieved from http://www.blueprintsprograms.com

Chandler, L.K., & Dahlquist, C.M. (2015). *Functional assessment: Strategies to prevent and remediate challenging behavior in school settings* (4th ed.). Upper Saddle River, NJ: Pearson Higher Education.

Chang, F., & Munoz, M.A. (2006). School personnel educating the whole child: Impact of character education on teachers' self-assessment and student development. *Journal of Personnel Evaluation in Education, 19,* 35–49.

Chitiyo, J. (2014). The wraparound process for youth with severe emotional behavioral disorders. *Journal of Research in Special Educational Needs, 14,* 105–109. doi: 10.1111/1471-3802.12008

Cihak, D., Fahrenkrog, C., Ayres, K.M., & Smith, C. (2010). The use of video modeling via a video iPod and a system of least prompts to improve transitional behaviors for students with autism spectrum disorders in the general education classroom. *Journal of Positive Behavior Interventions, 12,* 103–115.

Cihak, D.F., Kirk, E.R., & Boon, R.T. (2009). Effects of classwide positive peer "tootling" to reduce the disruptive classroom behaviors of elementary students with and without disabilities. *Journal of Behavioral Education, 18,* 267–278.

Clarke, S., Dunlap, G., Foster-Johnson, L., Childs, K.E., Wilson, D., White, R., . . . Vera, A. (1995). Improving the conduct of students with behavioral disorders by incorporating student interests into curricular activities. *Behavioral Disorders, 20,* 221–237.

Clarke, S., Worcester, J., Dunlap, G., Murray, M., & Bradley-Klug, K. (2002). Using multiple measures to evaluate positive behavior support: A case example. *Journal of Positive Behavior Interventions, 4,* 131–145.

Coffey, J.H., & Horner, R.H. (2012). The sustainability of schoolwide positive behavior interventions and supports. *Council for Exceptional Children, 78,* 407–422.

Cohen, R., Kincaid, D., & Childs, K.E. (2007). Measuring school-wide positive behavior support implementation: Development and validation of the benchmarks of quality. *Journal of Positive Behavior Interventions, 9,* 203–213.

Cole, C.L., & Bambara, L.M. (1992). Issues surrounding the use of self-management interventions in schools. *School Psychology Review, 21,* 193–201.

Cole, C.L., & Levinson, T.R. (2002). Effects of within-activity choices on the challenging behavior of children with severe developmental disabilities. *Journal of Positive Behavior Interventions, 4,* 29–37.

Collaborative for Academic, Social, and Emotional Learning. (2003). *Safe and sound: An education leader's guide to evidence-based social and emotional learning (SEL) programs.* Chicago, IL: Author.

Collaborative for Academic, Social, and Emotional Learning. (2012). *Effective social and emotional learning programs.* Chicago, IL: Author.

Colvin, B. (1993). *Managing acting-out behavior.* Eugene, OR: Behavior Associates.

Colvin, G., Sugai, G., Good, R.H., & Lee, Y. (1997). Using active supervision and precorrection to improve transition behaviors in an elementary school. *School Psychology Quarterly, 12,* 344–363.

Committee for Children. (2014). *Second Step: Skills for social and academic success.* Retrieved from http://www.cfchildren.org/second-step.aspx

Conroy, M.A., Asmus, J.M., Sellers, J.A., & Ladwig, C.N. (2005). The use of antecedent-based intervention to decrease stereotypic behavior in a general education classroom: A case study. *Focus on Autism and Other Developmental Disabilities, 20,* 223–230.

Conroy, M.A., Sutherland, K.S., Snyder, A.L., & Marsh, S. (2008). Classwide interventions: Effective instruction makes a difference. *Teaching Exceptional Children, 40,* 24–30.

Crone, D.A., Hawken, L.S., & Horner, R.H. (2015). *Building positive behavior support systems in schools: Functional behavioral assessment* (2nd ed.). New York, NY: Guilford Press.

Crone, D.A., Horner, R.H., & Hawken, L.S. (2003). *Responding to problem behavior in* schools: The Behavior Education Program. New York, NY: Guilford Press.

Curtis, R., Van Horne, J.W., Robertson, P., Karvonen, M. (2010). Outcomes of a school-wide positive behavioral support program. Professional School Counseling, 13(3), 159–164.

Dary, T., & Pickeral, T. (Eds.). (2013). School climate practices for implementation and sustainability. New York, NY: National School Climate Center.

Daunic, A.P., Smith, S.W., Robinson, T.R., Miller, M.D., & Landry, K.L. (2000). Implementing school-wide conflict resolution and peer mediation programs: Experiences in three middle schools. Intervention in School and Clinic, 36, 94–100.

Developmental Studies Center. (2014). Caring school community. Retrieved from http://www.devstu.org/caring-school-community

Devlin, S., Healy, O., Leader, G., & Hughes, B.M. (2011). Comparison of behavioral intervention and sensory-integration therapy in the treatment of challenging behavior. Journal of Autism and Developmental Disorders, 41, 1303–1320.

Didden, R., Korsilius, H., Van Oorsouw, W., & Sturmey, P. (2006). Behavioral treatment of challenging behaviors in individuals with mild mental retardation: Meta-analysis of single-subject research. American Journal on Mental Retardation, 111, 290–298.

Diken, I.H., & Rutherford, R.B. (2005). First Steps early intervention program: A study of effectiveness with Native American children. Education and Treatment of Young Children, 28, 444–465.

Domitrovich, C.E., Cortes, R.C., & Greenberg, M.T. (2007). Improving young children's social and emotional competence: A randomized trial of the Preschool "PATHS" curriculum. Journal of Primary Prevention, 28, 67–91.

Donnellan, A.M., LaVigna, G.W., Negri-Shoultz, N., & Fassbender, L.L. (1988). Progress without punishment: Effective approaches for learners with severe behavior problems. New York, NY: Teachers College Press.

Drummond, T. (1993). The Student Risk Screening Scale. Grants Pass, OR: Josephine County Mental Health Program.

DuBois, D.L., Holloway, B.E., Valentine, J.C., & Cooper, H. (2002). Effectiveness of mentoring programs: A meta-analytical review. American Journal of Community Psychology, 30, 157–197.

Dunlap, G., DePerczel, M., Clarke, S., Wilson, D., Wright, S., White, R., . . . Gomez, A. (1994). Choice making and proactive behavioral support for students with emotional and behavioral challenges. Journal of Applied Behavior Analysis, 27, 505–518.

Dunlap, G., Foster-Johnson, L., Clarke, S., Kern, L., & Childs, K.E. (1995). Modifying activities to produce functional outcomes: Effects on the problem behaviors of students with disabilities. Journal of The Association for Persons with Severe Handicaps, 20, 248–258.

Dunlap, G., Iovannone, R., Kincaid, D., Wilson, K., Christiansen, K., Strain, P.S., & English, C. (2010). Prevent-teach-reinforce: The school-based model of individualized positive behavior support. Baltimore, MD: Paul H. Brookes Publishing Co.

Dunlap, G., & Kern, L. (1996). Modifying instructional activities to promote desirable behavior: A conceptual and practical framework. School Psychology Quarterly, 11, 297–312.

Dunlap, G., Kern-Dunlap, L., Clarke, S., & Robbins, F.R. (1991). Functional assessment, curricular revision, and severe behavior problems. Journal of Applied Behavior Analysis, 24, 387–397.

Dunlap, G., Newton, J.S., Fox, L., Benito, N., & Vaughn, B. (2001). Family involvement in functional assessment and positive behavior support. Focus on Autism and Other Developmental Disabilities, 16, 215–221.

Durand, V.M. (1988). Motivational Assessment Scale. In M. Hersen & A.S. Belleck (Eds.), Dictionary of behavioral assessment techniques (pp. 309–310). New York, NY: Pergamon Press.

Durand, V.M. (1990). Severe behavior problems: A functional communication training approach. New York, NY: Guilford Press.

Durand, V.M., & Crimmins, D.B. (1988). Identifying the variables maintaining self-injurious behavior. Journal of Autism and Developmental Disorders, 18, 99–117.

Durand, V.M., & Merges, E. (2001). Functional communication training: A contemporary behavior analytic intervention for problem behaviors. Focus on Autism and Other Developmental Disabilities, 16, 110–119.

Dwyer, K., & Osher, D. (2000). Safeguarding our children: An action guide. Washington, DC: U.S. Department of Education and Justice, American Institutes for Research.

Eber, L., Hyde, K., & Suter, J.C. (2011). Integrating wraparound into a schoolwide system of positive behavior supports. Journal of Child and Family Studies, 20, 782–790.

Eber, L., & Nelson, C.M. (1997). Integrating services for students with emotional and behavioral needs through school-based wraparound planning. American Journal of Orthopsychiatry, 67, 385–395.

Elias, M.J., Zins, J.E., Weissberg, R.P., Frey, K.S., Greenberg, M.T., Haynes, N.M., . . . Shriver, T.P. (1997). Promoting social and emotional learning: Guidelines for educators. Alexandria, VA: Association for Supervision and Curriculum Development.

Ellingson, S.A., Miltenberger, R.G., Stricker, J., Galensky, T.L., & Garlinghouse, M. (2000). Functional assessment and intervention for challenging behaviors in the classroom by general classroom teachers. *Journal of Positive Behavior Interventions, 2,* 85–97.

Elliot, S.N. (1995, June). *Final evaluation report. The responsive classroom approach: Its effectiveness and acceptability.* Washington, DC: The Center for Systemic Education Change.

Ellis, E.S., & Worthington, L.A. (1994). *Research synthesis on effective teaching principles and the design of quality tools for educators* (Technical Report No. 5). Eugene: University of Oregon, National Center to Improve the Tools of Educators.

Epselage, D.L., & Swearer, S. (2003). Research on school bullying and victimization: What have we learned and where do we go from here? *School Psychology Review, 23,* 365–383.

Evans, I.M., & Meyer, L.H. (1985). *An educative approach to behavior problems: A practical decision model for interventions with severely handicapped learners.* Baltimore, MD: Paul H. Brookes Publishing Co.

Fairbanks, S., Sugai, S., Guardino, D., & Lathrop, M. (2007). Response to intervention: An evaluation of a classroom system of behavior support for second grade students. *Exceptional Children, 73,* 288–310.

Fenning, P., & Rose, J. (2007). Overrepresentation of African American students in exclusionary discipline the role of school policy. *Urban Education, 42,* 536–559.

Filter, K.J., McKenna, M.K., Benedict, E.A., Horner, R.H., Todd, A.W., & Watson, J. (2007). Check in/check out: A post-hoc evaluation of an efficient, secondary-level targeted intervention for reducing problem behaviors in schools. *Education and Treatment of Children, 30,* 69–84.

Fitzgerald, P.D., & Edstrom, L.V.S. (2006). Second Step: A violence prevention curriculum. In S.R. Jimmerson & M. Furlong (Eds.), *Handbook of school violence and school safety: From research to practice* (pp. 383–394). Mahwah, NJ: Lawrence Erlbaum Associates.

Fixsen, D.L., Naoom, S.F., Blase, K.A., Friedman, R.M., & Wallace, F. (2005). *Implementation research: A synthesis of the literature* (FMHI Publication #231). Tampa: University of South Florida, Louis de la Parte Florida Mental Health Institute, The National Implementation Research Network.

Flannery, D., Vazsonyi, A., Liau, A., Guo, S., Powell, K., Atha, H., . . . Embry, D. (2003). Initial behavior outcomes for the Peace-Builders universal school-based violence prevention program. *Developmental Psychology, 39,* 292–308.

Forness, S. (1990). Early detection and prevention of emotional and behavioral disorders: Developmental aspects of systems of care. *Behavioral Disorders, 21,* 226–240.

Forness, S.R., Kavale, K.A., MacMillan, D.L., Asarnow, J.R., & Duncan, B.B. (1996). Early detection and prevention of emotional or behavioral disorders: Developmental aspects of systems of care. *Behavioral Disorders, 21,* 226–240.

Foster-Johnson, L., Ferro, J., & Dunlap, G. (1994). Preferred curricular activities and reduced problem behaviors in students with intellectual disabilities. *Journal of Applied Behavior Analysis, 27,* 493–504.

Freeman, R., Eber, L., Anderson, C., Irvin, L., Horner, R., Bounds, M., & Dunlap, G. (2006). Building inclusive school cultures using school-wide positive behavior support: Designing effective individual support systems for students with significant disabilities. *Research and Practice for Persons with Severe Disabilities, 31,* 4–17.

Frey, K.S., Nolen, S.B., Schoiack-Edstrom, L.V., & Hirschstein, M.K. (2005). Effect of a school-based social-emotional competence program: Linking children's goals, attributions, and behavior. *Applied Developmental Psychology, 26,* 171–200.

Gann, C.J., Ferro, J.B., Umbreit, J., & Liaupsin, C.J. (2014). Effects of a comprehensive function-based intervention applied across multiple educational settings. *Remedial and Special Education, 35,* 50–60.

Gersten, R., Chard, D.J., & Baker, S. (2000). Factors enhancing sustained use of research-based instructional practices. *Journal of Learning Disabilities, 33,* 445–457.

Goh, A.E., & Bambara, L.M. (2012). Individualized positive behavior support in school settings: A meta-analysis. *Remedial and Special Education, 33,* 271–286.

Golly, A., Stiller, B., & Walker, H.M. (1998). First step to success: Replication and social validation of an early intervention program for achieving secondary prevention goals. *Journal of Emotional and Behavioral Disorders, 6,* 243–250.

Good, C.P., McIntosh, K., & Gietz, C. (2011). Integrating bullying prevention into school-wide positive behavior support. *Teaching Exceptional Children, 44,* 48–56.

Good, T.L., & Brophy, J.E. (2008). *Looking in classrooms* (10th ed.). New York, NY: Pearson.

Gottfredson, D.C. (1997). School-based crime prevention. In L. Sherman, D. Gottfredson,

D. Mackenie, J. Eck, P. Reuter, & S. Bushway (Eds.), *Preventing crime: What works, what doesn't, what's promising* (pp. 1–49). College Park: University of Maryland, Department of Criminology and Criminal Justice.

Gottfredson, G.D., & Gottfredson, D.C. (2001). What schools do to prevent problem behavior and promote safe environments. *Journal of Educational and Psychological Consultation, 12,* 313–344.

Grandy, S., & Peck, S.M. (1997). The use of functional assessment and self-management with a first grader. *Child and Family Behavior Therapy, 19,* 29–43.

Gray, C.A. (1998). Social Stories and comic strip conversations with students with Asperger syndrome and high-functioning autism. In E. Schopler & G.B. Mesibov (Eds.), *Asperger syndrome or high-functioning autism? Current issues in autism* (pp. 167–198). New York, NY: Kluwer Academic/Plenum Publishers.

Greenberg, M.T., Kusché, C.A., Cook, E.T., & Quamma, J.P. (1995). Promoting emotional competence in school-aged children: The effects of the PATHS curriculum. *Development and Psychopathology, 7,* 117–136.

Greenberg, M.T., Kusché, C., & Mihalic, S.F. (1998). *Promoting Alternative Thinking Strategies (PATHS): Book 10. Blueprints for violence prevention series.* Boulder: University of Colorado, Institute of Behavioral Science, Center for the Study and Prevention of Violence.

Greenwood, C.R., Delquandri, J., & Carta, J. (1997). *Together we can! Classwide peer tutoring to improve basic academic skills.* Longmont, CO: Sopris West Educational Services.

Gresham, E., Bao, M., & Cook, C.R. (2006). Social skills training for teaching replacement behaviors: Remediating acquisition deficits in at-risk students. *Behavioral Disorders, 3,* 363–377.

Gresham, F., & Elliot, S.N. (1990). *Social Skills Rating System.* Circle Pines, MN: American Guidance Service.

Gresham, F., & Elliott, S.N. (2008). *Social Skills Improvement System (SSIS) Rating Scales.* New York, NY: Pearson.

Gresham, F.M., Sugai, G., & Horner, R.H. (2001). Interpreting outcomes of social skills training for students with high-incidence disabilities. *Exceptional Children, 67,* 331–355.

Groden, J., & Le Vassuer, P. (1994). Cognitive picture rehearsal: A system to teach self-control. In K.A. Quill (Ed.), *Teaching children with autism: Strategies to enhance communication and socialization* (pp. 287–306). Albany, NY: Delmar Publishers.

Grossman, D.C., Neckerman, H.J., Koepsell, T.D., Liu, P., Asher, K.N., Beland, K., . . .

Rivara, F.P. (1997). Effectiveness of a violence prevention curriculum among children in elementary school: A randomized control trial. *Journal of the American Medical Association, 277,* 1605–1611.

Halle, J., Bambara, L.M., & Reichle, J. (2005). Teaching alternative skills. In L.M. Bambara & L. Kern (Eds.), *Individualized supports for students with problem behaviors: Designing positive behavior plans* (pp. 237–274). New York, NY: Guilford Press.

Hamre, B.K., & Pianta, R.C. (2001). Early teacher–child relationships and the trajectory of children's school outcomes through eighth grade. *Child Development, 72,* 625–638.

Handler, M.W., Rey, J., Connell, J., Their, K., Feinberg, A., & Putnam, R. (2007). Practical considerations in creating school-wide positive behavior support in public schools. *Psychology in Schools, 44,* 29–39.

Harding, M., Knoff, H.M., Glenn, R., Johnson, L., Schrag, H., & Schrag, J. (2008). *The Arkansas state improvement grant evaluation and outcome report to the U.S. Department of Education's Office of Special Education Programs: Improving student outcomes through the school-wide implementation of Project ACHIEVE's positive behavioral support systems.* Little Rock: Arkansas Department of Education.

Harvey, M.T., Lewis-Palmer, T., Horner, R.H., & Sugai, G. (2003). Trans-situational interventions: Generalization of behavior support across school and home environments. *Behavioral Disorders, 28,* 299–312.

Hawken, L.S., Adolphson, S.L., Macleod, S., & Schumann, J. (2009). Secondary-tier interventions and supports. In W. Sailor, G. Dunlap, & R. Horner (Eds.), *Handbook of positive behavior support* (pp. 395–420). New York, NY: Springer.

Hawken, L.S., & Horner, R.H. (2003). Evaluation of a targeted intervention within a schoolwide system of behavior support. *Journal of Behavioral Education, 12,* 225–240.

Hawken, L.S., MacLeod, K.S., & Rawlings, L. (2007). Effects of the behavior education program on office discipline referrals of elementary school students. *Journal of Positive Behavior Interventions, 9,* 94–101.

Heaviside, S., Rowand, C., Williams, C., & Farris, E. (1998). *Violence and discipline problems in U.S. public schools: 1996–1997* (NCES 98–030). Washington, DC: U.S. Department of Education, National Center for Education Statistics.

Henley, M. (2006). *Classroom management: A proactive approach.* Upper Saddle River, NJ: Pearson Education.

Hennessey, B.A. (2007). Promoting social competence in school-aged children: The effects of the Open Circle Program. *Journal of School Psychology, 45,* 349–360.

Hernandez, T.J., & Seem, S.R. (2004). A safe school climate: A systemic approach and the school counselor. *Professional School Counseling, 7,* 256–262.

Hobbs, N. (1975). *The futures of children.* San Francisco, CA: Jossey-Bass.

Horner, R.H., Albin, R.A., Sprague, J.R., & Todd, A.W. (2000). Positive behavior support. In M.E. Snell & F. Brown (Eds.), *Instruction of students with severe disabilities* (5th ed., pp. 207–243). Upper Saddle River, NJ: Prentice Hall.

Horner, R.H., & Carr, E.G. (1997). Behavioral support for students with severe disabilities: Functional assessment and comprehensive intervention. *Journal of Special Education, 31,* 84–104.

Horner, R.H., Carr, E.G., Strain, P.S., Todd, A.W., & Reed, H.K. (2002). Problem behavior interventions for young children with autism: A research synthesis. *Journal of Autism and Developmental Disorders, 32,* 423–446.

Horner, R.H., Day, H.M., & Day, I. (1997). Using neutralizing routines to reduce problem behaviors. *Journal of Applied Behavior Analysis, 39,* 601–614.

Horner, R.H., Dunlap, G., Koegel, R.L., Carr, E.G., Sailor, W., & Anderson, J. (1990). Toward a technology of "nonaversive" behavioral support. *Journal of The Association for Persons with Severe Handicaps, 15,* 125–132.

Horner, R.H., Sugai, G., & Anderson, C.M. (2010). Examining the evidence base for school-wide positive behavior support. *Focus on Exceptional Children, 42,* 2–14.

Horner, R.H., Sugai, G., Smolkowski, K., Eber, L., Nakasato, J., Todd, A.W., & Esperanza, J. (2009). A randomized, wait-list controlled effectiveness trial assessing school-wide positive behavior support in elementary schools. *Journal of Positive Behavior Interventions, 11,* 133–144.

Horner, R.H., Sugai, G., Todd, A.W., & Lewis-Palmer, T. (2000). Elements of behavior support plans: A technical brief. *Exceptionality, 8,* 205–215.

Horner, R.H., Sugai, G., Todd, A.W., & Lewis-Palmer, T. (2005). School-wide positive behavior support. In L. Bambara & L. Kern (Eds.), *Individualized supports for students with problem behaviors: Designing positive behavior support plans* (pp. 359–390). New York, NY: Guilford Press.

Horner, R.H., Todd, A.W., Lewis-Palmer, T., Irvin, L.K., Sugai, G., & Boland, J.B. (2004). The School-side Evaluation Tool (SET): A research instrument for assessing schoolwide

positive behavior support. *Journal of Positive Behavior Interventions, 6,* 3–12.

Horner, R.H., Vaughn, B.J., Day, H.M., & Ard, W.R., Jr. (1996). The relationship between setting events and problem behavior: Expanding our understanding of behavioral support. In L.K. Koegel, R.L. Koegel, & G. Dunlap (Eds.), *Positive behavioral support: Including people with difficult behavior in the community* (pp. 381–402). Baltimore, MD: Paul H. Brookes Publishing Co.

Huggins, P. (1995). *The ASSIST program—affective/social skills: Instructional strategies and techniques.* Seattle: Washington State Innovative Education Program.

Hunt, P., Staub, D., Alwell, M., & Goetz, L. (1994). Achievement by all students within the context of cooperative learning groups. *Journal of The Association for Persons with Severe Handicaps, 19,* 290–301.

Ialongo, N., Poduska, J., Werthamer, L., & Kellam, S. (2001). The distal impact of two first-grade preventive interventions on conduct problems and disorder in early adolescence. *Journal of Emotional and Behavioral Disorders, 9,* 146–160.

Individuals with Disabilities Education Improvement Act (IDEA) of 2004, PL 108-446, 20 U.S.C. §§ 1400 *et seq.*

Ingram, K., Lewis-Palmer, T., & Sugai, G. (2005). Function-based intervention planning: Comparing the effectiveness of FBA function-based and non-function-based intervention plans. *Journal of Positive Behavior Interventions, 7,* 224–236.

Irvin, L.K., Tobin, T.J., Sprague, J.R., Sugai, G., & Vincent, C.G. (2004). Validity of office discipline referral measures as indices of school-wide behavioral status and effects of school-wide behavioral interventions. *Journal of Positive Behavioral Interventions, 6,* 131–147.

Iwata, B.A., Dorsey, M.F., Silfer, K.J., Baumna, K.E., & Richman, G.S. (1994). Toward a functional analysis of self-injury. *Journal of Applied Behavior Analysis, 27,* 197–209.

Janney, R., Black, J., & Ferlo, M. (1989). *A problem-solving approach to challenging behaviors: Strategies for parents and educators of people with developmental disabilities and challenging behaviors.* Syracuse, NY: Syracuse University and Syracuse City School District.

Janney, R., & Snell, M.E. (2006). *Teachers' guides to inclusive practices: Social relationships and peer support* (2nd ed.). Baltimore, MD: Paul H. Brookes Publishing Co.

Janney, R., & Snell, M.E. (2013). *Teachers' guides to inclusive practices: Modifying schoolwork* (3rd ed.). Baltimore, MD: Paul H. Brookes Publishing Co.

Johnson, D.W., & Johnson, R.T. (1989). *Cooperation and competition: Theory and research.* Edina, MN: Interaction Book Co.

Johnson, D.W., & Johnson, R.T. (1995). *Teaching students to be peacemakers.* Edina, MN: Interaction Book Co.

Johnson, D.W., & Johnson, R.T. (1996). Conflict resolution and peer mediation programs in elementary and secondary school: A review of the research. *Review of Educational Research, 66,* 459–506.

Johnson, D.W., & Johnson, R. (2005). *Teaching students to be peacemakers* (4th ed.; teachers' manual). Edina, MN: Interaction Book Co.

Johnson, D.W., Johnson, R.T., & Dudley, B. (1992). Effects of peer mediation training on elementary school students. *Mediation Quarterly, 10,* 89–99.

Johnson, D.W., Johnson, R., Dudley, B., Ward, M., & Magnuson, D. (1995). The impact of peer mediation training on the management of school and home conflicts. *American Educational Research Journal, 32,* 829–844.

Johnson, D.W., Johnson, R.T., & Stanne, M.B. (2000). *Cooperative learning methods: A meta-analysis.* Minneapolis: University of Minnesota.

Johnson, R.T., & Johnson, D.W. (2002). Teaching students to be peacemakers: A meta-analysis. *Journal of Research in Education, 12,* 25–39.

Johnson-Gros, K.N., Lyons, E.A., & Griffin, R. (2008). Active supervision: An intervention to reduce high school tardiness. *Education and Treatment of Children, 31,* 39–53.

Joseph, G.E., & Strain, P.S. (2003). Comprehensive evidence-based social-emotional curricula for young children: An analysis of efficacious adoption potential. *Topics in Early Childhood Special Education, 23,* 65–76.

Kamps, D., Kravits, T., Stolze, J., & Swaggart, B. (1999). Prevention strategies for at-risk students and students with EBD in urban elementary schools. *Journal of Emotional and Behavioral Disorders, 7,* 178–188.

Kamps, D., Wills, H.P., Heitzman-Powell, L., Laylin, J., Szoke, C., Petrillo, T., & Culey, A. (2011). Class-wide function-related intervention teams: Effects of group contingency programs in urban classrooms. *Journal of Positive Behavior Interventions, 13,* 154–167.

Kartub, D.T., Taylor-Greene, S., March, R.E., & Horner, R.H. (2000). Reducing hallway noise: A systems approach. *Journal of Positive Behavior Interventions, 2,* 179–182.

Kavale, K.A., & Mostert, M.P. (2004). Social skills interventions for individuals with learning disabilities. *Learning Disabilities Quarterly, 27,* 31–43.

Kennedy, C.H., Long, T., Jolivette, K., Cox, J., Tang, J., & Thompson, T. (2001). Facilitating general education participation for students with behavior problems by linking positive behavior supports and person-centered planning. *Journal of Emotional and Behavioral Disorders, 9,* 161–172.

Kennedy, C.H., & Souza, G. (1995). Functional analysis and treatment of eye poking. *Journal of Applied Behavior Analysis, 28,* 27–37.

Kern, L., Bambara, L., & Fogt, J. (2002). Classwide curricular modification to improve the behavior of students with emotional or behavioral disorders. *Behavioral Disorders, 27,* 317–326.

Kern, L., & Clemens, N.H. (2007). Antecedent strategies to promote appropriate classroom behavior. *Psychology in the Schools, 44,* 65–75.

Kern, L., Delaney, B., Clarke, S., Dunlap, G., & Childs, K. (2001). Improving the classroom behavior of students with emotional and behavioral disorders using individualized curricular modifications. *Journal of Emotional and Behavioral Disorders, 9,* 238–239, 247.

Kern, L., Dunlap, G., Clarke, S., & Childs, K.E. (1994). Student-assisted functional assessment interview. *Assessment for Effective Intervention, 19,* 29–39.

Kern, L., Gallagher, P., Starosta, K., Hickman, W., & George, M. (2006). Longitudinal outcomes of functional behavior assessment-based intervention. *Journal of Positive Behavior Interventions, 8,* 67–78.

Kern, L., Mantegna, M.E., Vorndran, C.M., Bailin, D., & Hilt, A. (2001). Choice of task sequence to reduce problem behaviors. *Journal of Positive Behavior Interventions, 3,* 3–10.

Kern, L., O'Neill, R.E., & Starosta, K. (2005). Gathering functional assessment information. In L.M. Bambara & L. Kern (Eds.), *Individualized supports for students with problem behaviors* (pp. 129–164). New York, NY: Guilford Press.

Kern, L., & State, T. (2009). Incorporating choice and preferred activities into classwide instruction. *Beyond Behavior, 18,* 3–11.

Kern, L., Vorndran, C.M., Hilt, A., Ringdahl, J.E., Adelman, B.E., & Dunlap, G. (1998). Choice as an intervention to improve behavior: A review of the literature. *Journal of Behavioral Education, 8,* 151–169.

Kincaid, D., Childs, K., Blase, K.A., & Wallace, F. (2007). Identifying barriers and facilitators in implementing schoolwide positive behavior support. *Journal of Positive Behavior Interventions, 9,* 174–184.

Kincaid, D., Childs, K., & George, H. (2010). *School-wide Benchmarks of Quality–Revised.*

Unpublished instrument, University of South Florida, Tampa.

King-Sears, M.E., Janney, R., & Snell, M.E. (2015). *Teachers' guides to inclusive practices: Collaborative teaming* (3rd ed.). Baltimore, MD: Paul H. Brookes Publishing Co.

Knoff, H.M. (2008). *APPRAISE: Action plan for Project ACHIEVE implementation success and evaluation*. Little Rock, AR: Project ACHIEVE Press.

Knoff, H.M., & Batshce, G.M. (1995). Project ACHIEVE: Analyzing a school process for at-risk and underachieving students. *School Psychology Review, 24,* 579–603.

Koegel, L.K., Harrower, J.K., & Koegel, R.L. (1999). Support for children with developmental disabilities in full inclusion classrooms through self-management. *Journal of Positive Behavior Interventions, 1,* 26–34.

Kounin, J.S. (1970). *Discipline and group management in classrooms.* Austin, TX: Holt, Rinehart & Winston.

Lane, K.L., Gresham, F.M., & O'Shaughnessy, T.E. (2002). Serving students with or at risk for emotional and behavior disorders: Future challenges. *Education and Treatment of Children, 25,* 507–521.

Lane, K., Kalberg, J., Parks, R., & Carter, E. (2008). Systematic screening at the middle school level: Score reliability and validity of the Student Risk Screening Scale. *Journal of Emotional and Behavioral Disorders, 15,* 209–222.

Lane, K.L., Wehby, J., Menzies, H.M., Doukas, G.L., Munton, S.M., & Gregg, R.M. (2003). Social skills instruction for students at risk for antisocial behavior: The effects of small-group instruction. *Behavioral Disorders, 28,* 229–248.

Lassen, S.R., Steele, M.M., & Sailor, W. (2006). The relationship of school-wide positive behavior support to academic achievement in an urban middle school. *Psychology in the Schools, 43,* 701–712.

Learning First Alliance. (2001). *Every child learning: Safe and supportive schools—A summary.* Washington, DC: Author.

Lee, Y., Sugai, G., & Horner, R.H. (1999). Using an instructional intervention to reduce problem and off-task behavior. *Journal of Positive Behavior Interventions, 1,* 195–204.

Lequia, J., Machalicek, W., & Rispoli, M.J. (2012). Effects of activity schedules on challenging behavior exhibited in children with autism spectrum disorders: A systematic review. *Research in Autism Spectrum Disorders, 6,* 480–492.

Lewis, T.J., Colvin, G., & Sugai, G. (2000). The effects of pre-correction and active supervision on the recess behavior of elementary students. *Education and Treatment of Children, 23,* 109–121

Lewis, T.J., Powers, L.J., Kelk, M.J., & Newcomer, L.L. (2002). Reducing problem behavior on the playground: An investigation of the application of schoolwide positive behavior supports. *Psychology in the Schools, 39,* 181–190.

Lewis, T.J., Sugai, G., & Colvin, G. (1998). Reducing problem behavior through a schoolwide system of effective behavior support: Investigation of a schoolwide social skills training program and contextual interventions. *School Psychology Review, 27,* 446–460.

Loeber, R. (1991). Antisocial behavior: More enduring than changeable? *Journal of the American Academy of Child and Adolescent Psychiatry, 30,* 393–397.

Loeber, R., Green, S.M., Lahey, B.B., Frick, P.J., & McBurnett, K. (2000). Findings on disruptive behavior disorders from the first decade of the developmental trends study. *Clinical Child and Family Psychology Review, 3,* 37–60.

Lohrmann, S., Forman, S., Martin, S., & Palmieri, M. (2008). Understanding school personnel's resistance to adopting schoolwide positive behavior support at a universal level of intervention. *Journal of Positive Behavior Interventions, 10,* 256–269. doi:10.1177/1098300708318963

Loman, S., & Borgmeier, C. (2010). *Practical functional behavioral assessment training manual for school-based personnel.* Retrieved from http://archives.pdx.edu/ds/psu/11250

Long, N.J., & Newman, R.G. (1996). The four choices of managing surface behavior of students. In N.J. Long & W.C. Morse (Eds.), *Conflict in the classroom: The education of at-risk and troubled students* (5th ed., pp. 266–273). Austin, TX: PRO-ED.

Lovett, H. (1985). *Cognitive counseling and persons with special needs.* New York, NY: Praeger.

Lovett, H. (1996). *Learning to listen: Positive approaches and people with difficult behavior.* Baltimore, MD: Paul H. Brookes Publishing Co.

Lucyshyn, J.M., Kayser, A.T., Irvin, K.L., & Blumberg, E.R. (2002). Functional assessment and positive behavior support at home with families: Designing effective and contextually appropriate behavior support plans. In J.M. Lucyshyn, G. Dunlap, & R.W. Albin (Eds.), *Families and positive behavior support: Addressing problem behavior in family contexts* (pp. 97–132). Baltimore, MD: Paul H. Brookes Publishing Co.

Luiselli, J.K., Putnam, R.F., Handler, M.W., & Feinberg, A.B. (2005). Whole-school positive behavior support: Effects on student discipline problems and academic performance. *Educational Psychology, 25,* 183–198.

Luiselli, J.K., Putnam, R.F., & Sunderland, M. (2002). Longitudinal evaluation of behavior support intervention in a public middle school. *Journal of Positive Behavior Interventions, 4,* 182–188.

Luria, A.R. (1961). *The role of speech in the regulation of normal and abnormal behavior.* New York, NY: Liveright.

Maag, J.W. (2012). School-wide discipline and the intransigency of exclusion. *Children and Youth Services Review, 34,* 2094–2100.

MacSuga, A.S., & Simonsen, B. (2011). Increasing teachers' use of evidence-based classroom management strategies through consultation: Overview and case studies. *Beyond Behavior, 20,* 4–12.

Malloy, J., Cheney, D., & Cormier, G. (1998). Interagency collaboration and the transition to adulthood for students with emotional and behavioral disabilities. *Education and Treatment of Children, 1,* 303–320.

March, R.E., & Horner, R.H. (2002). Feasibility and contributions of functional behavioral assessment in schools. *Journal of Emotional and Behavioral Disorders, 10,* 158–171.

March, R.E., Horner, R.H., Lewis-Palmer, T., Brown, D., Crone, D., Todd, A.W., & Carr, E. (2000). *Functional Assessment Checklist: Teachers and Staff [FACTS].* Eugene: University of Oregon, Educational and Community Supports.

Marchant, M., Anderson, D.H., Caldarella, P., Fisher, A., Young, B.J., & Young, K R. (2009). Schoolwide screening and programs of positive behavior support: Informing universal interventions. *Preventing School Failure, 53,* 131–143.

Marchant, M.R., Solano, B.R., Fisher, A.K., Caldarella, P., Young, K.R., & Renshaw, T.L. (2007). Modifying socially withdrawn behavior: A playground intervention for students with internalizing behaviors. *Psychology in the Schools, 44,* 779–794.

Marquis, J.G., Horner, R.H., Carr, E.G., Turnbull, A.P., Thompson, M., & Behrens, G.A., ... Doolabh, A. (2000). A meta-analysis of positive behavior support. In R. Gersten, E.P. Schiller, & S. Vaughn (Eds.), *Contemporary special education research: Synthesis of the knowledge base on critical instructional issues* (pp. 137–178). Mahwah, NJ: Lawrence Erlbaum Associates.

Marzano, R.J., Marzano, J.S., & Pickering, D.J. (2003). *Classroom management that works: Research-based strategies for every teacher.* Alexandria, VA: Association for Supervision and Curriculum Development.

Marzano, R.J., Pickering, D.J., & Pollock, J.E. (2001). *Classroom instruction that works: Research-based strategies for increasing student achievement.* Alexandria, VA: Association for Supervision and Curriculum Development.

Mathews, S., McIntosh, K., Frank, J.L., & May, S.L. (2013). Critical features predicting sustained implementation of school-wide positive behavioral interventions and supports. *Journal of Positive Behavior Interventions, 16,* 168–178.

May, S., Ard, W., III, Todd, A.W., Horner, R.H., Glagow, A., Sugai, G., & Sprague, J.R. (2002). *School-wide information system.* Eugene: University of Oregon, Educational and Community Supports.

Mayer, G. (1995). Preventing antisocial behavior in the schools. *Journal of Applied Behavior Analysis, 28,* 467–478.

Mayer, G.R., Butterworth, T., Nafpaktitis, M., & Sulzer-Azaroff, B. (1983). Preventing school vandalism and improving discipline: A three-year study. *Journal of Applied Behavior Analysis, 16,* 355–369.

Mayer, G.R., & Sulzer-Azaroff, B. (2002). Interventions for vandalism and aggression. In M. Shinn, H. Walker, & G. Stoner (Eds.), *Interventions for academic and behavior problems II: Preventive and remedial approaches* (pp. 853–884). Bethesda, MD: National Association of School Psychologists.

McConnell, M.E., Cox, C.J., Thomas, D.D., & Hilvitz, P.B. (2001). *Functional behavioral assessment: A systematic process for assessment and intervention in general and special education classrooms.* Denver, CO: Love Publishing.

McCurdy, E.E., & Cole, C.L. (2014). Use of a peer support intervention for promoting academic engagement of students with autism in general education settings. *Journal of Autism and Developmental Disorders, 44,* 883–893.

McDonnell, J., Mathot-Buckner, C., Thorson, N., & Fister, S. (2001). Supporting the inclusion of students with moderate and severe disabilities in junior high school general education classes: The effects of classwide peer tutoring, multi-element curriculum, and accommodations. *Education and Treatment of Children, 24,* 141–160.

McGinnis, E. (2012). *Skill streaming the elementary school child: A guide for teaching prosocial skills. The Arnold P. Goldstein Approach* (3rd ed.). Champaign, IL: Research Press.

McGinnis, E., & Goldstein, A. (1990). *Skillstreaming in early childhood: Teaching prosocial skills to the preschool and kindergarten child.* Champaign, IL: Research Press.

McGinnis, E., & Goldstein, A. (1997a). *Skillstreaming the adolescent: New strategies and perspectives for teaching prosocial skills.* Champaign, IL: Research Press.

McGinnis, E., & Goldstein, A. (1997b). *Skillstreaming the elementary school child: New strategies and perspectives for teaching prosocial skills.* Champaign, IL: Research Press.

McIntosh, K., Bennett, J.L., & Price, K. (2011). Evaluation of social and academic effects of school-wide positive support in a Canadian school district. *Exceptional Educational International, 21,* 46–60.

McIntosh, K., Borgmeier, C., Anderson, C.M., Horner, R.H., Rodriguez, B.J., & Tobin, T.J. (2008). Technical adequacy of the Functional Assessment Checklist: Teachers and staff (FACTS) FBA interview measure. *Journal of Positive Behavior Interventions, 10,* 33–45.

McIntosh, K., Campbell, A.L., Carter, D.R., & Dickey, C.R. (2009). Differential effects of a tier two behavior intervention based on function of problem behavior. *Journal of Positive Behavior Interventions, 11,* 82–93.

McIntosh, K., Campbell, A.L., Carter, D.R., & Zumbo, B.D. (2009). Concurrent validity of office discipline referrals and cut points used in school-wide positive behavior support. *Behavioral Disorders, 34,* 100–113.

McIntosh, K., Filter, K.J., Bennett, J.L., Ryan, C., & Sugai, G. (2009). Principles of sustainable prevention: Designing scale-up of school-wide positive behavior support to promote durable systems. *Psychology in the Schools, 47,* 5–21.

McIntosh, K., Frank, J.L., & Spaulding, S.A. (2010). Establishing research-based trajectories of office discipline referrals for individual students. *School Psychology Review, 39,* 380–394.

McIntosh, K., Horner, R.H., & Sugai, G. (2009). Sustainability of systems-level evidence-based practices in schools: Current knowledge and future directions. In W. Sailor, G. Dunlap, G. Sugai, & R.H. Horner (Eds.), *Handbook of positive behavior support* (pp. 327–352). New York, NY: Springer.

McIntosh, K., Kauffman, A.L., Carter, D.R., Dickey, C.R., & Horner, R.H. (2009). Differential effects of a direct behavior rating intervention based on function of problem behavior. *Journal of Positive Behavior Interventions, 11,* 1–19.

McIntosh, K., Predy, L.K., Upreti, G., Hume, A.E., Turri, M.G., & Matthews, S. (2013). Perceptions of contextual features related to implementation and sustainability of school-wide positive behavior support. *Journal of Positive Behavior Intervention, 16,* 31–43.

McKinney, J., Montague, M., & Hocutt, A. (1998). A two year follow up study of children at-risk for developing SED: Initial results from a prevention project. In C. Liberton, K. Kutash, & R. Friedman (Eds.), *A system of care for children's mental health: Expanding the research base* (pp. 271–277). Tampa: University of South Florida, Research and Training Center for Children's Mental Health.

Meadan, H., Ostrosky, M.M., Triplett, B., Michna, A., & Fettig, A. (2011). Using visual supports with young children with autism spectrum disorder. *Teaching Exceptional Children, 43,* 28–35.

Medley, N.S., Little, S.G., & Akin-Little, A. (2008). Comparing individual behavior plans from schools with and without school-wide positive behavior support: A preliminary study. *Journal of Behavioral Education, 17,* 93–110.

Melton, G.B., Limber, S.P., Cunningham, P., Osgood, D.W., Chambers, J., Flerx, V., . . . Nation, M. (1998). *Violence among rural youth: Final report to the Office of Juvenile Justice and Delinquency Prevention.* Washington, DC: Office of Juvenile Justice and Delinquency Prevention.

Menzies, H.M., & Lane, K.L. (2011). Using self-regulation strategies and functional assessment-based interventions to provide academic and behavioral support to students at risk within three-tiered models of prevention. *Preventing School Failure, 55,* 181–191.

Merrell, K., Gueldner, B., Ross, S.W., & Isava, D. (2008). How effective are school bullying intervention programs? A meta-analysis of intervention research. *School Psychology Quarterly, 23,* 26–42.

Meyer, L.H., & Evans, I.M. (1989). *Nonaversive intervention for behavior problems: A manual for home and community.* Baltimore, MD: Paul H. Brookes Publishing Co.

Meyer, L., & Janney, R. (1989). User-friendly measures of meaningful outcomes: Evaluating behavioral interventions. *Journal of The Association for Persons with Severe Handicaps, 14,* 263–270.

Mihalic, S., Fagan, A., Irwin, K., Ballard, D., & Elliott, D. (2004). *Blueprints for violence prevention.* Boulder: University of Colorado, Institute of Behavioral Science, Center for the Study and Prevention of Violence.

Mitchell, B.S., Stormont, M., & Gage, N.A. (2011). Tier two interventions implemented within the context of a tiered prevention framework. *Behavioral Disorders, 36,* 241–261.

Moore, D.W., Anderson, A., & Kumar, K. (2005). Instructional adaptation in the management of escape-maintained behavior in a classroom. *Journal of Positive Behavior Interventions, 7,* 216–223.

Mount, B. (2000). *Person-centered planning: Finding directions for change using personal futures planning.* New York, NY: Graphic Futures.

Mount, B., & Zwernik, K. (1988). *It's never too early, it's never too late: A booklet about personal futures planning* (Report No. 421-88-109). St. Paul: Minnesota Governor's Planning Council on Developmental Disabilities.

Nakasato, J. (2000). Data-based decision making in Hawaii's behavior support effort. *Journal of Positive Behavior Interventions, 2,* 247–251.

Nansel, T.R., Overpeck, M., Pilla, R.S., Simons-Morton, B., & Scheidt, P. (2001). Bullying behaviors among US youth: Prevalence and association with psychological adjustment. *Journal of the American Medical Association, 285,* 2094–2100.

National Center for Education Statistics. (2006). *The condition of education: 2006.* Washington, DC: Author.

Nelson, J.R., Gonzalez, J.E., Epstein, M.H., & Benner, G.J. (2003). Administrative discipline contacts: A review of the literature. *Behavioral Disorders, 28,* 249–281.

Nelson, J.R., Martella, R., & Galand, B. (1998). The effects of teaching school expectations and establishing a consistent consequence on formal office disciplinary actions. *Journal of Emotional and Behavioral Disorders, 6,* 153–161.

Nelson, J.R., Martella, R.M., & Marchand-Martella, N. (2002). Maximizing student learning: The effects of a comprehensive school-based program for preventing problem behaviors. *Journal of Emotional and Behavioral Disorders, 10,* 136–148.

Newcomer, L.L., Freeman, R., & Barrett, S. (2013). Essential systems for sustainable implementation of Tier 2 supports. *Journal of Applied School Psychology, 29,* 126–147.

Newcomer, L.L., & Lewis, T.J. (2004). Functional behavioral assessment: An investigation of assessment reliability and effectiveness of function-based interventions. *Journal of Emotional and Behavioral Disorders, 12,* 168–181.

Northeast Foundation for Children. (2014). *About Responsive Classroom.* Retrieved from http://www.responsiveclassroom.org/about-responsive-classroom

Oakes, J. (1985). *Keeping track: How schools structure inequality.* New Haven, CT: Yale University Press.

Olweus, D. (1993). *Bullying at school: What we know and what we can do.* Cambridge, UK: Blackwell.

Olweus, D., Limber, S., & Mihalic, S. (2002). *Blueprints for violence prevention, book nine: Bullying prevention program.* Boulder: University of Colorado, Center for the Study and Prevention of Violence.

O'Neill, R.E., Albin, R.W., Storey, K., Horner, R.H., & Sprague, J.R. (2014). *Functional assessment and program development for problem behavior: A practical handbook* (3rd ed.). Stamford, CT: Cengage Learning.

O'Shaughnessy, T.E., Lane, K.L., Gresham, F.M., & Beebe-Frankenberger, M.E. (2003). Children placed at risk for learning and behavioral difficulties: Implementing a school-wide system of early identification and intervention. *Remedial and Special Education, 24,* 27–35.

Osher, D., & Dwyer, K. (2006). Safe, supportive, and effective schools: Promoting school success to reduce school violence. In S.R. Jimerson & M.J. Furlong (Eds.), *Handbook of school violence and school safety: From research to practice* (pp. 51–71). Mahwah, NJ: Lawrence Erlbaum Associates.

Osher, D., Dwyer, K., & Jackson, S. (2004). *Safe, supportive, and successful schools step by step.* Longmont, CO: Sopris West Educational Services.

Oswald, K., Safran, S., & Johanson, G. (2005). Preventing trouble: Making schools safer places using positive behavior supports. *Education and Treatment of Children, 28,* 265–278.

Painter, K. (2012). Outcomes for youth with severe emotional disturbance: A repeated measures longitudinal study of a wraparound approach of service delivery in systems of care. *Child Youth Care Forum, 41,* 407–425.

Peace Partners. (2014). *How Peace Builders works.* Retrieved from http://www.peacebuiders.com

Pearpoint, J., O'Brien, J., & Forest, M. (1998). *PATH, a workbook for planning possible futures: Planning alternative tomorrows with hope for schools, organizations, businesses, families.* Toronto, Canada: Inclusion Press.

Reed, H., Thomas E., Sprague, J.R., & Horner, R.H. (1997). The Student Guided Functional Assessment Interview: An analysis of student and teacher agreement. *Journal of Behavioral Education, 7,* 33–49.

Rhodes, J.E. (2008). Improving youth mentoring intervention through research-based practice. *American Journal Community Psychology, 41,* 35–42.

Rimm-Kaufman, S.E. (2006). *Social and academic learning study on the contribution of the responsive classroom approach.* Greenfield, MA: Northeast Foundation for Children.

Rispoli, M., Lang, R., Neely, L., Camargo, S., Hutchins, N., Davenport, K., & Goodwyn, F.

(2013). A comparison of within- and across-activity choices for reducing challenging behavior in children with autism spectrum disorders. *Journal of Behavioral Education, 22,* 66–83.

Robers, S., Kemp, J., Rathbun, A., & Morgan, R.E. (2014). *Indicators of school crime and safety: 2013* (NCES 2014-042/NCJ 243299). Washington, DC: National Center for Education Statistics, U.S. Department of Education, and Bureau of Justice Statistics.

Rock, M.L. (2005). Use of strategic self-monitoring to enhance academic engagement, productivity, and accuracy of students with and without exceptionalities. *Journal of Positive Behavior Interventions, 7,* 3–18.

Rosenshine, B. (1983). Teaching functions in instructional programs. *Elementary School Journal, 83,* 335–351.

Ross, S.W., & Horner, R.H. (2009). Bully prevention in positive behavior support. *Journal of Applied Behavior Analysis, 42,* 747–759.

Ross, S.W., & Horner, R.H. (2013). Bully prevention in positive behavior support: Preliminary evaluation of third-, fourth-, and fifth-grade attitudes toward bullying. *Journal of Emotional and Behavioral Disorders.* [Prepublished July 12, 2013] doi: 10.1177/1063426613491429

Ross, S.W., Horner, R.H., & Stiller, B. (2008). *Bully Prevention in Positive Behavior Support manual.* Eugene: University of Oregon, Educational and Community Supports.

Safran, S.P., & Oswald, K. (2003). Positive behavior supports: Can schools reshape disciplinary practices? *Exceptional Children, 69,* 361–373.

Schrumpf, F., Crawford, D., & Usadel, C. (1991). *Peer mediation: Conflict resolution in schools.* Champaign, IL: Research Press.

Scott, T.M., & Barrett, S.B. (2004). Using staff and student time engaged in disciplinary procedures to evaluate the impact of school wide positive behavior support. *Journal of Positive Behavior Interventions, 6,* 21–27.

Scott, T.M., Bucalos, A., & Liaupsin, C. (2004). Using functional assessment in general education settings: Making a case for effectiveness and efficiency. *Behavioral Disorders, 29,* 189–201.

Scott, T.M., & Caron, D.B. (2005). Conceptualizing functional behavior assessment as prevention practice within positive behavior support systems. *Preventing School Failure, 50,* 13–21.

Scott, T., & Eber, L. (2003). Functional assessment and wraparound as systemic school processes: Primary, secondary, and tertiary systems examples. *Journal of Positive Behavior Supports, 5,* 131–143.

Scott, T.M., & Hunter, J. (2001). Effective behavior support: Initiating school-wide support systems: An administrator's guide to the process. *Beyond Behavior, 11,* 13–15.

Scott, T.M., Liaupsin, C., Nelson, C.M., & McIntyre, J. (2005). Team-based functional behavior assessment as proactive public school process: A descriptive analysis of current barriers. *Journal of Behavioral Education, 14,* 57–71.

Scott, T.M., & Martinek, G. (2006). Coaching positive behavior support in school settings: Tactics and data-based decision making. *Journal of Positive Behavior Intervention, 8,* 165–173.

Scott, T.M., McIntyre, J.L., Liaupsin, C., Nelson, C.M., Conroy, M., & Payne, L.D. (2005). An examination of the relation between functional behavior assessment and selected intervention strategies with school-based teams. *Journal of Positive Behavior Interventions, 7,* 205–215.

Scott, T.M., Nelson, C.M., & Zabala, J. (2003). Functional behavior assessment training in public schools: Facilitating systemic change. *Journal of Positive Behavior Interventions, 5,* 216–224.

Scotti, J.R., Evans, I.M., Meyer, L.H., & Walker, P. (1991). A meta-analysis of intervention research with problem behavior: Treatment validity and standards of practice. *American Journal on Mental Retardation, 96,* 233–256.

Shogren, K.A., Faggella-Luby, M.N., Bae, S.J., & Wehmeyer, M.L. (2004). The effect of choice-making as an intervention for problem behavior: A meta-analysis. *Journal of Positive Behavior Interventions, 6,* 228–237.

Shores, R.E., Gunter, P.L., & Jack, S.L. (1993). Classroom management strategies: Are they setting events for coercion? *Behavioral Disorders, 18,* 92–102.

Shure, M.B. (1992). *I can problem solve (ICPS): An interpersonal cognitive problem-solving program* (3 volumes: preschool, kindergarten/primary grades, intermediate elementary grades). Champaign, IL: Research Press.

Shure, M.B. (2014). *"I Can Problem Solve" for schools.* Retrieved from http://www.thinkingchild.com

Shure, M.B., & Spivack, G. (1982). Interpersonal problem-solving in young children: A cognitive approach to prevention. *American Journal of Community Psychology, 10,* 341–356.

Simmons, D.C., Kuykendall, K., King, K., Cornachione, C., & Kame'enui, E.J. (2000). Implementation of a schoolwide reading improvement model: "No one ever told us it would be this hard." *Learning Disabilities Research and Practice, 15,* 92–100.

Simonsen, B., Britton, L., & Young, D. (2010). School-wide positive behavior support in an alternative school setting: A case study. *Journal of Positive Behavior Interventions, 12,* 180–191.

Simonsen, B., Fairbanks, S., Briesch, A., Myers, D., & Sugai, G. (2008). Evidence-based practices in classroom management: Considerations for research to practice. *Education and Treatment of Children, 31,* 351–380.

Simonsen, B., Myers, D., & Briere, D.E. (2011). Comparing a behavioral check-in/check-out (CICO) intervention to standard to practice in an urban middle school setting using an experimental group design. *Journal of Positive Behavior Interventions, 13,* 31–48.

Simonsen, B., Sugai, G., & Negron, M. (2008). Schoolwide positive behavior supports: Primary systems and practices. *Teaching Exceptional Children, 40,* 32–40.

Skiba, R.J. (2000). *Zero tolerance: Zero evidence: An analysis of school disciplinary practice* (Policy Research Report #SRS2). Bloomington: Indiana Education Policy Center.

Skiba, R., Boone, K., Fontanini, A., Wu, T., & Strassell, A. (2000). *Preventing school violence: A practical guide to comprehensive planning.* Bloomington: Indiana Education Policy Center.

Skiba, R.J., Horner, R.H., Chung, C.G., Rausch, M.K., May, S.L., & Tobin, T. (2011). Race is not neutral: A national investigation of African American and Latino disproportionality in school discipline. *School Psychology Review, 40,* 85–107.

Skiba, R.J., & Knesting, K. (2002). Zero tolerance, zero evidence: An analysis of school disciplinary practice. In G.G. Noam (Ed.), *Zero tolerance: Can suspension and expulsion keep school safe?* (pp. 17–43). San Francisco, CA: Jossey-Bass.

Skiba, R.J., & Peterson, R.L. (2000). School discipline at a crossroads: From zero tolerance to early response. *Exceptional Children, 66,* 335–346.

Skinner, C.H., Cashwell, T.H., & Skinner, A.L. (2000). Increasing tootling: The effects of a peer-monitored group contingency program on students' reports of peers' prosocial behaviors. *Psychology in the Schools, 37,* 263–270.

Slavin, R.E. (1991, February). Synthesis of research on cooperative learning. *Educational Leadership, 48,* 71–82.

Slavin, R.E., Madden, N.A., & Leavey, M.B. (1984). Effects of team assisted individualization on the mathematical achievement of academically handicapped and non-handicapped students. *Journal of Educational Psychology, 76,* 813–819.

Smith-Bird, E., & Turnbull, A.P. (2005). Linking positive behavior support to family quality-of-life outcomes. *Journal of Positive Behavior Interventions, 7,* 174–180.

Snell, M.E. (2006). What's the verdict: Are students with severe disabilities included in school-wide positive behavior support? *Research and Practice for Persons with Severe Disabilities, 31,* 62–65.

Snell, M.E., & Janney, R. (2005). *Teachers' guides to inclusive practices: Collaborative teaming* (2nd ed.). Baltimore, MD: Paul H. Brookes Publishing Co.

Snell, M.E., Voorhees, M.D., & Chen, L. (2005). Team involvement in assessment-based interventions with problem behavior. *Journal of Positive Behavior Interventions, 7,* 233–235.

Solomon, B.G., Klein, S.A., Hintze, J.M., Cressey, J.M., & Peller, S.L. (2012). A meta-analysis of school-wide positive behavior support: An exploratory study using single-case synthesis. *Psychology in the Schools, 49,* 105–121.

Solomon, D., Battistich, V., Watson, M., Schaps, E., & Lewis, C. (2000). A six-district study of educational change: Direct and mediated effects of the Child Development Project. *Social Psychology of Education, 4,* 3–51.

Sprague, J., Walker, H., Stieber, S., Simonsen, B., Nishioka, V., & Wagner, L. (2001). Exploring the relationship between school discipline referrals and delinquency. *Psychology in the Schools, 38,* 197–206.

Stoiber, K.C., & Gettinger, M. (2011). Functional assessment and positive support strategies for promoting resilience: Effects on teachers and high-risk children. *Psychology in the Schools, 48,* 686–706.

Strain, P.S., Wilson, K., & Dunlap, G. (2011). Prevent-teach-reinforce: Addressing problem behaviors of students with autism in general education classrooms. *Behavioral Disorders, 36,* 160–171.

Strauss, M.A. (1994). *Beating the devil out of them: Corporal punishment in American families and its effects on children.* Lexington, MA: Lexington Books.

Sugai, G., & Horner, R. (2002). The evolution of discipline practices: Schoolwide positive behavior supports. *Behavior Psychology in the Schools, 24,* 23–50.

Sugai, G., Horner, R.H., Dunlap, G., Hieneman, M., Lewis, T.J., Nelson, C.M., . . . Ruef, M. (2000). Applying positive behavior support and functional behavioral assessment in schools. *Journal of Positive Behavior Interventions, 2,* 131–143.

Sugai, G., Horner, R., & Todd, A. (2003). *Effective Behavior Support (EBS) Self-Assessment*

Survey: Version 2.0. Eugene: University of Oregon, Educational and Community Supports.

Sugai, G., Lewis-Palmer, T., Todd, A., & Horner, R. (2005, June). *SET: School-wide Evaluation Tool: Version 2.1.* Eugene: University of Oregon, Educational and Community Supports.

Sugai, G., O'Keefe, B.V., & Fallon, C.M. (2012). A contextual consideration of culture and school-wide positive behavior support. *Journal of Positive Behavior Interventions, 14,* 197–208.

Sugai, G., Sprague, J., Horner, R., & Walker, H. (2000). Preventing school violence: The use of office referral to assess and monitor school-wide discipline interventions. *Journal of Emotional and Behavioral Disorders, 8,* 94–101.

Sulzer-Azaroff, B., & Mayer, G.R. (1991). *Behavior analysis for lasting change.* Austin, TX: Holt, Rinehart & Winston.

Swanson, K.W. (2011). The effects of school-wide positive behavior support on middle school climate and student outcomes. *Research in Middle Level Education, 35*(4), 1–14.

Taylor-Greene, S.J., & Kartub, D.T. (2000). Durable implementation of schoolwide behavior support: The High Five Program. *Journal of Positive Behavior Interventions, 2,* 233–235.

Thorne, S., & Kamps, D. (2008). The effects of a group contingency intervention on academic engagement and problem behavior reduction with at-risk students. *Behavior Analysis in Practice, 2,* 12–18.

Thorson, S. (1996). The missing link: Students discuss school discipline. *Focus on Exceptional Children, 29,* 1–12.

Tobin, T.J., & Sugai, G.M. (1999). Using sixth-grade school records to predict school violence, chronic discipline problems, and high school outcomes. *Journal of Emotional and Behavioral Disorders, 7,* 40–53.

Tobin, T., Sugai, G., & Colvin, G. (1996). Patterns in middle school discipline records. *Journal of Emotional and Behavioral Disorders, 4,* 82–94.

Todd, A.W., Campbell, A.L., Meyer, G.G., & Horner, R.H. (2008). The effects of a targeted intervention to reduce problem behaviors: Elementary school implementation of Check In–Check Out. *Journal of Positive Behavior Interventions, 10,* 46–55.

Todd, A.W., Horner, R.H., & Sugai, G. (1999). Self-monitoring and self-recruited praise: Effects on problem behavior, academic engagement, and work completion in a typical classroom. *Journal of Positive Behavior Interventions, 1,* 66–76.

Todd, A.W., Horner, R.H., Sugai, G., & Sprague, J.R. (1999). Effective behavior support: Strengthening school-wide systems through a team-based approach. *Effective School Practices, 17,* 23–37.

Touchette, P.E., MacDonald, R.F., & Langer, S.N. (1985). A scatter plot for identifying stimulus control of problem behavior. *Journal of Applied Behavior Analysis, 18,* 343–351.

Tullis, C.A., Cannella-Malone, H.I., Basbigill, A.R., Yeager, A., Fleming, C.V., Payne, D., & Wu, P.F. (2011). Review of the choice and preference assessment literature for individuals with severe to profound disabilities. *Education and Training in Autism and Developmental Disabilities, 46,* 576–595.

Turnbull, A., Edmonson, H., Griggs, P., Wickham, D., Sailor, W., Freeman, R., . . . Warren, J. (2002). A blueprint for schoolwide positive behavior support: Implementation of three components. *Exceptional Children, 68,* 377–402.

Turnbull, A.P., Turnbull, R.R., III, Poston, D., Beegle, G., Blue-Banning, M., & Diehl, K., . . . Summers, J.A. (2004). Enhancing quality of life of families of children and youth with disabilities in the United States. In A.P. Turnbull, I. Brown., & H.R. Turnbull, III (Eds.), *Families and people with mental retardation and quality of life: International perspectives.* Washington, DC: American Association on Intellectual and Developmental Disabilities.

Umbreit, J., Lane, K.L., & Dejud, C. (2004). Improving classroom behavior by modifying task difficulty: Effects of increasing the difficulty of too-easy tasks. *Journal of Positive Behavior Interventions, 6,* 13–20.

U.S. Department of Education. (2001). *Exemplary and promising safe, disciplined and drug-free school programs.* Jessup, MD: U.S. Department of Education Publications Center.

U.S. Department of Education. (2014). *Guiding principles: A resource guide for improving school climate and discipline.* Washington, DC: Author.

Vandercook, T., York, J., & Forest, M. (1989). *MAPS: A strategy for building the vision.* Minneapolis: University of Minnesota, Institute on Community Integration.

Vaughn, B.J., & Horner, R.H. (1997). Identifying instructional tasks that occasion problem behaviors and assessing the effects of student versus teacher choice among these tasks. *Journal of Applied Behavior Analysis, 30,* 299–312.

Vaughn, S., Kim, A., Morris, C.V., Sloan, M., Hughes, M.T., Elbaum, B., & Sridhar, D. (2003). Social skills interventions for young children with disabilities: A synthesis of group design studies. *Remedial and Special Education, 24,* 2–15.

Vazsonyi, A.T., Belliston, L.M., & Flannery, D.J. (2004). Evaluation of a school-based, universal violence prevention program: Low-, medium-, and high-risk children. *Youth Violence and Juvenile Justice, 2,* 185–206.

Vincent, C.G., Randall, C., Cartledge, G., & Tobin, T.J., & Swain-Bradway, J. (2011). Toward a conceptual integration of cultural responsiveness and schoolwide positive behavior support. *Journal of Positive Behavior Interventions, 13,* 219–229.

Vincent, C.G., & Tobin, T.J. (2010). The relationship between implementation of schoolwide positive behavior support (SWPBS) and disciplinary exclusion of students from various ethnic backgrounds with and without disabilities. *Journal of Emotional and Behavioral Disorders, 19,* 217–232.

Wacker, D.P., Cooper, L.J., Peck, S.M., Derby, K.M., & Berg, W.K. (1999). Community-based functional assessment. In A.C. Repp & R.H. Horner (Eds.), *Functional analysis of problem behavior: From effective assessment to effective support* (pp. 32–56). Belmont, CA: Wadsworth.

Walker, B.A. (2010). Effective schoolwide screening to identify students at risk for social and behavioral problems. *Intervention in School and Clinic, 46,* 104–110.

Walker B., & Cheney, D. (2012). *The SAPR-PBIS™ manual: A team-based approach to implementing effective schoolwide positive behavior interventions and supports.* Baltimore, MD: Paul H. Brookes Publishing Co.

Walker, B., Cheney, D., Stage, S., & Blum, C. (2005). School-wide screening and positive behavior supports: Identifying and supporting students at risk for school failure. *Journal of Positive Behavior Interventions, 7,* 194–204.

Walker, H.M., Golly, A., McLane, J.Z., & Kimmich, M. (2005). The Oregon First Step to Success Replication Initiative: Statewide results of an evaluation of the program's impact. *Journal of Emotional and Behavioral Disorders, 13,* 163–172.

Walker, H., Hops, H., & Greenwood, C. (1993). *RECESS: A program for reducing negative aggressive behavior.* Seattle, WA: Educational Achievement Systems.

Walker, H.M., Horner, R.H., Sugai, G., Bullis, M., Sprague, J.R., Bricker, D., & Kaufman, M.J. (1996). Integrated approaches to preventing antisocial behavior patterns among school-age children and youth. *Journal of Emotional and Behavioral Disorders, 4,* 194–209.

Walker, H.M., Kavanaugh, K., Stiller, B., Golly, A., Severson, H.H., & Feil, E.G. (1998). First Step to Success: An early intervention approach for preventing school antisocial behavior. *Journal of Emotional and Behavioral Disorders, 6,* 66–80.

Walker, H.M., Ramsey, E., & Gresham, F.M. (2004). *Antisocial behavior in school: Evidence-based practices.* Belmont, CA: Wadsworth/Thomson Learning.

Walker, H., & Severson, H. (1992). *Systematic Screening for Behavior Disorders: User's guide and technical manual.* Longmont, CO: Sopris West Educational Services.

Walker, H., Severson, H., & Feil, E. (1995). *Early screening project: A proven child-find process.* Longmont, CO: Sopris West Educational Services.

Walker, H., Stiller, B., Golly, A., Kavanaugh, K., Severson, H.H., & Feil, E. (1997). *First Step to Success: Helping young children overcome antisocial behavior (an early intervention program for Grades K–3).* Longmont, CO: Sopris West Educational Services.

Warren, J.S., Bohanon-Edmonson, H.M., Turnbull, A.P., Sailor, W., Wickham, D., Griggs, P., & Beech, S.E. (2006). School-wide positive behavior support: Addressing behavior problems that impede student learning. *Education Psychology Review, 18,* 187–198.

Warren, J., Edmonson, H., Griggs, P., Lassen, S., McCart, A., Turnbull, A., & Sailor, W. (2003). Urban applications of school-wide positive behavior support: Critical issues and lessons learned. *Journal of Positive Behavior Interventions, 5*(2), 80–92.

Wehmeyer, M.L., & Schalock, R.L. (2001). Self-determination and quality of life: Implications for special education services and supports. *Focus on Exceptional Children, 33,* 1–16.

Wellesley Centers for Women. (2014). *Open Circle: Programming.* Retrieved from http://www.open-circle.org/programming/overview

Wong, C. (2013). *Social narratives (SN) fact sheet.* Chapel Hill: University of North Carolina, Frank Porter Graham Child Development Institute, The National Professional Development Center on Autism Spectrum Disorders.

Ysseldyke, J.E., & Christenson, S.L. (1987). *The Instructional Environment Scale: A comprehensive methodology for assessing an individual student's instruction.* Austin, TX: PRO-ED.

Zins, J.E., Weissberg, R.P., Walberg, H.J., & Wang, C. (Eds.). (2004). *Building academic success of social and emotional learning.* New York, NY: Teachers College Press.

APPENDIX A

Blank Forms

Team Meeting Agenda and Minutes

Team: _____ Date: _____

People present/role today: Absentees:

_____ _____ _____

_____ _____ _____

_____ _____ _____

_____ _____ _____

_____ _____ _____

Purpose of meeting: _____

Agenda items	Decisions/actions	Who and by when?
_____	_____	_____
_____	_____	_____
_____	_____	_____
_____	_____	_____
_____	_____	_____

Date: _____ Time: _____

Agenda items for next meeting:

1.

2.

3.

4.

Steps and Tools to Develop Individualized Positive Behavior Supports

Student: _____ Date initiated: _____

School: _____ Grade: _____

Members of positive behavior support team:

_____ _____

_____ _____

_____ _____

Steps and accompanying functional behavior assessment tools (Check box when completed.)

Step 1: Identify the Problem(s) and Decide on Priorities; Make a Safety Plan.

    Step 1A: Identify the Problem(s) and Decide on Priorities.
    ☐ Step 1A Worksheet: Problem Identification and Decisions About Priorities
    ☐ Team Meeting Agenda and Minutes (use at each team meeting)

    Step 1B (if necessary): Make a Safety Plan.
    ☐ Step 1B Worksheet: Safety Plan
    ☐ Incident Record

Step 2: Plan and Conduct the Functional Behavior Assessment.

    Step 2A: Gather Descriptive (Indirect) Information.
    ☐ Step 2A Worksheet: Student-Centered Functional Behavior Assessment Profile
    ☐ Student Schedule Analysis

    Step 2B: Conduct Direct Observations.
    ☐ Interval Recording or Scatter Plot
    ☐ Antecedent-Behavior-Consequence Observation

    Step 2C: Summarize Functional Behavior Assessment and Build Hypothesis Statement(s).
    ☐ Step 2C Worksheet: Summary of Functional Behavior Assessment and Hypothesis Statement(s)

    Step 2D (if necessary): Test Hypotheses.
    ☐ Team Meeting Agenda and Minutes (with plan for verifying hypotheses)
    ☐ Revision of Step 2C Worksheet

Step 3: Design an Individualized Positive Behavior Support Plan.
    ☐ Step 3 Worksheet: Positive Behavior Support Plan

Step 4: Implement, Monitor, and Evaluate the Positive Behavior Support Plan.
    ☐ Step 4 Worksheet: Implementing, Monitoring, and Evaluating the Positive Behavior Support Plan (decisions recorded on Team Meeting Agenda and Minutes)

Program-at-a-Glance

Student: _____ Date: _____

IEP goals (in a few words)	IEP accommodations and modifications
	Academic, social, and physical supports

Key: IEP, Individualized education program.

Step 1A Worksheet: Problem Identification and Decisions About Priorities

Student: _____ Date: _____

Describe each problem behavior as specifically as possible—what it looks like and sounds like, how intense it is, and how long each has been a problem. Estimate the frequency and duration of each behavior. Label the behaviors according to their level of priority.

Description of problem behaviors	Level of priority
1.	☐ Destructive ☐ Disruptive ☐ Distracting
2.	☐ Destructive ☐ Disruptive ☐ Distracting
3.	☐ Destructive ☐ Disruptive ☐ Distracting
4.	☐ Destructive ☐ Disruptive ☐ Distracting
5.	☐ Destructive ☐ Disruptive ☐ Distracting
6.	☐ Destructive ☐ Disruptive ☐ Distracting

Decision and rationale: Which behaviors should be priorities for intervention and why?

Is a Safety Plan needed immediately?   Yes   No

Teachers' Guides to Inclusive Practices: Behavior Support, Third Edition,
by Linda M. Bambara, Rachel Janney, and Martha E. Snell.
Copyright © 2015 by Paul H. Brookes Publishing Co., Inc. All rights reserved.

Student: _____ Date: _____

Behavior(s) that call for use of the Safety Plan:

Who will intervene in a serious behavior episode?

How to intervene and support the student during phases of the crisis cycle:

1. Trigger phase: Describe signals the student sends that indicate feeling threatened or uncomfortable. Describe antecedents known to trigger problems and how to eliminate them.

2. Escalation phase: Tell how to interrupt, redirect, and facilitate relaxation.

3. Crisis phase: Describe how to interrupt and protect the student and others.

4. Begin recovery phase: Describe how to avoid reescalating the behavior and continuing to reach full recovery.

5. Recovery phase: Describe any processing/reflecting that should be done with the student and how to reinstitute the positive behavior support plan.

   Directions for reporting and documentation: Give instructions for reporting the incident and completing and filing Incident Records.

Incident Record

Student: _____ Completed by: _____

Day: _____ Date: _____ Time: _____

Setting: _____

Class or activity: _____

Staff present: _____

Students present: _____

1. Describe what happened earlier in the day or just before the incident that may have led to the incident.

2. Describe the student's behavior and others' responses during the Trigger and Escalation phases.

3. Describe what the student and others did during the Crisis phase.

4. Describe the Begin Recovery and Recovery phases. Describe how the positive behavior support plan was reintroduced.

5. To what extent was the Safety Plan followed?   Fully   Somewhat   Very little

6. What is your hunch about the setting events or triggers of the behavior?

7. What is your hunch about the purpose of the behavior or how it is working for the student?

8. What might prevent or interrupt the behavior more effectively in the future? What suggestions do you have to improve the Safety Plan?

Teachers' Guides to Inclusive Practices: Behavior Support, Third Edition,
by Linda M. Bambara, Rachel Janney, and Martha E. Snell.
Copyright © 2015 by Paul H. Brookes Publishing Co., Inc. All rights reserved.

Student: _____   Date: _____

People providing initial information:

_____   _____

_____   _____

_____   _____

Directions: At a team meeting, summarize existing information about the student's problem behavior and begin to analyze the possible relationships among the behavior, the student's wants and needs, and the environment.

SECTION I: CLASSROOM CLIMATE

Directions: Review the Classroom Organization and Management Inventory (see Figure 3.1). Rate the extent to which each indicator is in place and the extent to which the target student understands and is responsive to expectations.

Ratings:
Good = The indicator is in place satisfactorily.
Fair = The indicator is partially in place but improvement is needed.
Poor = The indicator is in place to an unacceptable degree or not at all.

Indicator	Rating/comments	Improvement needed
Physical space		
Classroom procedures/routines		
Supervision/monitoring		
Classwide positive behavior support (PBS) system (clear expectations, contingent feedback)		
Active engagement		

SECTION II: QUALITY OF LIFE

Ratings:
Good = The indicator is in place satisfactorily.
Fair = The indicator is partially in place but improvement is needed.
Poor = The indicator is in place to an unacceptable degree or not at all.

Indicator	How is indicator in place?	Rating
Supportive people a. Family	a.	a.
b. Adults at school	b.	b.
c. Peers at school	c.	c.
d. Peers outside of school	d.	d.
Successful places and activities at school		
Successful places and activities at home and in the community		
Interests and preferences		
Opportunities to make age-appropriate choices		

Based on the quality-of-life indicators, list shortcomings that might be addressed in a PBS plan.

SECTION III: ACADEMICS AND COMMUNICATION

Academic strengths	Academic liabilities

Summarize the current fit between the student's educational programming and his or her academic strengths and liabilities.

Communication

What is the student's primary mode of communication (e.g., speech, signs, gestures, electronic devices), and how successful is the student in using it?

How does the student accomplish these communicative purposes?

1. *Get attention/help/interaction:*

2. *Get preferred activities or tangible items:*

3. *Avoid/escape attention/interaction:*

4. *Avoid/escape activity or item:*

5. *Calm self when agitated, stressed, angry, overstimulated:*

6. *Get sensory stimulation (e.g., when bored):*

SECTION IV: MEDICAL, HEALTH, AND SENSORY CONCERNS

Describe any health concerns or medication that may be affecting the student's mood or behavior:

Describe any sensory difficulties or needs:

List other important information about medical and health history:

SECTION V: TARGET BEHAVIORS AND PAST INTERVENTIONS

From Step 1A Worksheet, which behavior(s) will be targeted for intervention? Define the behaviors as clearly and specifically as possible. These are the definitions that will be used to collect any additional information and to develop the PBS plan.

Describe any current interventions for the behavior(s) (or attach any behavioral intervention plan that is currently in use).

What works to prevent or interrupt the behavior(s)?	What does not work to prevent or interrupt the behavior(s)?

SECTION VI: PRELIMINARY HUNCHES

Note: The team may want to complete the Student Schedule Analysis and several Incident Records (if they are being used to record incidents warranting use of a Safety Plan) before completing this section of the FBA Profile.

When this antecedent happens (setting event or trigger)	the student is likely to (target behavior)	and this consequence tends to occur	Therefore, the purpose of the behavior may be

SECTION VII: DECISIONS AND NEXT STEPS

1. Should any other people be interviewed to ensure that the information on this profile is complete and accurate?   Yes   No

   If "yes," then list others who should be interviewed:

2. Do quantifiable baseline data on the targeted behaviors need to be collected?   Yes   No

   If "yes," then when, where, and how will data be collected?

3. Is additional information needed to determine if the current hunches about the antecedents, consequences, and purposes of the behaviors are accurate?   Yes   No

   If "yes," then when, where, and how will data be collected?

Student Schedule Analysis

Student: _____   Staff who work with staff on a regular basis:

Date: _____   _____

_____

_____

Target behavior(s):

Time	Class/activity	Rating and behavior + = mild/rare − = excessive/often v = variable	Grouping i = independent 1:1 = one-to-one sg = small group lg = large group u = unstructured p = peer	Task type Paper/pencil Oral/listening Hands on Activity/routine Computer	Staff

From Meyer, L., & Janney, R. (1989). User-friendly measures of meaningful outcomes: Evaluating behavioral interventions. *Journal of The Association for Persons with Severe Handicaps, 14*(4), 267; adapted by permission.

In *Teachers' Guides to Inclusive Practices: Behavior Support, Third Edition,* by Linda M. Bambara, Rachel Janney, and Martha E. Snell (2015, Paul H. Brookes Publishing Co.)

Student: _____ Dates: _____

Target behaviors:

Used for: ____ Frequency count (tally each time behavior occurs within each interval)
____ Scatter plot (*Key:* ○ = one occurrence; ● = more than one occurrence)
____ Critical incident and use of Safety Plan (indicated by X)

Time	Activity	Monday		Tuesday		Wednesday		Thursday		Friday		Total	

Time	Activity	Monday		Tuesday		Wednesday		Thursday		Friday		Total	
Total problem behaviors/day													

	Monday/Tuesday	Wednesday/Thursday	Friday
Total per week			
Average per day			
Average per hour			

Teachers' Guides to Inclusive Practices: Behavior Support, Third Edition,
by Linda M. Bambara, Rachel Janney, and Martha E. Snell.

Antecedent-Behavior-Consequence Observation

Student: _____   Date: _____

Setting: _____   Observer: _____

Class/subject: _____

Target behaviors (see Step 2A Worksheet: Student-Centered Functional Behavior Assessment Profile for observable definitions of behaviors)

Time	Antecedents (What was going on before the behavior? What was being said and done?)	Behavior (What did the student do?)	Consequences (What happened after the behavior? How did people react?)	Hypothesis (About the function of the behavior)

Teachers' Guides to Inclusive Practices: Behavior Support, Third Edition,
by Linda M. Bambara, Rachel Janney, and Martha E. Snell.
Copyright © 2015 by Paul H. Brookes Publishing Co., Inc. All rights reserved.

Antecedent-Behavior-Consequence Checklist

Date/ period	Activity/setting	Setting event	Antecedent	Behavior	Consequence
Start: End:	☐ Arrival ☐ Math ☐ Physical education ☐ Music ☐ Reading ☐ Language arts/writing ☐ Lunch ☐ Science ☐ Recess ☐ Library ☐ Snack ☐ Art ☐ Social studies ☐ Departure	☐ Lack of sleep ☐ Missed breakfast ☐ Teacher absent ☐ Half day ☐ Snow day ☐ Schedule change ☐ Not feeling well ☐ _____ ☐ _____ ☐ _____	☐ Teacher direction ☐ Presentation of task ☐ Peer interactions ☐ Nonpreferred activity ☐ _____ ☐ _____ ☐ _____	☐ ☐ ☐ ☐ ☐ ☐	☐ Verbal redirection ☐ Paraeducator assisted with activity ☐ Escape from activity ☐ Did not complete the activity ☐ Delayed the activity ☐ _____ ☐ _____ ☐ _____
Start: End:	☐ Arrival ☐ Math ☐ Physical education ☐ Music ☐ Reading ☐ Language arts/writing ☐ Lunch ☐ Science ☐ Recess ☐ Library ☐ Snack ☐ Art ☐ Social studies ☐ Departure	☐ Lack of sleep ☐ Missed breakfast ☐ Teacher absent ☐ Half day ☐ Snow day ☐ Schedule change ☐ Not feeling well ☐ _____ ☐ _____ ☐ _____	☐ Teacher direction ☐ Presentation of task ☐ Peer interactions ☐ Nonpreferred activity ☐ _____ ☐ _____ ☐ _____	☐ ☐ ☐ ☐ ☐ ☐	☐ Verbal redirection ☐ Paraeducator assisted with activity ☐ Escape from activity ☐ Did not complete the activity ☐ Delayed the activity ☐ _____ ☐ _____ ☐ _____
Start: End:	☐ Arrival ☐ Math ☐ Physical education ☐ Music ☐ Reading ☐ Language arts/writing ☐ Lunch ☐ Science ☐ Recess ☐ Library ☐ Snack ☐ Art ☐ Social studies ☐ Departure	☐ Lack of sleep ☐ Missed breakfast ☐ Teacher absent ☐ Half day ☐ Snow day ☐ Schedule change ☐ Not feeling well ☐ _____ ☐ _____ ☐ _____	☐ Teacher direction ☐ Presentation of task ☐ Peer interactions ☐ Nonpreferred activity ☐ _____ ☐ _____ ☐ _____	☐ ☐ ☐ ☐ ☐ ☐	☐ Verbal redirection ☐ Paraeducator assisted with activity ☐ Escape from activity ☐ Did not complete the activity ☐ Delayed the activity ☐ _____ ☐ _____ ☐ _____

Sources: Kern, O'Neill, & Starosta, 2005; Loman & Borgmeier, 2010.

In *Teachers' Guides to Inclusive Practices: Behavior Support, Third Edition,* by Linda M. Bambara, Rachel Janney, and Martha E. Snell. Copyright © 2015 by Paul H. Brookes Publishing Co., Inc. All rights reserved.

Directions: Summarize the functional behavior assessment (FBA) information that has been gathered from all sources to build hypothesis statement(s) about targeted problem behaviors. If the student has appropriate alternative behaviors that serve the same purpose as the problem behavior (alternative behaviors may be nonexistent or very weak), then describe those behaviors. Then determine if any data are missing or team members disagree or are uncertain about their hypotheses. Make a plan for further data collection and verification of hypotheses if necessary.

Student: _____ Date of initial summary: _____ Revision date, if necessary: _____

People completing this form:

_____   _____

_____   _____

_____   _____

Duration: On average, how long does the behavior occur?

Frequency: On average, how often does the behavior occur?

1. Per hour? _____ Per day? _____ Per week? _____
2. Per hour? _____ Per day? _____ Per week? _____
3. Per hour? _____ Per day? _____ Per week? _____
4. Per hour? _____ Per day? _____ Per week? _____

Describe chains of antecedents (both setting events and triggers) that predict the target behavior will occur, observable definitions of the target behaviors, and consequences that seem to be maintaining the behavior. Then hypothesize about the function or purpose of the target behavior(s).

When this happens (setting events and/or triggers)	the student does or is likely to (describe target behavior[s])	and results in these maintaining consequences	Therefore, the function of the behavior may be
Setting event: Trigger(s):			
Setting event: Trigger(s):			

Setting event: Trigger(s):			

2. Describe alternative behaviors that the student has demonstrated (the behaviors may be very weak) that may serve the same function as the problem behavior(s).

3. Are additional data needed to build hypothesis statement(s)?   Yes   No

   Is Step 2D: Test Hypotheses needed to confirm or refute hypotheses?   Yes   No

   If "yes," then use the Team Meeting Agenda and Minutes form to plan how, when, and by whom further FBA data collection or verification tests will be conducted. Decide on a date for the next team meeting, at which this worksheet will be revised.

Student: _____   Date: _____

Team members designing this plan:

Behavior hypotheses (when this happens [antecedents], the student does this [target behavior], and results in [consequences and presumed function of behavior])

Goals

Increase	Decrease

Interventions and support strategies to be implemented

Preventing (antecedent changes)		Teaching replacement and other desired skills	Responding to alternative skills and problem behaviors
Alter setting event	Alter trigger(s)		

Preventing (antecedent changes)		Teaching replacement and other desired skills	Responding to alternative skills and problem behaviors
Alter setting event	Alter trigger(s)		

Is Safety Plan still needed?   Yes   No

If so, attach Safety Plan that has been revised and updated as needed.

Step 4 Worksheet: Implementing, Monitoring, and Evaluating the Positive Behavior Support Plan

Student: _____   Date: _____

Directions: Use the Team Meeting Agenda and Minutes form to list issues, decisions made, and actions to be taken in order to put the positive behavior support (PBS) plan into place, monitor its use, evaluate its effects, and make needed revisions. The first set of issues listed below relates to putting the plan into place and requires immediate consideration. The second set of issues relates to monitoring and evaluation of the plan and will require ongoing consideration at future team meetings.

Issues for immediate consideration (check boxes as issues are addressed):

☐ Materials to be made, purchased, or adapted

☐ Communicating with others who need to know about the plan

☐ Developing and sharing teaching plans for replacement skills and other alternative academic or social-communication skills

☐ The schedule for putting various intervention strategies of the plan into place

☐ In-service training, coaching, or modeling needed for team members and other staff

☐ A system for monitoring whether the plan is being used as designed (Are prevention, teaching, responding, and safety management strategies being consistently used?)

☐ Team meeting schedule

Issues for ongoing consideration as the plan is implemented:

☐ How often the use and effects of the PBS plan will be evaluated and revised as necessary

☐ The rate of improvement in targeted behaviors and the use of alternative skills that are acceptable

☐ Parents, teachers, and other relevant people's judgments about the plan's effectiveness, efficiency, and appropriateness for the student and the context, as well as their comfort level in implementing the plan

☐ The student's feedback about the acceptability of the interventions and progress toward his or her goals

APPENDIX B

Resources on Behavior Support

SCHOOLWIDE POSITIVE BEHAVIOR SUPPORT AND SYSTEMS-CHANGE STRATEGIES

Baker, B., & Ryan, C. (2014). *The PBIS team handbook: Setting expectations and building positive behavior.* Minneapolis, MN: Free Spirit Publishing.

Boynton, M., & Boynton, C. (2007). *The educator's guide to assessing and improving school discipline programs.* Alexandria, VA: Association for Supervision and Curriculum Development.

Colvin, G. (Ed.). (2007). *Seven steps for developing a proactive schoolwide discipline plan: A guide for principals and leadership teams.* Thousand Oaks, CA: Corwin Press.

Crone, D.A., Hawken, L.S., & Horner, R.H. (2015). *Building positive behavior support systems in schools: Functional behavioral assessment* (2nd ed.). New York, NY: Guilford Press.

Dwyer, K., & Osher, D. (2000). *Safeguarding our children: An action guide.* Washington, DC: U.S. Departments of Education and Justice, American Institutes for Research.

Osher, D., Dwyer, K., & Jackson, S. (2004). *Safe, supportive, and successful schools step by step.* Longmont, CO: Sopris West Educational Services.

Sprague, J.R., & Golly, A. (2004). *Best behavior: Building positive behavior in school.* Longmont, CO: Sopris West Educational Services.

Sprague, J.R., & Walker, H.M. (2005). *Safe and healthy schools: Practical strategies.* New York, NY: Guilford Press.

Stormont, M.A., Lewis, T.J., Becknew, R.S., & Johnson, N. (2007). *Implementing positive behavior support systems in early childhood and elementary settings.* Thousand Oaks, CA: Corwin Press.

Walker, H.M., Ramsey, E., & Gresham, F.M. (2004). *Antisocial behavior in school: Evidence-based practices.* Belmont, CA: Wadsworth/Thomson Learning.

Young, E.L., Caldarella, P., Richardson, M.J., & Young, K.R. (2012). *Positive behavior support in secondary schools: A practical guide.* New York, NY: Guilford Press.

TIER II INTERVENTIONS (INCLUDING CLASSROOM MANAGEMENT AND BULLYING PREVENTION)

Conroy, M.A., Sutherland, K.S., Snyder, A.L., & Marsh, S. (2008). Classwide interventions effective instruction makes a difference. *Teaching Exceptional Children, 40,* 24–30.

Crone, D.A., Hawken, L.S., & Horner, R.H. (2010). *Responding to problem behavior in schools: The behavior education program.* New York, NY: Guilford Press.

Debnam, K.J., Pas, E.T., & Bradshaw, C.P. (2012). Secondary and tertiary support systems in schools implementing school-wide positive behavioral interventions and supports: A preliminary descriptive analysis. *Journal of Positive Behavior Interventions, 14,* 142–152.

Good, C.P., McIntosh, K., & Gietz, C. (2011). Integrating bullying prevention into schoolwide positive behavior support. *Teaching Exceptional Children, 44,* 48–56.

Knoster, T.P. (2014). *The teacher's pocket guide for effective classroom management* (2nd ed.). Baltimore, MD: Paul H. Brookes Publishing Co.

Lane, K.L., Cook, B.G., & Tankersley, M. (Eds.). (2013). *Research-based strategies for improving outcomes in behavior.* New York, NY: Pearson.

Lewis, T., & Rose, C. (2013). *Addressing bullying behavior through school-wide positive behavior supports.* Arlington, VA: Council for Exceptional Children. Retrieved from http://cecblog.typepad.com/files/addressing-bullying-behavior-through-school-wide-positive-behavior-support.pdf

Ross, S.W., Horner, R.H., & Higbee, T. (2009). Bully prevention in positive behavior support. *Journal of Applied Behavior Analysis, 42,* 747–759.

Ross, S.W., Horner, R.H., & Stiller, B. (2009). *Bully prevention in positive behavior support.* [Curriculum manual developed for intervention implementation.] Eugene, OR: Educational and Community Supports. Retrieved from http://www.pbis.org/common/cms/files/pbisresources/2013_02_18_FINAL_COVR_MANUAL_123x.pdf; http://www.pbis.org/common/cms/files/pbisresources/bullyprevention_ES.pdf; http://www.pbis.org/common/cms/files/pbisresources/BullyPrevention_PBS_MS.pdf

Stiller, B., Nese, R.N.T., Tomlonovich, A., Horner, R., & Ross, S. (2013). *Bullying and harassment prevention in positive behavior support: Expect respect.* Eugene, OR: Educational and Community Supports. Retrieved from http://www.pbis.org/common/cms/files/pbisresources/PBIS_Bullying_Behavior_Apr19_2011.pdf

INDIVIDUALIZED POSITIVE BEHAVIOR SUPPORT PLANNING AND IMPLEMENTATION

Bambara, L., & Kern, L. (Eds.). (2005). *Individualized supports for students with problem behaviors: Designing positive behavior plans.* New York, NY: Guilford Press.

Bambara, L.M., & Knoster, T.P. (2009). *Designing positive behavior support plans* (2nd ed.). Washington, DC: American Association on Intellectual and Developmental Disabilities.

Brown, F., Anderson, J.L., & De Pry, R.L. (Eds.). (2015). *Individual positive behavior supports: A standards-based guide to practices in school and community settings.* Baltimore, MD: Paul H. Brookes Publishing Co.

Carr, E.G., Levin, L., McConnachie, G., Carlson, J.I., Kemp, D.C., & Smith, C.E. (1994). *Communication-based intervention for problem behavior: A user's guide for producing positive change.* Baltimore, MD: Paul H. Brookes Publishing Co.

Chandler, L.K., & Dahlquist, C.M. (2014). *Functional assessment: Strategies to prevent and remediate challenging behavior in school settings.* New York, NY: Pearson.

Crimmins, D., Farrell, A.F., Smith, P.W., & Bailey, A. (2007). *Positive strategies for students with behavior problems.* Baltimore, MD: Paul H. Brookes Publishing Co.

Dunlap, G., Iovannone, R., Kincaid, D., Wilson, K., Christiansen, K., Strain, P., & English, C. (2010). *Prevent-teach-reinforce: The school-based model of individualized positive behavior support.* Baltimore, MD: Paul H. Brookes Publishing Co.

Koegel, L.K., Koegel, R.L., & Dunlap, G. (Eds.). (1996). *Positive behavioral support: Including people with difficult behavior in the community.* Baltimore, MD: Paul H. Brookes Publishing Co.

Riffel, L.A. (2011). *Positive behavior support at the tertiary level: Red zone strategies.* Thousand Oaks, CA: Sage Publications.

Scott, T.M., Liaupsin, C., & Nelson, C.M. (2001). *Behavior intervention planning: Using the outcomes of functional behavioral assessment.* Longmont, CO: Sopris West Educational Services.

TOOLS AND HANDBOOKS FOR FUNCTIONAL BEHAVIOR ASSESSMENT

Bambara, L., & Kern, L. (2005). *Individualized supports for students with problem behaviors: Designing positive behavior plans.* New York, NY: Guilford Press.

Carr, E.G., Levin, L., McConnachie, G., Carlson, J.I., Kemp, D.C., & Smith, C.E. (1994). *Communication-based intervention for problem behavior: A user's guide for producing positive change.* Baltimore, MD: Paul H. Brookes Publishing Co.

Colvin, B. (1993). *Managing acting-out behavior.* Eugene, OR: Behavior Associates.

Crone, D.A., & Horner, R.H. (2003). *Building positive behavior support systems in schools: Functional behavioral assessment.* New York, NY: Guilford Press. (Includes the Functional Behavioral Assessment Interview [FBAI], the Functional Assessment Checklist for Teachers and Staff [FACTS], and the Functional Assessment Observation Form.)

Durand, V.M., & Crimmins, D.B. (1988). *The Motivation Assessment Scale (MAS) administration guide.* Topeka, KS: Monaco & Associates.

Kern, L., Dunlap, G., Clarke, S., & Childs, K.E. (1994). Student-assisted functional assessment interview. *Assessment for Effective Intervention, 19,* 29–39.

Loman, S., & Borgmeier, C. (2010). *Practical functional behavioral assessment training manual for school-based personnel.* Retrieved from http://archives.pdx.edu/ds/psu/11250

Newcomer, L. (2010). *Functional assessment linking FBA to function-based intervention plans.* Unpublished manuscript. Retrieved from http://rpdc.mst.edu/media/center/rpdc/documents/newcomerfba08.pdf

Newcomer, L.L., & Lewis, T.J. (2004). Functional behavioral assessment: An investigation of assessment reliability and effectiveness of function-based interventions. *Journal of Emotional and Behavioral Disorders, 12*(3), 168–181.

O'Neill, R.E., Albin, R.W., Storey, K., Horner, R.H, & Sprague, J.R. (2014). *Functional assessment and program development for problem behavior: A practical handbook* (3rd ed.). Stamford, CT: Cengage Learning. (Includes the Functional Assessment Interview [FAI] and the Student-Directed FA Interview [SFAI].)

Wacker, D.P., Cooper, L.J., Peck, S.M., Derby, K.M., & Berg, W.K. (1999). Community-based functional assessment. In A.C. Repp & R.H. Horner (Eds.), *Functional analysis of problem behavior: From effective assessment to effective support* (pp. 32–56). Belmont, CA: Wadsworth.

CONFLICT MANAGEMENT, PROBLEM SOLVING, AND PEER MEDIATION

The Collaborative for Academic, Social, and Emotional Learning (CASEL). (2003). *Safe and sound: An education leader's guide to evidence-based social and emotional learning (SEL) programs.* Chicago, IL: Author. Available at http://www.casel.org

Flaxman, E. (Ed.). (2001). *Evaluating school violence programs.* (Urban Diversity Series No. 113. ERIC Clearinghouse on Urban Education). New York, NY: Teachers College Press.

Johnson, D.W., & Johnson, R.T. (1995). *Teaching students to be peacemakers.* Edina, MN: Interaction Book Co.

Johnson, D.W., & Johnson, R.T. (1996). Conflict resolution and peer mediation programs in elementary and secondary schools: A review of research. *Review of Educational Research, 66,* 459–506.

Mihalic, S., Irwin, K., Elliott, D., Fagan, A., & Hansen, D. (2001, July). *Blueprints for violence prevention* (OJJDP Juvenile Justice Bulletin). Washington, DC: U.S. Department of Justice, Office of Juvenile Justice and Delinquency Prevention. Retrieved from http://www.ncjrs.gov/html/ojjdp/jjbul2001_7_3/contents.html

Schrumpf, F., Crawford, D., & Usadel, C. (1991). *Peer mediation: Conflict resolution in schools.* Champaign, IL: Research Press.

RESOURCES FOR RESEARCH-BASED INFORMATION, PLANNING, TRAINING, AND TECHNICAL ASSISTANCE IN POSITIVE BEHAVIOR SUPPORT

Alliance for School Mental Health. (2006). *PBIS school-family-community- partnership toolkit.* Long Island, NY: Author. Available from the Office of PBIS, District 75, NYC Public Schools, 400 First Avenue, New York, NY 10010.

Association for Positive Behavior Support—http://www.apbs.org/

Beach Center on Disability. (2007). *Family research instruments and toolkits.* Retrieved from http://www.beachcenter.org/families/family_research_toolkit.aspx

Bouffard, S.M., & Stephen. N. (2007). *Promoting family involvement in middle and high schools.* Reston, VA: National Association of Secondary School Principals. Retrieved from https://www.nassp.org/portals/0/content/56645.pdf

Caspe, M., & Lopez, M.E. (2006). *Lessons from family-strengthening interventions: Learning from evidence-based practice.* Cambridge, MA: Harvard Family Research Project. Retrieved from http://www.hfrp.org/publications-resources/browse-our-publications/lessons-from-family-strengthening-interventions-learning-from-evidence-based-practice

Center for Effective Collaboration and Practice at American Institutes for Research—http://cecp.air.org

Center for the Study and Prevention of Violence Institute of Behavioral Science, University of Colorado Boulder—http://www.colorado.edu/cspv

Collaborative for Academic, Social, and Emotional Learning—http://www.casel.org

Educators for Social Responsibility—http://www.engagingschools.org

Illinois Positive Behavior Interventions and Supports Network—http://www.pbisillinois.org

Kansas Institute for Positive Behavior Support—http://www.kipbsmodules.org

Kentucky Commissioner of Education's Parents Advisory Council. (2007). *The missing piece of the proficiency puzzle: Recommendations and a rubric for involving families and community in improving student achievement.* Lexington: Kentucky Department of Education.

National Association of School Psychologists—http://www.nasponline.org

National Network of Partnership Schools at Johns Hopkins University, Center on School, Family, and Community Partnerships—http://www.csos.jhu.edu/P2000/center.htm

National Information Center for Children and Youth with Disabilities—http://www.parent centerhub.org/nichcy-resources

National Parental Information Resource Center Coordination Center—http://www.nationalpirc.org

National Wraparound Initiative—http://www.rtc.pdx.edu/nwi

Positive Behavioral Interventions and Support OSEP Technical Assistance Center—http://pbis.org

Public Education Network. (2004). *School-parent compact: Action guide for parent and community leaders.* Washington, DC: Author.

University of Kansas, Center on Developmental Disabilities, Positive Behavior Support—http://uappbs.apbs.org

Index

Tables and figures are indicated by *t* and *f*, respectively.